JUSTICES AND JOURNALISTS

Justices and Journalists examines whether justices are becoming more publicity conscious and why that might be happening. The book discusses the motives of justices "going public" and demonstrates that the justices have become more newsworthy over the last decade.

The book describes the interactions justices have (and have had) with the journalists who cover them. These interactions typically are not discussed publicly by justices or journalists. The book explains why justices care about press and public relations, how they employ external strategies to affect press portrayals of themselves and their institution, and how and why journalists participate in that interaction.

Drawing on the papers of Supreme Court justices in the nineteenth and twentieth centuries, the book examines these interactions throughout the history of the Court. It also includes a content analysis of print and broadcast media coverage of Supreme Court justices covering a forty-year period from 1968 to 2007.

Richard Davis is a professor of political science at Brigham Young University. He is the author or co-author of several books on media and American politics, including *Electing Justice: Fixing the Supreme Court Nomination Process* (2005), *Decisions and Images: The Supreme Court and the Press* (1994), *The Web of Politics* (1999), *Campaigning Online* (2003, with Bruce Bimber), and *New Media and American Politics* (1998, with Diana Owen). He is past chair of the political communication section of the American Political Science Association.

Justices and Journalists

THE U.S. SUPREME COURT AND THE MEDIA

RICHARD DAVIS

Brigham Young University

CAMBRIDGE
UNIVERSITY PRESS

CAMBRIDGE UNIVERSITY PRESS
Cambridge, New York, Melbourne, Madrid, Cape Town, Singapore,
São Paulo, Delhi, Dubai, Tokyo, Mexico City

Cambridge University Press
32 Avenue of the Americas, New York, NY 10013-2473, USA

www.cambridge.org
Information on this title: www.cambridge.org/9780521704663

First published 2011

Printed in the United States of America

A catalog record for this publication is available from the British Library.

Library of Congress Cataloging in Publication data

Davis, Richard, 1955–
Justices and journalists : the U.S. Supreme Court and the media / Richard Davis.
    p. cm.
Includes bibliographical references and index.
ISBN 978-0-521-87925-5 (hardback) – ISBN 978-0-521-70466-3 (pbk.)
1. Law in mass media.   2. Mass media – Law and legislation – United States.
3. United States. Supreme Court – Officials and employees.   4. Judges – United States.
I. Title.
K487.M43D38   2011
347.73'2634 – dc22   2010031683

ISBN 978-0-521-87925-5 Hardback
ISBN 978-0-521-70466-3 Paperback

To my family, for their unfailing support
through good times and bad

Contents

Foreword

Adam Liptak

In the late summer of 2010, Justice Stephen Breyer embarked on an extraordinary publicity tour.

He had just published a book called *Making Our Democracy Work: A Judge's View*, which was earnest and dry and worthy. It would have vanished without a trace had its author not sat on the Supreme Court.

Thus it was Justice Breyer's status, rather than his message, that propelled him onto the airwaves. Over a month or so, he appeared on CNN's *Larry King Live*, on PBS's *Newshour* and *Charlie Rose*, on NPR's *Fresh Air* and *Morning Edition*, on ABC's *Good Morning America*, on the NBC *Nightly News*, and on C-SPAN.

Justice Breyer was also profiled in *The New Yorker* and interviewed by, among others, the Associated Press, Bloomberg News, and *The Washington Post*.

And he appeared at countless discussions sponsored by the Aspen Institute, the National Constitution Center, book stores, law schools, libraries, and civic groups from coast to coast.

In many of these forums, there was the usual tension between journalist and subject, with the former pressing provocatively for fresh and newsworthy comments and the latter seeking to convey an array of stock talking points.

For the most part, Justice Breyer stuck to his main themes, and even a connoisseur of Supreme Court interviews would have difficulty distinguishing what he told, say, Charlie Rose from what he told Larry King.

Over and over again, Justice Breyer stressed that public support for the court is important so that even unpopular decisions are obeyed. The Supreme Court is not, he added more than once, made up of nine "junior varsity politicians."

But Justice Breyer got the occasional offbeat question, too.

He announced that he would attend the next State of the Union address, even as some of his colleagues expressed reservations about it in light of the comments President Obama directed at them in January 2010.

Chief Justice John G. Roberts Jr. called the event a "political pep rally." Justice Samuel A. Alito Jr., who had appeared to be mouthing the words "not true" as President Obama characterized the decision in *Citizens United v. Federal Election Commission*, said in October that "I doubt I will be there in January" of 2011.

Justice Breyer told Larry King, apropos a controversy in the news at the time, how he had felt seeing a flag burned in the Vietnam era.

"I had a physical reaction of revulsion," Justice Breyer said. "I couldn't stand it."

He seemed perplexed when C-SPAN's Brian Lamb asked him about an unfounded rumor.

"Some conservative talk show over the last month said Justice Breyer wants – I got to be careful, because I don't remember the quote, but the essence of it was – that you are in favor of incorporating Sharia law," Lamb proposed.

"I don't know where that one came from," Justice Breyer said. Lamb pressed on.

"I can't remember ever saying anything," a befuddled Justice Breyer responded. "I think maybe there was some issue on this in England. Maybe they're mixing it up with England. My wife is English."

Asked by George Stephanopoulos on *Good Morning America* about a Florida pastor's plan to burn the Qu'ran, Justice Breyer mused about Justice Oliver Wendell Holmes's 1919 opinion in *Schenck v. United States*.

"With the Internet, you can say this," Justice Breyer said. "Holmes said it doesn't mean you can shout 'fire' in a crowded theater. Well, what is it? Why? Because people will be trampled to death. And what is the crowded theater today? What is the being trampled to death?"

The answer, Justice Breyer said, "will be answered over time in a series of cases which force people to think carefully."

Two kinds of criticism followed this last exchange. Some said Justice Breyer seemed to be prepared to revisit settled First Amendment principles. After all, if flag burning is constitutionally protected, ought not the burning of religious books be protected as well?

Others noted that Justice Breyer had been imprecise in his paraphrase of Justice Holmes, who wrote that "the most stringent protection of free speech would not protect a man in falsely shouting fire in a theatre and causing a panic." The omission of the word "falsely" does alter Justice Holmes's meaning; the addition of the word "crowded," which seems part of the collective memory, less so.

Dahlia Lithwick, *Slate*'s lively and astute Supreme Court correspondent, said the exchange was illuminating for another lesson.

"If they signify anything," she wrote, "Breyer's strange musings about Qu'ran burning illustrate the danger of allowing Supreme Court justices to go on live television for their book tours."

Justice Breyer's book tour is thus a vivid example of the phenomenon Richard Davis explores in this book – the varied, fitful, and strategic ways in which many Supreme Court justices are interacting with the press and exposing themselves to the public.

Some of it seems a matter of temperament. Justice Breyer, like Justice Antonin Scalia, is outgoing. By contrast, as Richard Davis notes, Justice David H. Souter managed to complete almost two decades on the court without granting an on-the-record interview and appearing only very occasionally in public.

Of course, many justices teach and lecture at law schools, judicial conferences, and bar associations, generally on bland topics. But they tend to be more selective in engaging with journalists.

Such interviews generally are granted to advance an agenda. Sometimes it is to help sell a book, though that did not seem to be a central goal for Justice Breyer. Sometimes it is an effort to persuade the public about a larger point. Justices Breyer and Scalia, singly and together, for instance, have made their cases in public for their opposing views of how the Constitution should be interpreted.

But the most important theme in the justices' recent appearances is one aptly identified by Professor Richard Davis in this fascinating and comprehensive book. "Justices in the twenty-first century," he writes, "are using publicity to defend the institution."

Justice Breyer, for his part, has said that the Supreme Court's legitimacy is enhanced by allowing the public to see the justices as committed, careful, and apolitical. Working with and through the press may be necessary to convey that message.

But the justices generally remain wary of reporters. Among Richard Davis' most interesting findings are how closely and critically the justices have followed press coverage of the court.

Justice Harry A. Blackmun even kept an annotated copy of the American Society of Newspaper Editors' code of ethics in his files. The provisions he highlighted suggested that the justice believed the press had at least occasionally treated the code as merely aspirational.

Chief Justice Earl Warren took a different approach, writing thank-you notes to reporters whose work had pleased him. I have yet to receive such a note.

Adam Liptak is the Supreme Court correspondent of *The New York Times*.

Preface

One Sunday morning, Justice Antonin Scalia of the U.S. Supreme Court faced a phalanx of reporters as he left Mass at the Cathedral of the Holy Cross in Boston. A reporter asked Scalia, a devout Catholic, whether he should be considered impartial in matters of church and state given his religious affiliation and devotion. Scalia responded with a hand gesture that is unfamiliar to most Americans but is considered indecent by some Italians. The *Boston Herald* covered the incident, called the gesture obscene, and even included a photograph of Scalia making the gesture. Offended by the newspaper's characterization of his action, Scalia wrote a letter to the editor defending himself and defining the gesture as not obscene but merely expressive of his lack of concern for the reporter's question.[1]

Scalia's church-steps encounter with the press followed on the heels of another news story about Scalia from earlier that month. In a question-and-answer session after a speech in Switzerland, Scalia had commented on the Bush administration's detainment of suspected terrorists, a topic that was closely related to a case pending before the Court. Criticism about Scalia's comments quickly followed, and a public effort was made to get the outspoken justice to recuse himself from the case. Scalia refused, initiating another round of publicity.[2]

These were not isolated incidents. Scalia became newsworthy because of his hunting trip with then–Vice President Dick Cheney while a case involving Cheney was before the Court, his stint as grand marshal of New York's Columbus Day parade that sparked protests from gay rights groups, and an apology he gave to two reporters after a federal marshal protecting Scalia demanded they erase tape recordings of his speeches because of Scalia's prohibition of recordings of his public appearances.[3] In the Cheney case, newspaper editorials urged Scalia to recuse himself from participation in the case, which he again declined to do.

Nor has Scalia been unique among Supreme Court justices in receiving press attention in recent years. Like Scalia's, this notice from the press has been as much personal as jurisprudential. Justice Sonia Sotomayor became the object of attention not only for her frequent questioning from the bench as a new justice but also for her salsa dancing. In 2006, David Souter attracted press attention when a group of anti–eminent domain activists protested *Kelo v. City of New London* in front of Souter's New Hampshire home and urged that his hometown seize his home under eminent domain.[4]

Several justices have sparked news stories with their involvement in two legal issues involving the Court. One is the role of the judiciary in American government. Justices Ruth Bader Ginsburg and Sandra Day O'Connor (while the latter was still on the bench) gave speeches defending the independence of the judiciary in the wake of Bush administration actions challenging federal courts.[5] In a May 2006 speech, Ginsburg called a Republican proposal to set up an inspector general over the Courts "a scary idea." She added that "the judiciary is under assault in a way that I haven't seen before."[6] The other issue was whether justices should consider foreign court decisions in their decision-making process. Although some justices, such as Scalia, have argued that the Court should not use foreign court decisions as precedents, others, including Justice Steven Breyer, have publicly defended the process. Indeed, Justices Scalia, Breyer, Anthony Kennedy, and Ginsburg have sparred publicly about that issue in speeches and public forums.[7]

Nor was Scalia alone in commenting on cases while the Court has been considering them. In an interview with Joan Biskupic of *USA Today*, Ruth Bader Ginsburg criticized her colleagues for their questions and statements during an oral argument for a case involving a strip search of a thirteen-year-old girl by school administrators. Ginsburg, who said the male justices did not understand the trauma the thirteen-year-old girl had gone through during the ordeal, was commenting after the oral argument but before the Court had ruled on the case.[8]

The justices appear to have shed their camera shyness. In a remarkable departure from the policy of his predecessor, soon after becoming chief justice, John Roberts appeared on a broadcast network news program, ABC News' *Nightline*. He used the occasion to discuss the Supreme Court as an institution, although he also answered questions about his family. Moreover, Roberts gave two press conferences in his first year as chief justice. Chief Justice William Rehnquist gave that same number during his entire nineteen years as chief.[9]

Yet by the end of his term, even Rehnquist became more visible on television than he had been throughout the majority of his tenure as a justice. He sat for an interview with C-SPAN founder Brian Lamb and allowed his speeches to be aired by C-SPAN. Clarence Thomas appeared on CBS News' *60 Minutes* to promote his autobiography. Antonin Scalia followed a year later with his own *60 Minutes* interview to talk about his new book on lawyers and judges.[10]

The justices also make news when they give televised speeches. Formerly, justices typically banned television cameras and even audio recording devices from the room while they spoke. That was David Souter's policy while he was on the Court.[11] However, justices increasingly are allowing television cameras to record their speeches. The recording of a speech allows reporters to know exactly what was said in order to quote the justice and write the story. Also, broadcast reporters obviously can use video or audio clips in news broadcasts, thus making the story more broadcast worthy.

Now it is easier for justices to make news when they speak – and they do. In one speech, Anthony Kennedy criticized how senators questioned Supreme Court nominees. He also dismissed the notion of activist justices with the comment that "an activist court is a court that makes a decision you don't like."[12] John Roberts gained attention when he criticized President Barack Obama in a question-and-answer session with University of Alabama law students. Fully aware that his remarks were being recorded on C-SPAN and that he would make news, Roberts questioned whether the justices should even show up at the State of the Union speech with "one branch of government standing up, literally surrounding the Supreme Court, cheering and hollering while the court – according to the requirements of protocol – has to sit there expressionless."[13] Thomas made a similar statement that made national news when he explained in a speech to law students why he rarely attends State of the Union addresses. "I don't go because it has become so partisan and it's very uncomfortable for a judge to sit there," Thomas said. He added that "one of the consequences is now the court becomes part of the conversation, if you want to call it that, in the speeches."[14]

In fact, most of the justices – John Roberts, John Paul Stevens, Antonin Scalia, Stephen Breyer, Ruth Bader Ginsburg, Samuel Alito, and Sonia Sotomayor – sat for television interviews on C-SPAN during the first decade of the twenty-first century. By contrast, appearances by justices in the previous half century were rare. For example, only two justices gave a few television interviews in the 1950s and 1960s.

GOING PUBLIC?

Is something going on here? Are U.S. Supreme Court justices "going public"? Have the justices decided to become more visible to attract the attention of the press and the public? Has there been a conscious decision to raise their public profile? If so, why?

Any such change at the Court would appear to be a significant departure from the past. It also would alter general expectations about the behavior of justices. Former *New York Times* reporter Linda Greenhouse, who covered the Court for many years, once commented: "I see a Court that is quite blithely oblivious to the needs of those who convey its work to the outside world. . . . "[15] That is how the Court is generally perceived.

Yet another journalist suggested that a change already has occurred. Tony Mauro, who also covered the Court for a long time, concluded that John Roberts was "lifting the veil, ever so slightly" and that, as a result of Roberts' example, "a new somewhat more open climate seems to be unfolding at the nation's highest court."[16] As mentioned earlier, in Roberts' first year as chief justice, he appeared on broadcast television, held press conferences, and sat for interviews. All of that was a radical departure from his predecessor in terms of relations with the press. Roberts may have been an impetus for change on the part of other justices as well. Soon after he arrived on the Court a few months after Roberts, Samuel Alito gave an on-the-record interview to his hometown newspaper, and other justices began to give on-the-record interviews rather than the off-the-record interviews that had been more common.[17]

However, there is evidence that the justices' approach to publicity was changing even before Roberts arrived. Two years prior to Roberts' arrival at the Court, Stephen Breyer and Sandra Day O'Connor sat for an interview with the ABC News show *This Week*. The year before that, O'Connor published an autobiography. Antonin Scalia appeared on several televised forums early in 2005 while Rehnquist was still chief justice.[18]

Even though the timing of the change in public exposure, or Roberts' possible role in stimulating it, may be debatable, the fact remains that Supreme Court justices, whom one would expect not to "go public," seem to be doing just that. Yet the incidents beg the question: What incentive do they have to do so? As schoolchildren know, the justices have no constituency to court for reelection; they enjoy lifetime tenure – and that tenure is designed to insulate them from public response to their decisions and enhance their independence.[19] One would assume that the lack of any necessity to "go public" would translate into a continued low public profile, with exceptions such as retirement, death, serious illness, or, in the rare case, scandal.

Moreover, it is not easy for a justice to "go public" as compared with an elected official. For one thing, justices do not have the regular electoral process that offers them an opportunity to gain public attention. There is no electoral link to the public, as exists with members of Congress or the president.

Constitutionally, they do not depend on the public for their position on the Court. In fact, the Constitution's framers designed judicial selection in a manner that excluded not only the public (i.e., through elections) but also the public's direct representatives (the House of Representatives). The president (elected by a set of elite electors) and senators (at that time, elected by the state legislatures) were themselves distant from the public. Moreover, once in office, they can only be removed for violating "good behavior." A Supreme Court justice has never been removed from office, and only one (Samuel Chase in 1803) has even been impeached.

In theory, the justices have little or no connection with the general public. Formally, they need not gauge public opinion when they make decisions. As a result, one would expect them to have little connection with the press. Hence, if they are unconcerned about public opinion, why would they need to even take account of press coverage of their decisions, much less attempt as individuals to get that coverage? Because the extent of their external constituency would seem to be the legal community, which is charged with implementing legal policy set by the Court, why would they need to communicate with any other constituency or even communicate with the legal community through means other than their written opinions?

Yet, as indicated earlier, justices today do interact with the press.[20] That interaction goes beyond being covered by the press for their judicial actions either collectively or individually. It also includes sitting for interviews with reporters, delivering speeches the press will cover, writing books or cooperating with others writing books about them, and participating in forums they know will receive press attention. Moreover, studies of the Court's interaction with the press demonstrate that the justices do follow press coverage of their own decisions and other actions and structure the Court's institutional relationship with the press to maximize press coverage in ways that reinforce the institution's legitimacy.[21] Nor is this interaction necessarily recent. Scholarly evidence of the press' interaction with the Court dates back to at least the 1960s.[22]

However, recent behavior by many of the justices prompts important questions: What would a justice gain by expressing himself or herself to the public, particularly beyond opinion writing? Why go public? Also, is this new behavior? Are the justices today suddenly "going public" in a way foreign to their predecessors? If so, what recent forces have contributed to the changed nature of justices' relations with reporters? These questions will be addressed in these pages.

The structure of the book is as follows: The first chapter describes why and how justices act as strategic actors in their relations with external constituencies, particularly the press and the public. It also offers several hypotheses that will be tested in this study. Chapter 2 reviews general expectations of judicial behavior vis à vis the press and then offers explanations of recent factors that might contribute to a shift in justices' attitudes toward the press and the public. The next three chapters address the second question – that is, the extent to which justices in the past have engaged in public relations, particularly via the press, and whether the current justices are acting differently from their predecessors. Beginning with the Jay Court in 1790 and moving through the nineteenth and twentieth centuries, these chapters review interactions with reporters and editors as well as attempts by justices to affect press coverage, public policy, and public opinion through both their judicial activities and their extrajudicial efforts. Chapter 6 consists of the results of a content analysis of press coverage of the justices during a forty-year period – 1968 to 2007. The final chapter centers on twenty-first-century justices and the recent efforts by justices to "go public." In addition, the chapter discusses the implications of justices' public profiles for the justices individually and the Court as a powerful institution of American government in the twenty-first century. It discusses three main questions: What are the effects of the behaviors of the justices on the Court as an institution? What are the effects on the role of the Court as an arbiter of decision making? Finally, if the justices are emerging from their monastic-style existence, what are the implications for their future interactions with other political players, particularly the public?

JUSTICES AND JOURNALISTS

1

External Strategies

In 1989, the Court issued an opinion in *Webster v. Reproductive Health Services*, which upheld most of the provisions of a Missouri law imposing increased regulations on abortion. The much-anticipated decision had been viewed as the death knell for the *Roe* case. Since 1973, four new justices had joined the Court, and three of them were considered to be unsympathetic to *Roe*. That change tipped the expected *Roe* supporters on the Court from seven to four, robbing *Roe* supporters of the majority they had enjoyed.

However, as chief justice and a friend of Sandra Day O'Connor, William Rehnquist suspected that O'Connor's vote was not solid. When the justices met in their conference to discuss *Webster*, Rehnquist spoke first and advocated a position with which he did not fully agree – that the Court should modify the *Roe* standard rather than overturn the decision.[1] This was not easy for Rehnquist. He had been one of the two justices voting against the majority in *Roe* in 1973. Personally, he strongly advocated overturning *Roe*. But he also knew that without O'Connor in agreement, there would be no majority for at least eroding *Roe*. Rehnquist hoped O'Connor would agree with Rehnquist on most of the provisions of the Missouri statute, even if she was unwilling to go further with him to overturn *Roe*. Rehnquist's attempt to compromise on a core principle indicated his willingness to engage in strategic behavior to achieve his broader objective.

Rehnquist's act was hardly novel among Supreme Court justices. This story demonstrates the dilemmas underlying the motivations that drive Supreme Court justices. Are they primarily focused on expressing their views in opinions, or are they seeking to woo other justices to form a majority around some measure of their views, if not their full expression? What is their primary motivation in their interactions with each other as well as with those beyond the Court?

MODELS OF JUDICIAL MOTIVATIONS AND BEHAVIOR

The question of why justices would "go public" really is one about motivations of justices. In terms of judicial motivations, scholars of the U.S. Supreme Court have focused primarily on the act of voting. Because voting is the most common act by justices, as well as the most public act in which they engage, it makes sense that their individual decisions on cases would dominate the study of judicial reasons for their actions. The predominant model in that study has been the social-psychological or attitudinal approach. The key premise of this model is that justices' votes in conference reflect their own attitudes.[2] C. Herman Pritchett posited this model with the thesis that personal attitudes adequately explain how a justice approaches individual decisions regarding granting writ or deciding a case.[3] Whether a justice joins the majority, writes a concurrence, or issues a dissenting opinion is determined by the individual justice's personal interpretation of the U.S. Constitution, statutes, and previous Court decisions.

At first glance, the attitudinal model seems to fit neatly the situation of U.S. Supreme Court justices. Because they appear to answer to no constituency, are highly unlikely to be removed for any opinion they write, and are equal to each other justice in terms of voting, they can act as solitary players lacking incentives to do anything but express their own personal preferences in their opinions. In fact, one might suggest that other political players, particularly the public, expect them to engage in just such behavior.

Yet historical analysis of the justices' papers, as well as occasional glimpses of individual justices' public behavior in switching sides on issues, sometimes over a relatively short period of time, suggests that the attitudinal model may not be as exhaustive an explanation as one might think. For example, in 1940, the Court declared that a state could coerce children of Jehovah's Witnesses to recite the Pledge of Allegiance. Three years later, in the wake of extensive public criticism from scholars and newspaper editorial boards, the Court majority switched dramatically in the opposite direction.[4] Did the justices who switched sides view the Constitution differently in that short time frame, or were they influenced by outside pressures?

History shows us that the Court often shifts direction when personnel change. Most famously, justices appointed by President Franklin D. Roosevelt in the late 1930s and early 1940s replaced predecessors who opposed the constitutionality of New Deal programs, thus resulting in an end to the judicial debate about the constitutionality of New Deal programs. The effect of personnel change also has been in evidence more recently. In 2003, the Court, by 5 – 4, upheld bans on corporate campaign spending. Seven years later, again by a vote of 5 to 4, the Court reversed itself after Sandra Day O'Connor, who supported the ban, was replaced by Samuel Alito, who opposed it. Similarly, the Court overturned a partial birth abortion ban and then upheld it three years later. Again, the switch was from O'Connor to Alito.[5]

Justices also genuinely change their minds over time or when they are faced with arguments from the other justices. As an example of the former, Justice John Paul Stevens transformed from an advocate of the death penalty early in his Court tenure to a vocal critic by the end.[6] As for the latter, Justice Robert Jackson once admitted, "I myself have changed my opinion after reading the opinions of the other members of this Court. . . . I sometimes wind up not voting the way I voted in conference because the reasons of the majority didn't satisfy me."[7]

These changes would support the attitudinal model; that is, justices change their minds, and therefore their votes, over time. But other evidence suggests that, at least at times, attitudes may be secondary to other motivations by justices. In 1954, Stanley Reed agreed to join the Court's opinion in *Brown v. Board of Education*, thus making the decision unanimous, explaining to his colleagues that "Well, if you are all going to vote that way, I'm not going to stand out."[8] Similarly, in 1968, Justice Hugo Black changed his mind on a case involving union voting rules to avoid dissenting alone.[9] Black dissented on the case in conference but, like Reed, was uncomfortable in his role as the sole dissenter on the case. He wrote a note to Justice William O. Douglas, informing him that "I am still of the opinion that a union like this one needs rules to prevent indiscriminate candidacies for offices where the incumbent has such heavy duties. . . . " Yet Black admitted that "[s]ince this is so surely a matter of judgment, however, I am not willing to dissent alone. Consequently I acquiesce provided all the others go along."[10] Black's personal attitudes regarding the issue became of less importance than his desire not to be publicly voting alone.

Perhaps a more frequent example is when an opinion writer is willing to compromise his or her personal preferences in order to win over, or maintain, the support of other justices who constitute a potential coalition. A nineteenth-century justice wrote to his colleague that he could not agree with one section of his colleague's majority opinion and "that I fear, unless it can be a good deal tempered, I shall have to deliver a separate opinion on the lines of the enclosed memorandum." The justice even added that he knew that, without his support, the majority opinion would become a minority one. The opinion writer compromised and incorporated the language necessary to hold his wavering colleague.[11] Explaining this practice, Antonin Scalia related that the writer of a majority opinion has to "craft it in a way that as many people as possible will jump on, which means accepting some suggestions – stylistic and otherwise – that really you don't think. . . . are best, but nonetheless, in order to get everybody on board, you take them."[12] Justice Tom Clark described his own approach: "If one was assigned to write, he might go around and talk, as I did, to the doubtful justice, who was on the fence, asking 'Now, what do you think? How should this be written?' And you'd try to get him to come along with you."[13]

In accordance with the attitudinal approach, a justice could abandon strategy and write whatever he or she wanted. In 1994, Antonin Scalia was assigned the Court's opinion in *Holder v. Hall*. However, Scalia reached far beyond what the majority had agreed on when he used the majority opinion to criticize the 1965 Voting Rights Act. As a result, he lost the opinion assignment and ended up joining a concurrence by Thomas. Taking the attitudinal approach may be personally satisfying, but there can be a cost in terms of shaping the Court's decisions.[14]

The flip side of that relationship occurs when a justice who agrees with the position of an opinion chooses to join it, if there is some tweaking by the author, rather than express his or her own personal preferences separately. For example, one justice wrote to another, attaching a summary of his views on an opinion being written by the latter, and urged his colleague to incorporate his views into the latter's opinion. In return, the first justice promised that he would forego writing on his own and join the second justice's opinion. He added: "If you feel that you could agree with me, I think you would find no difficulty in making some changes in your opinion which would make it unnecessary for me to say anything."[15] Similarly, when he disagreed with the majority, Louis Brandeis would write a memorandum to the other justices explaining that he had not decided whether to dissent but was willing to negotiate with the majority for his support. That tactic sometimes led to the other justices compromising with Brandeis to obtain his vote. At other times, Brandeis ended up writing a dissent.[16]

Another example is the assignment of cases. The chief justice, or a senior associate justice when the chief justice is in the minority, often assigns a case to the justice in the majority who is the shakiest member of the narrow majority coalition to keep that individual from defecting to the minority and reversing the direction of the Court.[17] John Paul Stevens admitted that he assigned opinions to the weakest member of the minority because "it might be wiser to let that person write the opinion." For instance, Stevens assigned the *Lawrence v. Texas* decision to Anthony Kennedy to keep Kennedy in the majority.[18] According to the attitudinal model, the assigning justice would seek an opinion that matches his or her personal attitudes. Yet that is not the practice when the goal is to hold together a majority.

Some scholars, then, have questioned whether the attitudinal model best explains judicial decision making. Lee Epstein and Jack Knight argue that a judicial strategy approach is more prominent today.[19] Lawrence Baum has argued that many times justices do express their personal attitudes in decisions, but at other times they seem to act in strategic ways that may not reflect their personal preferences, but allow them to accomplish their desired outcomes.[20] Baum refers to another, competing model in the analysis of judicial behavior: the strategic model.

The strategic model posits that the justices employ strategies in their case acceptance, voting, and opinion writing that will produce a policy outcome that most closely matches their own.[21] Unlike the attitudinal model, the strategic model carries a rational choice perspective that describes the justices as rational actors operating within a political context they attempt to navigate and manipulate. According to Epstein and Knight, justices are "strategic actors who realize that their ability to achieve their goals depends on a consideration of the preferences of others, of the choices they expect others to make, and of the institutional context in which they act."[22]

The strategic model is not an exhaustive explanation of judicial voting. In many cases, justices do not act in a strategic manner; they simply express their personal preferences and leave it at that. Rather, the model suggests that justices can engage in this behavior and sometimes do. Indeed, they use certain tactics, such as bargaining, personal friendship, and sanctions on other justices, to achieve their own policy preferences through opinions.[23]

JUSTICES AS STRATEGIC EXTERNAL ACTORS

Whether or not the strategic model is supplemental to the attitudinal model in judicial voting, its explanatory value may be more powerful when applied to areas of behavior other than voting. This would include the justices' relationship with constituents beyond the Court, such as the presidency and Congress.[24] But it would also apply to the Court's relationship with the public.

Admittedly, there are those who contend that the attitudinal model still prevails, even in the realm of the Court's interaction with public opinion. Brenner and Whitmeyer argue that the strategic model does not extend to the Court's relationship with the public and offer examples in which justices could not have been acting strategically because of the nature of some of their decisions. These include high-profile cases when the justices opposed public opinion on issues such as school desegregation, school prayer, and the rights of the accused.[25]

Brenner and Whitmeyer are referring to an historical debate regarding whether the Court is fundamentally majoritarian or counter-majoritarian.

On one hand, scholars have pointed to the Court's opinions that have been reflective of public opinion.[26] Robert McCloskey concluded that "the Court has seldom lagged far behind or forged far ahead of America."[27] Indeed, it is not difficult to find examples of the Court mirroring public will. The Court's shift on the New Deal in the late 1930s often is cited.[28] However, many similar examples are available: Decisions regarding the legality of opposition to World War I, Japanese internment during World War II, and the death penalty all closely matched public opinion at the time. Even a controversial case like *Brown v. Board of Education* may be an example of majoritarianism, as the case actually leaned toward the view of the majority of the public at the time.[29] The *Planned Parenthood v. Casey* decision is another example. The Court's decision hewed closely to extant public opinion on abortion, which tended to a middle ground on the issue rather than agreement with either the pro-choice or pro-life camps. Indeed, the opinion of the three justices in the plurality even acknowledged that they were responding to the public's acceptance of the *Roe* decision.[30]

Scholars have pointed out the Court's willingness to issue specific counter-majoritarian decisions and pursue counter-majoritarian trends, at least temporarily.[31] Moreover, the perception left by critics of the Court is of an institution increasingly driven by counter-majoritarian tendencies. From Franklin Roosevelt in the 1930s to Richard Nixon in the 1960s to George W. Bush in the 2000s, presidents have used their "bully pulpits" to label the Court as heedless of public opinion and anxious to employ judicial activism to further the justices' own policy ends.

Yet another view is that although the Court does differ from public opinion at times (and in doing so attempts to shape that opinion), it is still calibrating its actions in terms of its perception of the will of the public. This attitude is suggested in a letter one justice wrote about how the justices navigate public opinion. Justice Wiley Rutledge told a correspondent: "We here cannot allow our judgment to be swayed by the anticipated unpopularity of our views, but this does not mean either that we can be unconscious of that probability.... "[32] Barry Friedman argues that the justices participate in and even stimulate an ongoing public debate about the interpretation of the Constitution. Rather than being aloof from the public, they are regularly gauging public sentiment to ensure that they do not stray far from it even as they attempt at times to lead it.[33] This approach conforms at least partly to the strategic approach, because it allows that the justices may strike out in terms of decisions that move beyond public opinion, but also recognizes they do not do so naively.

One explanation for judicial concern about public opinion is the need to build diffuse support among the public, which then translates into acceptance of and compliance with individual decisions, particularly when they are counter-majoritarian.[34] The solution would seem to be simple enough: The justices could issue only majoritarian decisions. However, the solution is not so simple, because the link between individual decisions and diffuse support for the Court is debatable.[35] On the one hand, confidence in the Supreme Court fell after abortion and flag burning cases in 1989. On the other hand, despite broad public dissatisfaction with the *Bush v. Gore* decision, that case did not damage public support for the institution.[36]

Rather, building diffuse support would seem to rest on broader factors than whether the public is in agreement with any individual decision. The key to creating diffuse support rests not only in what the Court does but also in how it frames and then communicates what it does. The object of such communication is the general public. Gregory A. Caldeira and James L. Gibson suggest that when the justices "anchor their decisions in legal, not political, values and symbols," the public responds with diffuse support.[37]

Clearly, those symbols are not communicated casually, but by design. They cannot be left to chance, because too many other factors would combine to undermine some merely inadvertent communication of diffuse support-building values and symbols. These countervailing forces include publicly stated opposition to individual decisions of the Court by affected parties (including not only the parties to the case but also various interest groups); politically driven criticisms of the Court's general direction by Congress, presidents, or interest groups; general public misunderstanding of the Court decisions due to inaccurate press coverage; or even lack of knowledge by the public of Court opinions as a consequence of the relatively low level of press attention paid to Court actions.

The need for a strategy of public relations stems from the constitutional status as well as the historical experience of the Court. The Court lacks the enforcement mechanism that would allow it to carry out its own decisions regardless of the reaction of other political institutions or the public. Therefore, the Court relies on public deference to achieve general compliance with its decisions. However, as mentioned earlier, the Court lacks direct linkages to the public, as is present for presidents and members of Congress. Those linkages would facilitate public relations and therefore enhance public deference and compliance.

The absence of such linkages is a two-edged sword in the sense that the distance from the public enhances the mystique of the Court. If familiarity breeds contempt, then that aloofness may produce deference. In contrast, if other players seek to shape the Court's image, the Court has no automatic mechanism for rebuttal. If the justices attempted to engage in the traditional

methods of public rebuttal (e.g., press conferences, interviews, photo opportunities), the public would consider such actions unseemly, and the justices'
efforts could be counterproductive to the aim of enhancing public deference.

For example, recent presidents have used the State of the Union address to
criticize the Court directly or indirectly. In 2004 and 2005, President George
W. Bush decried "activist judges" whom he charged were shaping public
policy against the public's will. In 2010, President Barack Obama criticized
a specific decision – *Citizen's United v. F.E.C.* – that significantly altered
the role of corporate money in electoral campaigns. While the justices who
were present sat impassively during the Bush addresses, Samuel Alito shook
his head and mouthed "not true" after Obama's remark. A debate ensued
about whether Alito had acted appropriately. The justice gave no subsequent
explanation of his action, even though he was specifically asked by the press
to do so.[38]

Therefore, the Court may be affected by public opinion when that opinion is shaped by others. This includes presidents, Congress, and interest
groups, among others. However, at the same time, the Court is at a severe
disadvantage in responding to others' image-making efforts regarding the
Court. The justices are constrained by the Court's own norms (partly driven
by that same public opinion) in their attempts to shape the public's opinion
of their institution, as well as of themselves as members of that institution.

Historical examples suggest the justices do act to remake negative public
opinion to save the institution's power and that failure to do so can have long-
term consequences for the Court's role. In the early 1800s, in the midst of
bitter attacks by Jeffersonian Republicans, as well as the problem of current
justices involving themselves in partisan politics, Chief Justice John Marshall
attempted to recast the public image of the Court from that of a divided,
partisan body to a united, nonpolitical institution.[39] Again in the 1850s, aboli-
tionists portrayed the Court as a pro-slavery institution dominated by Southern
interests to undermine its legitimacy as a policy maker on the issue of slavery.
This time there was no John Marshall present to save the Court. The result
was a general lack of public acceptance for the Dred Scott case and a seeming
willingness on the part of the public to allow the post–Civil War Congress to
weaken the Court's power over Reconstruction.[40] Conversely, the Court acted
in its own defense eighty years later when President Franklin Roosevelt sought
to mold an image of the Court as a group of policy makers rather than neutral
adjudicators of law to build public support for his eventual Court-packing
plan. The justices took action to save the Court through a public defense of
their institution as well as an eventual acceptance of Roosevelt's economic
views.[41]

In each case, the image of the Court was tarnished – sometimes briefly and sometimes over a lengthy period of time – by the efforts to paint it as possessing certain negative characteristics. The 1850s and 1860s Court suffered powerful attacks from other national political players who accused the justices of overt bias in their decision making on the slavery issue. That Court was one of the weakest in history and ultimately produced a long period where deference to the Court was suspended. The New Deal–era Court was forced to fight back with both public statements asserting its efficiency and a change in voting patterns that more closely reflected the public's will. The danger to the Court of the creation of a public image diminishing the Court is real. The justices must engage in their own public relations strategies to prevent others from setting that image for them, an image that likely will not conform to their own desired one.

As discussed earlier, whether individual decisions shape long-term public opinion about the Court is questionable. Given the uncertainty of scholars, the justices cannot expect that their decisions will not affect public opinion of the institution. Hence, strategic external relations would appear necessary if it is the case that public opinion can be shaped by the justices, either through written opinions or via other means.

A variant of the strategy model then would posit that the justices engage not only in strategic internal negotiations with each other but also in external strategic behavior – that is, public relations – to achieve certain desired objectives such as institutional support for the Court. In this approach, the justices are external strategic actors who view the public as an important constituency and seek the public's diffuse support for the institution. They act strategically to preserve the institution from external threats.

As indicated previously, these strategic public relations acts do not exist in a vacuum. The justices are aware that the Court at any time may come under attack by various groups in society or even from other political players, such as the Congress or the presidency, who seek to use the Court for their own purposes. Such moves regarding the Court have been frequent in the Court's history as various players find political gain in taking on the justices. The Jefferson Republicans sought to undermine the Court in the early 1800s. Both pro- and antislavery forces assailed the Court in the pre–Civil War period. The Radical Republicans in the immediate aftermath of the war continued the assault. New Deal advocates joined in during the 1930s. More recently, both liberals and conservatives have criticized the Court in the past quarter century when decisions moved in directions they have opposed.

How do the justices engage in public relations in the face of external threats? The most obvious means is through written opinions. One example is the policy of public unanimity that John Marshall, as chief justice, enacted to shield the justices from attacks by Jefferson Republicans. Again in 1974, the justices were directly threatened with noncompliance by President Richard Nixon, who claimed he would abide by a split decision regarding the Watergate tapes. Joined by three Nixon appointees, the Court responded with a unanimous opinion opposing Nixon's position.[42]

The justices believe that their written opinions can affect how the public responds, not only to the Court's own policy resolution in the case at hand but also to the Court itself. They are sensitive to the effects their decisions have on public opinion and their own institution's role, as well as to the imperatives of "selling" their actions to a sometimes skeptical public. One example was the Court's handling of the segregation cases in the mid-1950s. In 1955, Justice Felix Frankfurter reminded his colleagues of their position when he admonished that "how we do what we do in the Segregation cases may be as important as what we do."[43]

Another means for response has occurred outside the realm of judicial opinions. This has included public letters, testimony to Congress, and speeches. An example of the use of public letters was the effort by Charles Evans Hughes, chief justice during the New Deal era when Roosevelt's Court-packing plan potentially undermined the independence of the Court. With the intent of shaping debate about the Court-packing plan, Hughes issued a public letter to Senator Burton K. Wheeler, Senate Judiciary Committee chair, refuting Roosevelt's claims about the Court.[44] An example of the role of congressional testimony is the regular appearance by select justices before Congress to discuss the judiciary's budget. Occasionally, the justices have used this forum to express institutional needs that could be met through legislation. The use of speeches is demonstrated by the examples discussed in the preface – that is, public addresses by Ruth Bader Ginsburg and Sandra Day O'Connor designed to blunt congressional Republican criticism of the Court.

The small size of the Court enhances the ability of the justices to engage in joint actions to preserve the institution in the face of some external menace. The advantage of small size is maintained by a norm of secrecy, the violation of which would expand the number of players involved in the Court's inner workings. As Brenner and Whitmeyer note, secrecy "lessens criticism of . . . Court actions, lessens the ability of outsiders to work the Court strategically, and garners the Court more mystery and respect."[45] This norm is usually maintained even in the face of competing individual-oriented goals.

The justices' public relations strategy is not wholly institutional. Justices may possess individual goals that are not necessarily shared by their colleagues. Even if others also possess those goals, justices still pursue them largely in a solitary fashion. These may include objectives such as influencing colleagues on the bench, affecting public policy debate generally, shaping (or reshaping) public opinion about an individual justice, or illuminating a justice's views beyond what is possible in joint opinions or opinions addressing a particular case.

On January 21, 2010, when the Court announced its decision in *Citizens United v. Federal Elections Commission,* John Paul Stevens read his dissent from the bench.[46] In fact, Stevens' reading of his dissent took twice as long as Anthony Kennedy's announcement of the majority opinion.[47] Was Stevens merely expressing himself, or was more going on? Stevens himself has suggested in the past that there is more to the act of reading a dissent than the mere expression of a contrary view. He once explained to a journalist that the reading of dissents by justices in the courtroom is a way to make sure the dissent does not get lost among the other news of the day.[48]

Such behavior is not limited to the bench. Various justices, particularly recent ones, have written books and articles for the general public, and others have given speeches to various public, nonlegal groups. As discussed previously, recent justices have conducted press interviews, participated in public forums, and delivered televised speeches. These may serve the purpose of defending the institution's power, but they also may serve a justice's individual purposes. For instance, near the end of his tenure, John Paul Stevens sat for an interview with Jeffrey Rosen during which Stevens elaborated at length on his role as a dissenter on the Court and spoke about his reaction to issues such as presidential power, abortion, and affirmative action.[49]

An individual justice's strategy may be primarily policy related. A justice may seek to change the opinions of colleagues, either directly through press messages or indirectly through press messages communicated to other political players who in turn shape colleagues' views. Alternately, the object of persuasion may be primarily or wholly external to the Court. A justice may seek to shape public opinion about a topic related to the Court, such as the role of the judiciary or the nature of constitutional interpretation. A justice also may wish to affect the actions of public policy makers outside the Court's current jurisdiction in areas such as foreign affairs or domestic policy. For example, Justice Louis Brandeis was called a "deeply involved reformer."[50] Brandeis sought to shape public policy in a number of areas including labor relations, civil liberties, and Zionism.

These public strategy objectives may be wholly personal in nature. One personal goal would be to shape historical perceptions of a justice's role on the Court, particularly at the end of his or her career. In 1994, Harry Blackmun used an interview at the time of his retirement to explain his own personal opposition to the death penalty despite the fact that he had voted frequently to uphold the practice.[51] Shortly before retiring, John Paul Stevens sat for several press interviews at the end of his Court career and explained his views and actions on a range of high-profile topics relative to the Court.[52]

Another goal would be to achieve popularity with the press. Conservatives have deemed this the "Greenhouse Effect," referring to Linda Greenhouse, who served as the *New York Times* reporter at the Court for two decades. The argument is that some justices like to see themselves spoken of positively in the newspapers and tilt their extrajudicial behavior, as well as their opinions, to achieve that goal.[53] Recent justices who have been accused of succumbing to the Greenhouse Effect are Sandra Day O'Connor, Anthony Kennedy, and Harry Blackmun – all Republicans who were perceived as conservatives when they joined the Court but became more moderate the longer they served. Although the movement of some conservatives to the left is clear, the question of whether it is caused by a desire for popularity with the press remains. And the shifting on the part of some Republican justices does not explain why just as many others – Rehnquist, Scalia, Burger, and Thomas – made no such move. Lawrence Baum suggests the difference is between those justices who have come to Washington to serve on the Court and those who were already in Washington. The former, he argues, are more susceptible to the Greenhouse Effect.[54] Two justices who would test Baum's hypothesis are Samuel Alito and John Roberts. One would expect Roberts to have remained to the right, while Alito would have shifted toward the left. However, after several years on the Court, there has been no evidence of Alito's expected ideological movement.

Another individual objective would be to achieve higher office, particularly the chief justiceship or the presidency or vice presidency. Throughout the history of the Court, a majority of justices have had some experience in political office prior to coming onto the Court. Nor have they been wholly immune to considering their position on the Court as a stepping-stone for another office. This includes movement while on the Court – from associate to chief – as well as from the Court to president or vice president or a prominent cabinet position. Appointment as chief is not a remote prospect for many associate justices. Four of the chief justices in the twentieth century had previously served as associate justices before their appointments, including, most recently, William Rehnquist. In the twenty-first century, Antonin Scalia, Anthony Kennedy, and Sandra Day O'Connor all were discussed as possible chief justice nominees.

Another motive could be to triumph in a personal conflict occurring on the Court. In the 1940s, Hugo Black and Robert Jackson engaged in a public feud about Black's refusal to recuse himself in a case and Black's efforts to undermine Jackson's possible appointment as chief justice. Several years earlier, Black, who was a brand-new justice, had been the subject of a press campaign by other justices to malign him as an incompetent member of the Court.[55]

The conflict may be ideological and not just personal. Are justices inclined to widen internal conflict to an external audience to win ideological or personal conflicts among themselves?[56] This may have occurred during the late 1980s and early 1990s, when pro-choice justices perceived that a pro-life majority was poised to erode *Roe v. Wade* and began to use speeches to criticize the majority. It may have happened again in the early 2000s, when Antonin Scalia went public to express his dissatisfaction about having to issue continual dissents from majority opinions written by swing justices such as Anthony Kennedy and Sandra Day O'Connor.[57]

PURSUING EXTERNAL STRATEGIES

Just as there may be multiple motivations for engaging in the pursuit of external strategies, there are also multiple methods for implementing those strategies. The external product with which justices are most commonly identified is the written opinion. This is particularly true when the justices act in concert to pursue institutional strategies. Court opinions like *Brown v. Board of Education* and *Roe v. Wade* intentionally reshaped public policy. Other opinions emerged in an atmosphere of external threat to the institution, including *Marbury v. Madison* (1803), *West Coast Hotel v. Parrish* (1937), and *United States v. Nixon* (1974). Each majority opinion was intended to address a challenge to the Court's power by the executive branch at a discrete point in U.S. history.

Moreover, those opinions are directed not just at the legal community. They also are intended to reach the public. Chief Justice Earl Warren urged his fellow justices to write opinions that laypeople could understand. He admonished that "opinions should be short, readable by the lay public, non-rhetorical, unemotional and, above all, non-accusatory."[58] Years later, John Roberts made the same point in a speech, saying that opinions should be accessible to the intelligent layperson and should not be lengthy and densely written, but accessible to the intelligent layperson and comprehensible to the public.[59]

Opinions also become important for individualistic external strategies. A dissenting opinion provides a justice with the opportunity to make a public statement separating him- or herself from the majority's will. Antonin Scalia characterized it as "you say what you want, and if somebody doesn't want to join it, who cares?"[60] The public nature of that separation may be intended as a message not only for fellow justices but also for the legal community and perhaps even for the general public at large. During the deliberations over *Brown v. Board of Education*, as well as subsequent cases involving race relations, the majority of the justices were sensitive to the possible actions of Southern justices, including Stanley Reed and Tom C. Clark, who might dissent from the majority opinion and offer moral support to the South's resistance.[61]

Even a concurring opinion can be an individualistic action designed to further an external strategy by announcing a separation from the Court's rationale while still agreeing with the overall outcome. In fact, concurring opinions may be even stronger signs of an individual-oriented public relations effort because they may be unnecessary to achieve the basic ends of the justice in terms of results, although not necessarily the rationale of the decision. Obviously, the justice has an audience with whom he or she wishes to communicate, requiring the justice to explain him- or herself even after he or she has ostensibly won. This could include communication with interest groups who seek to understand why a justice has voted in an unpredictable fashion or with a president who appointed the justice and may be unhappy with the appointee's decision.

Within an individual opinion, the direction or rationale is not the only consideration in conveying an external message. The tone of the language and the method of delivery also are highly significant. A tone of frustration and anger with the majority that borders on personal criticism will receive more press and public attention, as well as the notice of colleagues, than a mild-mannered content that merely takes issue with the direction of the Court's opinion. Also, a justice who delivers a dissenting or concurring opinion in full from the bench during an opinion announcement period (particularly when the opinion includes pointed criticism of other justices) signals to the press the intensity of feeling on the issue and the presence of profound conflict within the usually secretive conference room.

Still other methods within the confines of traditional judicial activity could include the acceptance of certain cases for hearing, the scheduling of argument, questioning in oral arguments, and the timing of decisions. In 1856, the Court delayed its decision in Dred Scott to avoid influencing the presidential elections that year.[62] In 1990, the Court declared that Congress' attempt to criminalize flag burning was unconstitutional. The decision was issued three days before Flag Day.[63]

These methods all fall within the heading of standard judicial activity. Justices could blunt criticism of using these tools for external public relations strategies by asserting that they are merely doing their job. They could reasonably claim that no strategic activity is involved. Rather, they are merely performing their assigned tasks.

However, there are still other available methods that do go beyond the norm of judicial behavior. These extrajudicial activities are not essential to their constitutional or statutory duties. Nevertheless, we know that justices engage in them. One such method is speeches. Speeches fall into two categories, one of which could be construed as efforts designed merely to engage the legal community. These include addresses to bar associations, federal appellate district conferences, law schools, and legal workshops. In recent years, several justices, such as Sandra Day O'Connor, Stephen Breyer, and Anthony Kennedy, have spoken at workshops sponsored by the Aspen Institute, and Samuel Alito, Clarence Thomas, and Antonin Scalia have been invited speakers at the Federalist Society.[64] Justices are frequent visitors to law schools throughout the nation.

The second category is different. Those consist of speeches beyond the legal community. These audiences may include college students, interest groups and associations, and even the press. For instance, during his three years on the Court in the 1960s, Arthur J. Goldberg gave numerous speeches to legal groups, as other justices often did. However, Goldberg also spoke to various other groups, including the Jewish Center for the United Nations, the American Israel Public Affairs Committee, and B'nai B'rith. These speeches often veered beyond traditional legal subjects for justices. Goldberg discussed racial discrimination, business-labor relations, U.S. foreign policy toward the Soviet Union and China, and peace in the Middle East. He even gave speeches to press groups, including the American Society of Newspaper Editors. In that speech, Goldberg admonished the press to do a better job in supplying the public with "accurate and comprehensive news coverage."[65]

Whether speaking to a legal group or some other audience, a justice typically understands that a much larger audience is accessible, particularly if the speech is televised. Justices can and do make news through such speeches. Indeed, they seek to do so. William O. Douglas once wrote to a reporter in 1948 that he had decided upon coming to the Court that he would not cease speaking out on national issues: "I cannot stand mute on important questions that transcend political or judicial considerations."[66] A few justices have sought to limit press access to their speeches to control the dissemination of their message. Others, however, have appeared in public knowing that their words would reach a larger audience than those physically present.

Still other methods are available to justices. However, they are more problematic because they delve into the realm of explicit press relations. These include direct contacts with journalists via press conferences and interviews.

Justices rarely hold press conferences. Typically, those only occur when a justice comes to the Court or leaves it. Because of the proscription on press conferences in terms of judicial norms, they have limited utility to a justice as a tool for external strategy. However, press interviews are a different story. Justices only infrequently make themselves available for on-record interviews, although several have granted on-record interviews in recent years. But they are willing to give off-the-record interviews to journalists.[67]

Justices, then, have various motives for developing and implementing public relations strategies. All of the justices share an institutional motive to protect the institution's power and, by extension, their own. Many also would seem to possess individual motives that would propel them to engage in external relations. Moreover, they possess the means to pursue institutional or individual public relations strategies, although those mechanisms are more limited than those available to an elected official.

Have those motives become more important in recent years? Do the justices have more cause to speak to the public today than their predecessors did? Could one of those motivations be that some justices "go public," which would seem to propel other justices to defend themselves or their views in public?

Finally, are those means for going public becoming more available to them as well? It would appear that more opportunities for carrying out external strategies are available today than a half century ago. Thirty years ago, C-SPAN was a new cable network focused on covering the proceedings of the U.S. House of Representatives. Television appearances by justices occurred rarely before the existence of this new public affairs cable network. Today, justices can appear regularly on C-SPAN through interviews and televised speeches and forums. The expansion of television networks and individual programs has provided access to television. Moreover, the programming of this new network conforms more closely to the justices' concerns about media outlets respecting the dignity of the Court.

Yet have those motivations and means actually changed in nature in recent years, as indicated by the possible extrajudicial public incidents discussed earlier? Alternately, perhaps the justices are not taking any actions on themselves but are merely being covered more by journalists who are fascinated by the Court.

It is important to note that the justices are hardly monolithic in their approach to the possession and employment of external strategies. The motive and the perception of the opportunity may vary across justices. Moreover, some may possess both but still conclude that it is not appropriate for them to engage in such behavior. Although Antonin Scalia, Stephen Breyer, John Roberts, and others have been willing to talk to the press in various ways, others have not. During a nineteen-year term in office, David Souter gave no on-record interviews and appeared infrequently in public forums.

Beyond the question of what is going on and how it fits historical patterns is another question about what all of this means. If this is a new phenomenon (or even just a reiteration of past practice), what are the implications for the Court's role in American government? Will higher profile justices lead to more or less capability for the Court to fulfill its role as arbiter in the American legal and political system?

These questions lead to several hypotheses that will be addressed in this book:

1. In an attempt to retain institutional power (and with it individual power), many of the justices at times have engaged in strategic external relations throughout the Court's history.
2. Those strategic external relations have been employed both for institutional and individual uses.
3. Strategic external relations have been used for individual purposes when:
    a. Justices anxious for higher office desire personal publicity to attain that office.
    b. Policy-oriented justices want to use the Court as a forum to shape larger policy debates.
    c. Retiring justices attempt to define their own legacies.
    d. Justices seek to send messages to each other that will change their colleagues' behavior.
4. The extent of use of strategic external relations for institutional purposes has varied over time depending on the existence of severe external threats to the Court from other political players and the extent of the justices' desire to settle public policy debates.

Before beginning to address these hypotheses, it is important to understand the contemporary forces that have affected justices' relations with the press and the public. Chapter 2 details those forces that have propelled the justices toward openness and offers explanations for the current Court's approaches to external relations.

2

The Pressure to Go Public

In 1990, the Supreme Court press corps held its traditional reception for a new justice joining the Court. That new justice, David Souter, mingled with reporters at the off-record session. At the end of the reception, however, Souter turned to the press corps and said: "Well, thank you for this. I enjoyed it. Let's do it again when I retire."[1]

The notion that a powerful individual in the shaping of public law and policy would not interact with the press throughout his tenure in office may seem shocking to most Americans, except when that person is a U.S. Supreme Court justice. In fact, Souter's attitude, in juxtaposition with his power, expresses the paradox for the Court. Although the justices desire to convey the image that they are above politics, in fact, as members of the third branch of government, they have a significant role in shaping public policy. That role places them in the midst of public policy debates and requires them to promote that desired image of distance to preserve their public policy role. Otherwise, they would be treated like other policy actors and lose their status as resolvers of public policy conflicts.

Formally, the justices' public approach to the press can be explained by a code of judicial ethics, which limits judicial behavior off the bench. Although U.S. Supreme Court justices technically are not bound by that code, they usually consider themselves constrained by it nonetheless. Their adherence to judicial ethics codes stems from their position at the pinnacle of the judicial system in the United States. As the most visible participants in the judicial system, they consider themselves models of behavior for their colleagues in lower federal and state courts.

However, written codes do not fully explain what the justices are doing in their relations with the press and the public. That explanation lies much deeper and speaks to the Court's basic position in American government. In short, that position is, by nature, precarious. As Alexander Hamilton wrote, the Court lacks the power of enforcement: "It may truly be said to have neither Force nor Will, but merely judgment."[2] The Court lacks coercive power to enforce its decisions. Therefore, public deference to the Court is the most powerful weapon in the justices' arsenal.

That deference stems from both the Court's stability as an institution during more than two hundred years of history, but also through its overt use of symbolism. The Court's stability as an institutional icon (including adherence to precedent, relative avoidance of public disputes among members, and typical caution in engaging in institutional conflict) has enhanced the Court's role as arbiter of political conflicts. Moreover, the Court's use of symbols – the Court's building, the cult of the robe, the raised bench – contributes to a sense of authority that legitimates the expectation of deference. Jeffrey Rosen has explained that "[e]verything about the Court's majestic rituals – from the white marble palace to the black robes – is designed to minimize the human element and to convey the impression that the Court's opinions are, if not the word of God, the impersonal pronouncements of a Delphic oracle."[3]

Public deference also emanates from the Court's ability to adapt to the changing climates of American politics and public opinion. During World War II, the Court acquiesced to the Roosevelt administration's popular plans for Japanese internment camps. Changes in some state abortion laws became evidence to Harry Blackmun and the Court's majority that society accepted more liberal abortion laws and that the Court should as well. David Souter used public opinion again nearly twenty years later to justify upholding the *Roe* decision on abortion while carving out a middle position between the pro-choice and pro-life camps.[4]

Still another reason for that deference is an approach exemplified by Souter's statement at his press reception. That is the avoidance of the appearance by the justices of influence over politicians or the public in political matters or even any involvement in politics. The traditional dearth of news conferences, press statements, on-the-record interviews, photo opportunities, or other mechanisms of overt public relations reinforces the conception of the justices as towering above such petty concerns as the current state of public opinion.

This does not mean the justices do not get attention from the press. Indeed, the Court can receive extensive ink and broadcast time when it issues decisions on highly controversial issues. Rather, it means that, historically, justices have attempted to divert such attention away from themselves personally and toward their products – the written opinions they issue. As a result, the justices traditionally have dwelt in an environment of relative anonymity as individuals.

Whereas the president enjoys widespread name and face recognition and congressional leaders are fairly well known because of their constant presence in the news, Supreme Court justices, particularly by contrast, are relatively invisible.

Typically, most of the general public cannot name any of them. (In fact, only half of the pubic knows there are nine justices. About one in five thinks there are ten or more.) Individual justices typically do worse. A 2006 FindLaw national survey found that only 43 percent of Americans could name a Supreme Court justice.[5] A Zogby poll in 2006 found that only 11 percent of Americans could name Samuel Alito as the newest Supreme Court justice five months after he had been confirmed. A year later, John Roberts was known by only 15 percent of Americans. But that number was still higher than the 13 percent who could recognize Roberts' predecessor, William H. Rehnquist.[6] However, by 2009, only 11 percent could recognize Roberts. Not surprisingly, the justice with the highest name recognition was Clarence Thomas (14 percent), whereas none of the other associate justices cracked the double digits. Only 1 percent could recognize John Paul Stevens (who had served for thirty-four years), Anthony Kennedy (twenty-one years), and Stephen Breyer (fifteen years).[7]

Some justices remain fairly anonymous throughout their tenure on the Court. For example, both Stevens and Breyer had the same amount of name recognition (1 percent) in 1995 that they had in 2009. In that year, 1995, Breyer had only been on the Court for one year, but Stevens had served for twenty years and still was unknown by virtually all Americans. In 1995, only 8 percent of Americans could name William Rehnquist as a member of the Court, even though he had been chief justice for nine years.[8]

Traditionally, name recognition by the general public has risen at two points in a justice's career. One is when he or she comes onto the Court. That happens because there is still some residual name recognition from the confirmation process. The other is when a justice retires or even nears retirement and speculation ensues about his or her pending departure from the Court. John Paul Stevens received the most news coverage of his career early in 2010 when he gave interviews suggesting he would retire soon.

Despite the plethora of information sources today – cable news channels, the Internet, talk radio, et cetera – if anything, the public's level of knowledge about the justices seems to have declined during the past several decades. In 1970, 22 percent of the public could name the chief justice at that time (Warrren Burger).[9] Burger had been in office for only one year. Thirty-five years later, John Roberts was recognized by only 16 percent of the public in his first year.

THE CHANGE

As discussed earlier, a change seems to have occurred in the public visibility of Supreme Court justices. From Antonin Scalia to Ruth Bader Ginsburg to Stephen Breyer, justices appear to have become more public figures during the past several years. What factors may be pressuring the justices to become more public? Several have played a role in raising the public profile of current justices. They include the judicial selection process; several high-impact, and therefore high public interest, decisions of the Court; changes in journalism; the celebrity culture in American society; and the role of television.

JUDICIAL SELECTION

One source of pressure is the nature of the modern judicial selection process. Traditionally, the judicial nomination process was the high point in a Supreme Court justice's public profile. The announcement of the presidential appointment, as well as the Senate's confirmation hearings and final vote, filled news media accounts for each new justice appointed to the Court. An appearance at the White House (sometimes in the Rose Garden or perhaps in the East Room) drew the new nominee into the usual saturation media coverage accorded the president. The high drama of the confirmation hearings attracted television cameras and tables filled with reporters from various news organizations taking notes on the proceedings.

Yet when the confirmation process ended, that extensive news coverage also stopped. The nominee retreated into a job shielded from (and even by) the press. One notable exception was the 1981 nomination of Arizona Supreme Court Justice Sandra Day O'Connor as the first female U.S. Supreme Court justice. Not surprisingly given the unique nature of her appointment, O'Connor's early days on the Court attracted greater-than-normal press and public attention for a new justice, although it was still miniscule compared with that accorded other political figures.

Then the Robert Bork nomination occurred. Although controversial nominations were not new in American political history, the Bork nomination established a new precedent. First, the whole process extended over a much longer period than any previous twentieth-century nomination. The Bork nomination meant that subsequent nomination processes would be longer than those in the pre-Bork era.[10] During that lengthy period, interest groups became major players in the confirmation process. This included not just the usual participants such as the American Bar Association but also a coalition of interest groups, many of which had never before taken a position on a

Supreme Court nomination. The Bork nomination also occurred at a time when ideological legal groups were beginning to evolve. On the left, Alliance for Justice formed in 1979, and People for the American Way appeared about two years later. On the right came the Federalist Society, 1982; the American Center for Law & Justice, 1990; and the Institute for Justice, 1991. These groups became new and formidable players in the Supreme Court nomination process, particularly because presidents paid attention to them during the nominee selection stage and senators cooperated with them during the confirmation process.

Not only were more groups involved but the tactics of opponents also ventured into new territory. These groups not only lobbied senators on prospective confirmation votes but they also turned to media strategies. Full-page newspaper advertisements excoriated Bork and urged readers to write to their senators to oppose the nominee. Television advertisements featuring actor Gregory Peck warned that Bork would set back the cause of civil rights. Given the intensity of the conflict, the amount of news coverage far exceeded that accorded recent Supreme Court nominations. As a result, public consciousness of a nominee was raised to new heights.

Yet only four years later, the Clarence Thomas nomination garnered even more public attention. One factor was Thomas' role as only the second African American nominated for the Court. Another was the tenuous nature of the ideological balance on the Court and Thomas' role in switching Justice Thurgood Marshall's seat from a liberal bastion to a conservative one. The abortion issue also hinged on Marshall's replacement, as Marshall was one of a dwindling group of justices in the *Roe* majority in 1973. All of these factors guaranteed widespread opposition to the appointment. Nevertheless, the conventional wisdom was that, despite a large number of opposition votes, Thomas eventually would be confirmed.

However, the second stage of the hearings following Anita Hill's charges of sexual harassment turned the confirmation story from an ideological news angle to a more titillating one involving sex and employer-employee relations. With its competing story lines of sexual harassment by an employer or a "high-tech lynching" by a disgruntled employee aided by the press, depending on who was believed, the second stage of the Judiciary Committee hearings garnered saturation media coverage. Although Thomas, unlike Bork, did take his seat on the Court, questions of whether the nomination process had irrevocably changed lingered long afterward. Subsequent nominations have not featured the soap-opera drama of the second round of Senate Judiciary Committee hearings in the Thomas confirmation process, but they have included traits found in both the Bork and Thomas nominations – a lengthy process stretching over months rather than weeks or days, elongated televised confirmation hearings, lobbying by various interest groups, and frequent public opinion polls measuring the public's views of the nominee.

Yet the Bork and Thomas nominations may well have accelerated a trend that was already occurring. Nomination processes had become increasingly contentious during the nearly twenty-year-period since the Bork nomination. Thurgood Marshall's nomination in 1967 as associate justice engendered widespread opposition from Southern senators. Justice Abe Fortas' nomination for chief justice foundered in 1968 when Fortas withdrew his name amid charges of cronyism with President Lyndon Johnson and the prospect of a Republican filibuster in the Senate. Similarly, Nixon appointee Judge Clement Haynsworth failed to win confirmation in 1969, as did the following Nixon appointee, G. Harrold Carswell, in 1970.

At the same time, highly political efforts were under way to create appointments on the Court in order to shape it to the liking of successive administrations. Lyndon Johnson essentially compelled Justice Tom C. Clark to retire when he appointed Clark's son, Ramsey, as U.S. attorney general. Clark's retirement allowed Johnson to appoint the first African American to the court, Thurgood Marshall, and to shift the Court from the somewhat more conservative Clark to the decidedly more liberal Marshall. Then the Nixon administration successfully forced Fortas to resign from the Court in 1969 under an ethical cloud.[11]

When appointments could not be made, the next tactic was intimidation of sitting justices. In 1970, the Nixon administration persuaded Representative Gerald Ford, then the House minority leader, to instigate impeachment charges against William O. Douglas. Although the effort was unsuccessful, as the administration knew it would be, it signaled to Douglas, as well as to other justices, that the administration was willing to "play hardball" with the Court. Ironically, it was Ford, later as president, who accepted Douglas' reluctant retirement and appointed his successor, John Paul Stevens.

Regardless of the starting point, Supreme Court judicial selection is a process that is no longer elite driven, with senators acquiescing to the president's choice, as was true for most of the twentieth century. Rather, it is a process that includes the press, a multitude of concerned interest groups, and the public. Nominees who emerge from that process, if they emerge at all, have been scrutinized by the press and opposition groups while they have become well-known figures through news stories and television confirmation hearing appearances during a several-month-long period. They may retreat into anonymity subsequently as they join the bench, but the previous anecdotes suggest that in the future that may no longer be the case.

HIGH-PROFILE CASES

The Court seems to have enjoyed a consistently high profile during the past half century or so because of the types of decisions it has rendered on controversial social policy issues. In 1954, the *Brown v. Board of Education* decision elicited widespread attention as a landmark case on a topic of intense public conflict. But that was only the beginning of a succession of social policy related issues that have reached the Court. As a result, the Court has become the final arbiter on a wide range of issues that intensely affect people's lives. This has been true in the last half of the twentieth century and also in the early years of the twenty-first. These include school desegregation, school busing, affirmative action, abortion, gay rights, and the right to die, among others. These issues – where they send their children to school, whether they can get employment or a promotion, and whether a woman can obtain an abortion – either directly affect millions of Americans or indirectly affect many others who view them as symbols of increased social tolerance or rapid moral decline.

The Court's public profile has occurred partly because of its entrance into public debate on these issues that carry their own public importance, even prior to the Court's attention to them. Each time the Court makes decisions on already high-profile issues, the Court's profile increases as well. These range from *Lawrence v. Texas* in 2003 (gay rights) to *Columbia v. Heller* in 2008 (gun control) to *Citizens United v. FEC* in 2010 (campaign finance). That attention to the Court is manifested in brief but often-intense press coverage of the Court's actions. When other players comment as well, the story continues further. For example, the Court's action in *Citizens United* was additionally publicized by President Obama's pointed criticism of it during a State of the Union address a week after the decision was announced.

Nor do the issues necessarily diminish once the Court has ruled. Instead, the Court's decisions spark public action. The *Brown* case led to massive resistance in the South but also to dramatic shifts within the Democratic Party to embrace civil rights and isolate its former base of white Southerners. The *Roe* case similarly created the pro-life movement and affected state and national legislation, presidential campaigns, and the judicial nomination process for years to come. The continued public turmoil produced successive cases on these topics, thus further intertwining the Court with these high-profile issues. In turn, that repeated intersection enhanced press and public attention to the Court's work and the ideological leanings of the justices as well as of Supreme Court nominees.

The public impression may be that these cases are all the Court attends to. The Court's willingness to handle these cases places it in the public spotlight once again regarding that particular issue each time the Court addresses it. The public perceives the Court as a powerful public policy maker. A 1987 poll found that 59 percent believed the Court plays a very important role in national policy making. However, even though the Court handles some high-profile issues and is perceived as a highly significant player, and therefore a potentially controversial policy player, approval of the Court also remains high, particularly compared with other institutions of government.[12]

CHANGES IN JOURNALISM

In the latter half of the twentieth century, the Court dealt with a changed media environment. One of those changes was journalists' treatment of the Court. When journalists began to adopt a "new journalism" in the 1960s and 1970s advocating more scrutiny of public officials, the adversarial role of the press, and a penchant for investigative journalism in the style of Watergate's Bob Woodward and Carl Bernstein, the Court did not emerge unscathed. It was touched to a lesser extent than other institutions such as the presidency and the Congress, yet it was not unaffected.

The Brethren, an account of the Burger Court, appeared in 1979. The provocative book, co-authored by Woodward and fellow *Washington Post* reporter Scott Armstrong, was an inside look at the Burger Court by an icon in American journalism who had uncovered Watergate. Unlike the vast majority of books about the Court, *The Brethren* treated the highest court as primarily a political institution and the justices themselves as individuals adopting political methods to achieve their goals. The book followed the justices as they decided controversial cases from 1969 to 1974. Those years were pivotal in the Court's jurisprudence as it decided cases regarding executive power, abortion, school busing, and freedom of the press.

Through anonymous sources, Woodward and Armstrong revealed the justices' attempts to lobby one another, their personal animosities toward each other, and the influences of current events and public opinion on their decisions. It was a rare inside look at a secretive institution and exposed the justices as political players as much as legal arbiters. Woodward purposely sought to portray the justices as human beings who, despite the official public image of the Court, were driven by personal passions and strong political considerations. The aim of *The Brethren* was not totally new. William O. Douglas once admitted that "we're not entirely rational in our decisions."[13] But such candor was rare. Woodward sought to make transparent what Douglas had alluded to. He also encouraged other journalists to do the same. In fact, Woodward publicly chastised other reporters for not being aggressive enough in covering the Court. He hoped to shape future coverage of the Court by asserting that "the courts are a political institution and we [the press] don't cover them as such."[14]

Like *All the President's Men*, *The Brethren* had a significant impact on journalists. Following Woodward's lead, some other reporters began to view the Court as an institution full of individuals with political goals. At the *New York Times*, Stuart Taylor paid close attention to the justices' speeches, not just their decisions. Similarly, ABC News reporter Tim O'Brien sought to scoop his peers by digging for unreleased information he could report on. Richard Carelli, an Associated Press reporter, explained once that he felt the personal context of a justice's opinion was important for the public to understand:

> When Justice Stevens writes an opinion about parental rights, we can put in the story that this author is himself the adoptive parent of two children. It adds something for the readers, an appreciation of where this guy is coming from.[15]

Not all reporters shared the Woodward and Armstrong approach. Many opposed it and viewed it as unnecessary to do their job. Some believed that even if they received a draft of an opinion before it was circulated, they should not use it. Nor would they go out of their way to obtain such information.[16] Justice Lewis Powell referred to this camp of Supreme Court reporters when he commented that they "deserve a great deal of credit for not making efforts to ascertain information that would be very easy to obtain if one put his or hand to doing so...."[17]

The Brethren may have emboldened some of the justices to be more open about themselves and their colleagues. During the 1980s, Harry Blackmun became increasingly candid about his colleagues. He used one speech to assess publicly each of their personalities. In addition, he speculated on how his colleagues would vote in the *Webster* case before the Court had even heard oral arguments. Blackmun said: "Will Roe v. Wade go down the drain? I think there's a very distinct possibility that it will, this term. You can count the votes." Similarly, John Paul Stevens used a high-profile speech to express his despair about the rightward shift of the Court.[18]

The publication of *The Brethren* concerned some of the justices as a serious breach of the institution's use of secrecy to protect itself from external criticism. Warren Burger, particularly, was angry about the leaks that emanated from the Court in the writing of *The Brethren*, and he convinced the other justices to institute new guidelines on clerks' interaction with reporters. However, eventually the book paved the way for similar journalistic accounts of the Court.

One group that may be following Woodward's lead in the twenty-first century is the blogosphere.[19] The justices, the nomination process, and the Court itself have all become regular blog topics. Some of the leading political bloggers are attorneys, such as John Hindraker and Scott Johnson of *Powerline*, or law school professors, such as Glenn Reynolds, *Instapundit*; Hugh Hewitt; and Eugene Volokh, *The Volokh Conspiracy*. In addition, other bloggers specializing in the Supreme Court have acquired a niche within the blogger community. Their approach focuses on personalities along with cases. One example is SCOTUS blog, which offers texts of cert petitions and opinions, transcripts of oral arguments, and extensive discussion of judicial selection. It also occasionally discusses the personalities on the bench. Dahlia Lithwick at *Slate* goes even further in focusing on the individual justices, commenting on Alito, Roberts, and Scalia's new vigor in oral argument questioning, calling John Paul Stevens the "court's last negotiator and bridge builder," and noting that Antonin Scalia's "hide is tougher than a rhino's."[20]

CELEBRITY CULTURE

Another factor is a celebrity culture that makes known personalities the substance of news.[21] This ranges from sports figures to entertainment stars to politicians. The application of the celebrity culture to politics was even a theme of the 2008 presidential campaign, with Senator John McCain criticizing the rock star status of Barack Obama. Attention to Obama was not the only evidence of celebrity status of politicians. Politicians grace the covers of entertainment magazines as well as tabloids. On talk shows, they sit in the same seats as entertainment celebrities and are interviewed in similar ways by talk show hosts as they discuss their families, their favorite books, and even their top-ten lists.

Supreme Court justices have enjoyed some celebrity status in Washington. They have long been on the social register and gain notice at Washington social functions. But that celebrity status typically has not extended to the nation at large. As indicated earlier, most justices are virtually unknown to the American public. Supreme Court justices do not make the top-ten lists of celebrities, or even the top one hundred.

However, to the extent that there have been exceptions to that rule, they have occurred within the last quarter century. A couple of the justices in recent years – Sandra Day O'Connor and Clarence Thomas – acquired something like a celebrity status, again, at least for Supreme Court justices. O'Connor did so for being the first woman justice on the Court. Thomas' notoriety arose from confirmation hearings that gained a level of saturation media coverage unknown to such hearings before or since. The hearings made Thomas a well-known celebrity, and that celebrity status was reinforced when Thomas and his wife appeared on the cover of *People* magazine. Thomas also has been active in giving speeches across the nation, often attracting opposition from various organizations and the resulting news attention.[22]

With most Americans unable to recall the name of a single justice, the status of justices is far from that of entertainment or sports celebrities. Nor is it likely to reach such heights. Yet in comparison with their predecessors, some of the justices do get more attention, and that attention appears to be personal and not just job related.

THE INFLUENCE OF TELEVISION

Confirmation hearings in the latter half of the twentieth century were characterized by a new feature – television coverage. When television appeared in the 1950s, Americans embraced the new medium. So did politicians. President Dwight Eisenhower made the televised press conference a staple of White House communications. Congress also invited television cameras to cover congressional hearings in the 1950s and 1960s. Floor coverage took longer. The U.S. House allowed broadcasting of floor proceedings in 1978, which created the C-SPAN network. The U.S. Senate followed eight years later.[23]

Because television cameras covered committee hearings, they also altered the judicial selection process. Prior to television, the Senate Judiciary Committee typically did not hold hearings on Supreme Court nominees. When they did, the nominee usually was not invited to testify. When William O. Douglas was confirmed to the Court in 1939, he waited patiently outside the committee room to be called for questioning until he was told that the Senate Judiciary Committee had no questions for him.[24]

Also, those confirmation processes, which lacked Senate Judiciary Committee hearings and television cameras, occurred within days or weeks (and sometimes hours) of a presidential nomination. Hence, there was little opportunity for most Supreme Court nominees to become well known outside Washington through that process. The exceptions were the controversial nominations such as Louis Brandeis and John J. Parker, which only confirmed the rule.

Yet national media coverage of nominations, particularly live television coverage of confirmation hearings, changed the process from one that was elite driven to one that was mass oriented. With that change came the need for the White House to "sell" the Supreme Court nominee to the public to garner public approval, interest group quiescence, and eventual Senate confirmation. Similarly, the opposition to a nominee employed the news media, including television, to blunt the White House's efforts. These efforts range from televised testimony against a nominee (such as that of Anita Hill) to televised press conferences and photo ops to television ads (such as those run against Robert Bork) urging Americans to oppose the nomination.[25]

Celebrity culture is intertwined with the emergence of television. Discussion of television as a cutting-edge technology may seem odd today. After all, television's breakthrough in reaching a mass audience in the United States occurred a half century ago. However, the Court has been slow to embrace television. The early exposure to television for the justices was the issue of cameras in the courtroom, which the justices addressed in the 1960s. At the time, they were fearful of the effects of television cameras on the ability of the judicial process to work. Jurors would be more inclined to be influenced by public opinion, they reasoned. In fact, potential jurors might even be more difficult to locate in the first place. The presence of the cameras would inhibit witnesses while emboldening attorneys who would play to the court of public opinion rather than the Court. In *Estes v. Texas*, Tom C. Clark declared for the Court that "television, in its present state and by its very nature, reaches into a variety of areas in which it may cause prejudice to an accused."[26]

In extrajudicial statements, justices have expressed similar sentiments when considering television in their own courtroom. William O. Douglas wrote to the Judicial Council of California expressing his gratitude for its decision to ban broadcasting from state courtrooms. Douglas stated that "the courtroom should be a quiet, dignified place, not under the extra tensions of a theatrical production."[27] In recent years, each confirmation hearing has included a question about televising the Court's public sessions, and each nominee has expressed qualified support for the idea. However, after justices go onto the Court, their opinions seem to shift. Antonin Scalia said that he was in favor of cameras in the courtroom when he first joined the Court but later said "I am less and less so. . . ."[28] Despite congressional opening of its doors to television cameras, the Supreme Court has rejected continual pleading from broadcast organizations, particularly C-SPAN, to allow television broadcasting of oral arguments or decision announcements. Even after three justices sat for a mock televised Court session, no change was made.[29]

The justices' resistance was understandable. For the justices, allowing television coverage was not merely about the placement of a camera at a discreet location in the courtroom. Rather, such coverage represented the collapse of their strategy of placing public attention on their products – their written opinions – rather than on themselves. Justices would become celebrities, particularly in today's celebrity culture. Unlike the print media, where the occasional interaction with print journalists could be masked through background interviews, television offered no such anonymity. Broadcast journalists wanted pictures. A justice interviewed for a television news story, or who actually sat for a fully taped interview, would be publicly identified. And even worse, regular television broadcasts of the Court's public sessions would magnify public awareness of the justices as individuals.

The demand for the Court to bow to the television age increased when state courts began to open their sessions to television coverage. Television cameras became smaller and more inconspicuous and seemed less obtrusive to the judicial process, particularly if the jury remained hidden outside camera range. When federal courts experimented with television coverage, the Supreme Court did not seem far behind. However, the Court bucked the trend and remained closed to cameras.

That reluctance to have the Court on camera also was extended to the justices themselves. Prior to the 1980s, the justices almost never appeared on television. Even on the rare occasions when they were did, they demanded control. William O. Douglas wrote to a local television reporter in 1974 that he asked not to be taped when he was speaking extemporaneously or answering questions. He allowed taping when he was giving a prepared speech. He said he made that distinction because unethical reporters would take his statements out of context.[30]

But most of the justices have adapted to cameras, at least with regard to themselves. So far they have not budged on the issue of television coverage of their institution's formal activities, such as decision announcements or oral arguments, but they have opened up to the idea of television coverage of themselves. Indeed, as mentioned earlier, justices have become frequent speakers or interview subjects on C-SPAN and even in other settings.

This change has come in two ways. First, the justices are allowing television cameras to record their speeches. The justices are routinely covered by television cameras as they appear before various types of audiences: law school student groups, legal organizations, and bar associations. C-SPAN also has created a program called "America and the Courts" that regularly features televised speeches by Supreme Court justices. Usually these speeches do not make the national news. But, unlike in the past, television cameras would be there to record the events if they did.

Justices also are participating in televised forums, including debates with each other. Scalia, Breyer, and O'Connor participated in a televised "constitutional conversation" at the National Archives three months before O'Connor retired in 2005. During the session, the three justices sparred genially about constitutional interpretations. The appearance was unusual in that three justices appeared on camera simultaneously. Breyer and Scalia also have appeared together in several settings, including at a televised forum at the Supreme Court building. The two justices used the occasion to express their differences on interpreting the Constitution and their proper approach to judging.[31] It is ironic that the justices relate that they do not debate issues in their conferences (rather that they merely state their positions and vote), but they have become willing to conduct public debates with each other. Admittedly, the topics are not the same. They have not used such forums to discuss current cases. However, they have debated issues related to how they do their job.

Second, televised interviews appear to have become more routine. As discussed previously, television appearances by the justices seem to have increased in the 1980s and the 1990s. Those appearances usually occurred on C-SPAN. C-SPAN became the kind of respectful venue for justices' television appearances that overrode their fear of publicity. In the 1990s and early 2000s, Brian Lamb was able to persuade several justices, including William Rehnquist, Antonin Scalia, and Sandra Day O'Connor, to sit for interviews broadcast on the network.

In 2009, C-SPAN interviewed all of the current justices of the Supreme Court and posted the video and transcripts of those interviews on its Web site. The interview content avoided current cases. However, the interviews did offer human perspectives on the justices. They discussed what it was like on their first day at the Court and their childhoods. Ruth Bader Ginsburg talked about her mother's death on the day she graduated from high school and revealed that her mother's death "was one of the most trying times in my life, but I knew that she wanted me to study hard and get good grades and succeed in life so that's what I did."[32] Antonin Scalia admitted that cert petitions are the most uninteresting part of a justice's job and that he hates Fourth Amendment cases.[33]

Yet the justices have ventured beyond C-SPAN. Stephen Breyer appeared on the *Larry King Live* program. Sandra Day O'Connor, Antonin Scalia, and Stephen Breyer were interviewed by Charlie Rose on his PBS interview program; William Rehnquist even appeared on the program three times.[34] The justices are not necessarily avoiding television; they are just selective about which venues they use.

Still another explanation stems from the justices themselves. Like any other group of people, the justices vary in their personalities. Some, such as Antonin Scalia, Stephen Breyer, and Sonia Sotomayor, are extroverts who seem to enjoy the limelight. Byron White and David Souter, by contrast, were iconoclasts who not only made no effort to attract publicity, but they actually shunned it. Those who are extroverts may relish the opportunity to speak out in forums, speeches, and even in interviews.

One example of the extrovert is Antonin Scalia. Scalia is a popular social figure in Washington. He enjoys socializing with Katherine Graham and Phyllis Schafly. A Washington magazine noted that "unlike many of the other justices, who by virtue of age or health or personal inclination prefer only the most limited social lives conducted over sedate dinners in private homes, Scalia circulates happily and easily in Washington's more public social swirl."[35] Indeed, Scalia seems limited by the stage of the courtroom in the Supreme Court building. He is animated in oral argument and appears to enjoy mixing comedy and pathos in his oral argument questioning. Similarly, the sharp tone of his opinions also begs for a broader audience than those situated in the courtroom or even the legal community poring over his written words. With the celebrity culture, the presence of television, and the nature of some of their personalities, it should not be a surprise that some justices, like Scalia, would venture out of the Court's previous norms and become more visible.

THE COURT AS AN OBJECT OF PUBLIC ATTENTION

The justices themselves have taken on controversial social issues, each of which enhances their public profile. Had the Court not taken on abortion, gay rights, affirmative action, the right to die, and so on, they would not have garnered the press attention they have received during the past quarter century. Admittedly, the justices' own official actions have led to press and public notice. Nor was this effort unintentional, particularly for justices who seek to shape public policy.

But external forces also are pushing the justices to "go public." Justices today are selected through a confirmation process that is longer, more controversial, and more public than ever before. They exist within a celebrity culture that emphasizes personalities, including those in politics. Additionally, they are faced with the demands of television to make themselves more visible to the public (even though they continue to resist applying that change to their formal roles), and journalists' approaches to the Court have shifted toward covering the justices as individuals and the Court itself as more of a political institution. All of these factors have placed pressure on the justices to become more open to the press and the public and to develop external relations strategies that will help them navigate through a political and social environment affected by media.

Clearly, the increased attention that justices have received, and may even solicit, is not comparable to that accorded the president or party leaders in Congress. Justices still do infrequently what the president, presidential candidates, members of Congress, governors, and other politicians do constantly – hold press conferences, sit for on-record interviews, issue dozens of press releases, and hire individual press relations staffs, among other practices. Moreover, it is necessary to emphasize that not all recent justices have abandoned the traditional avoidance of extrajudicial attention. For the vast majority of his time on the Court, John Paul Stevens avoided on-the-record interviews, public forums, or controversial speeches. Again, David Souter was a recluse compared with some of his colleagues. Whether there will continue to be recluses in the future is an open question.

A change seems to have occurred. Antonin Scalia explained in a television interview why he had altered his approach to publicity:

[T]hat's one reason I've sort of come out of the closet and – in recent months – done more interviews and allowed my talks to be televised more than I did formerly. I've sort of come to the conclusion that the old common law tradition of judges not making public spectacles of themselves and hiding in the grass has just broken down. It's no use, I'm going to be a public spectacle whether I come out of the closet or not. . . . [36]

If the other justices are like Scalia and have decided that they, too, will get publicity no matter whether they "go public" or not, then does this suggest a unprecedented and dramatic change in justice-journalist relations? To answer that question, it is necessary to go back in time to examine how justices and journalists interacted in earlier days. Have justices in the past "gone public" as well? Did they follow the press and use that press attention as justices seem to today? The next three chapters answer those questions.

3

The Early Years

On February 1, 1790, Chief Justice John Jay convened the first session of the newly created United States Supreme Court. The justices, properly attired in black and red robes, sat on a high bench before spectators who included the mayor of New York, the sheriff, New York judges, and a host of other dignitaries. However, only when the fourth of the six newly appointed justices arrived the next day did the Court actually begin its business. What business the Court had to conduct was primarily ceremonial. After only ten days, the Court adjourned for six months.[1]

But the session did receive press notice. One newspaper reported that the new body's first meeting attracted more attention than "any other event connected with the new Government." Stories about the new Court were printed in newspapers throughout the nation.[2] Such extensive press coverage of the Court would not be a regular occurrence, however. From the origins of the Court, the justices have received press coverage when newspapers felt the Court was newsworthy. The press thoroughly covered the landmark case of *Marbury v. Madison* in 1803. One national newspaper devoted three of its issues to coverage of the decision, and two others devoted two.[3] A New York newspaper, anticipating the case of *Gibbons v. Ogden*, said that "[i]nquiries are hourly made respecting the anxiously-looked-for decision of the Supreme Court in this important case."[4]

Yet even in the beginnings of the Court, news coverage of the justices was overshadowed by that of other institutions. When John Marshall became the new chief justice in February 1801, few people attended the ceremony, and the press largely ignored it. Instead, newspapers of the day were filled with news about the House of Representatives voting on who the new president would be – Thomas Jefferson or Aaron Burr.[5]

JUSTICES' POLITICAL BACKGROUNDS

In many ways, press relations of the justices were much as they are today. Press attention to the Court was dwarfed by the press' preoccupation with the other national government branches. In others ways, though, there were stark differences. One of those differences was the justices' previous familiarity with the press because of the positions they had held prior to joining the Court. Unlike today's justices, many early justices were as much politicians as jurists. The first chief justice, John Jay, had limited judicial experience; he had served briefly as chief justice of the state of New York immediately following national independence. However, he did have a comprehensive political background. Prior to his appointment as chief justice, he had served as minister of Spain for the new country and then later as secretary of foreign affairs for the Confederation Congress. He had been a member of the Continental Congress and a member of the Council of Safety for New York.[6]

Jay's lack of significant judicial experience before joining the highest court in the new nation was not unusual. Judicial positions existed in the new states, but such experience was not a prerequisite for appointment to the U.S. Supreme Court. In fact, some of the most prominent members of the new Court had little or no judicial experience. Justice James Wilson was a prominent lawyer who was an active participant in the shaping of the U.S. Constitution at the Federal Convention in 1787, but he had never served as a judge. Justice William Paterson also had been a member of the Continental Congress and a delegate to the Federal Constitutional Convention and had served as a U.S. senator and state attorney general. Again, his career had not included a position as a judge. James Iredell had served as a judge in North Carolina, but only for a short time. His most prominent position had been state attorney general.[7] During the period from 1812 to 1823, the justices on the Marshall Court included four who had been state supreme court justices. However, that court also included five who had been legislators, including two who had been speakers of their respective state legislatures.[8]

Some of the early justices did have substantial judicial experience. Chief Justice John Rutledge, an associate justice from 1789 to 1791, had served on the South Carolina Court of Chancery. Prior to his recess appointment as chief justice in 1795, Rutledge spent four years as chief justice of the South Carolina Court of Common Pleas and Sessions. Justice Samuel Chase was a chief justice of the Maryland Supreme Court; Justice James Blair was a judge in Virginia for more than a decade before his appointment to the Supreme Court; and Chief Justice Oliver Ellsworth served five years as a Connecticut state judge.[9]

But even these justices had substantial political careers as well. Rutledge was president and then governor of South Carolina, in addition to his service in the Continental Congress and at the Constitutional Convention in 1797. Chase spent twenty years in the Maryland General Assembly and was Maryland's representative in the Continental Congress. Blair served in the Virginia House of Burgesses and as a member of the governor's advisory council, and Ellsworth served in the Continental Congress as a delegate to the Federal Convention in 1787 and was a U.S. senator from Connecticut for seven years.

The point is not that men of significant judicial experience could not have been selected. The federal district courts were new, but each state had its own judicial system, including a state supreme court. They had existed for more than a dozen years prior to the creation of the U.S. Supreme Court. Moreover, state courts had been active in defining the role of the judicial branch at the state level prior to the ratification of the U.S. Constitution.[10] That experience should have made state court justices the prime candidates for the U.S. Supreme Court. Some were drawn from those ranks, but the early justices seemed to be those like Jay, Marshall, and Wilson, who had experience in national government (or the creation of the national government).

Of course, Supreme Court service in those early years was not necessarily viewed as the pinnacle of one's career. In fact, a Supreme Court justice-ship was not considered an attractive position in the first place. Government compensation repelled some nominees who felt they could not live on a jus-tice's salary. Initially, justices received no compensation for expenses and had no money for staff.[11] Turnover was high for the original Court, particularly because justices were required to spend many weeks and months riding their circuits to preside over trial courts. Their sense of service had to be strong enough to endure the rigors of serving as a Supreme Court justice. James Iredell wrote that "the duty will be severe."[12] The most physically taxing part of the job was the circuit riding. The Judiciary Act of 1789 mandated that the justices personally preside over circuit court trials. The combination of a large geographical area to cover, as well as the then-current state of poor roads and lodgings in the new country, made circuit riding an onerous task for justices. One justice described how he traveled nineteen hundred miles to cover one circuit. Some nominees declined appointment because of this expected duty. Others suffered health problems that may have hastened their resignations or deaths.[13]

Nor was service on the Supreme Court viewed as a barrier to supplemental political service. While serving as the first chief justice, John Jay served as a foreign affairs advisor to President George Washington.[14] Jay even negotiated the controversial Jay Treaty, which sparked large-scale protests and contributed to the partisan cleavage between Federalists and Republicans. Similarly, the second chief justice, Oliver Ellsworth, led a delegation to France to negotiate with Napoleon's government on U.S. shipping. Early Court justices also provided private counsel to the president and Congress. Both John Jay and Oliver Ellsworth offered advisory opinions to the Washington administration on legal matters as well as other issues. The justices also commented on pending legislation in Congress and even wrote drafts of bills.[15]

The justices' service off the bench was not limited to official government positions or advising. Some of them became involved in electoral politics. Oliver Ellsworth allowed his name to be put forward as a candidate for president while he was chief justice. He lost to John Adams. In 1828, while serving on the Court, Justice Smith Thompson ran for governor of New York to help John Quincy Adams carry the state.[16] John Jay twice ran for governor of New York while serving as chief justice. He was denied election the first time (1792) because of a technicality, but he was elected in 1795 and left the Court that year.

Election to public office in the 1790s was a different process than it would be two centuries later. Candidates, even those not on the Supreme Court, usually did not campaign publicly. However, in the case of Jay, a campaign did take place, but Jay did little publicly to support his own campaign. Nevertheless, Jay met with the same kind of partisan criticism any other gubernatorial candidate would have received. One opponent wrote a pseudonymous newspaper essay addressed to "Timothy Tickler, C-J-of the U-S-." The essay accused Jay of having "an overweening ambition" and "a cold heart."[17] In an era of pseudonymous essays hurling charges back and forth during the campaign, Jay responded with a rare public letter asserting that he was not the author of any published newspaper essays.[18]

Other justices did not run for office themselves but campaigned on behalf of others. Samuel Chase stumped for and against various candidates. He campaigned for his cousin, who was running as a presidential elector in 1800. He spoke against a Maryland candidate running for the state legislature.[19] He also delivered speeches in the 1800 presidential election, campaigning vigorously for the unsuccessful reelection bid of John Adams. Chase's politicking drew attacks from the Republican press supporting Thomas Jefferson for president. One paper charged it was a "spectacle to see Chase mounted on a stump, with a face like a full moon, vociferating in favor of the present President."[20] In 1828, Justice Bushrod Washington attended a Virginia political convention for John Quincy Adams. The same year, Justice Joseph Story wrote a book review criticizing the democratic forces that were about to prevail in the presidential election. In fact, during that election year, only one of the justices avoided political involvement in the presidential campaign.[21]

NOT POLITICALLY SEPARATE AND DISTINCT

Service on the Supreme Court during its early years did not mean that justices
were separated from politics. Even in the physical arrangements for the Court,
that sense of distance was not present. The Supreme Court building today is
a majestic structure that sits across First Street, N.E., from the U.S. Capitol
building. Like the White House, the Court sits apart from the Capitol. However, it was not until 1935 that the Court possessed its own building. After the
seat of government moved to Washington in 1800, no separate facilities were
provided for the Court. Instead, the Court met in a committee room under
the House of Representatives chamber. The Court spent most of its history
in a courtroom in a basement underneath the Senate chambers in the U.S.
Capitol building. The facilities were so cramped that the justices had to put
on their robes in front of the assembled audience.[22] Justices had no offices;
they worked from their homes.

Nor was the Court perceived as separate by others in national government.
Both Federalists and Republicans viewed the Court as a vehicle for further-
ing their own political agendas. The Republicans, who faced a Federalist-
dominated Supreme Court long after they had taken control of the White
House and Congress, considered the Court as a primarily political institution.
"The constitution . . . is a mere thing of wax in the hands of the judiciary,
which they may twist and shape into any form they please," lamented Thomas
Jefferson in a letter to Spencer Roane.[23] A Tennessee paper wrote about the
Court after *McCulloch v. Maryland*, complaining that the Supreme Court
was "above the law and beyond the control of public opinion."[24] The *Niles
Weekly Register*, one of the most influential newspapers in the country, condemned that decision as a blow against the sovereignty of the states.[25] Justices
generally were viewed as partisans. The Federalist judges, including Supreme
Court justices, were viewed as extensions of the Federalist administrations of
Washington and Adams. They became representatives of the administration
to the people as they traveled their circuits espousing Federalist philosophy
and explaining the new Constitution and administration to the voters.[26]

PRESS COVERAGE OF THE EARLY COURT

The combination of judicial and political experience, as well as continued
political involvement by some while on the Court, meant that early justices
were well acquainted with political institutions and the coverage of them by
the press. Indeed, the early Court was an object of frequent press attention
when the justices issued major decisions. And those decisions were frequent

because issues of the day regarding the nature of the federal relationship and the power of the federal government were still in flux. The Court shaped that early nature, setting precedents that would be followed for generations. The justices themselves, as well as other political players in Philadelphia, Washington, and across the nation, knew that the Court was establishing precedents. That recognition enhanced the salience of its rulings and public and press interest in those decisions. For example, the Court's decision in *McCulloch v. Maryland* was anxiously awaited in the press and even called "great" before the case was heard.[27]

The justices were aware of the larger political environment that was shaping the power of the new Court. They were conscious of the tenuous nature and newness of their institution and their ultimate reliance on the public for support in sustaining the Court's claim as a co-equal branch and an arbiter of what was and was not constitutional. They also knew that these early cases offered an opportunity for the Court to establish its role in the public mind. John Marshall explicitly used the *Marbury* decision in 1803 to educate the public on the role of the Court and the nature of constitutional government.[28]

At the same time, the early Court also received press attention in the early 1800s because its position as the last bastion of Federalism was widely known.[29] Federalist judges appointed by Washington and Adams continued on the Court long after their party had disintegrated. The Court's reaction to Republican administrations guaranteed coverage because it seemed to promise conflict between the Court and the presidency and Congress. The Court, at times, did not disappoint. The early Court issued a series of opinions favoring the national government over state's rights – the Federalist position over the Republican one. *Fairfax's Devisee v. Hunter's Lessee* (1813), *Martin v. Hunter's Lessee* (1816), *McCulloch v. Maryland* (1819), and *Cohens v. Virginia* (1821) all came in quick succession and solidified the federal government's role vis-à-vis the states. Each of those decisions was praised by the Federalist press and generally roundly condemned by Republicans.[30]

The Court of that day was not viewed as above censure by critics. Court opinions were the subject of intense criticism by opponents, primarily Republicans who viewed justices like Chase, Marshall, and Washington as hopeless partisans bent on continuing Federalist Party policy from their perch on the Court. In the immediate aftermath of *McCulloch v. Maryland* in 1819, some Republican newspapers, particularly in Virginia, launched a print attack on Marshall, the Court, and the decision. The most extensive coverage came from a nearly three-month series of essays in the *Richmond Enquirer*. Written by prominent Virginian Republicans, the essays were blatantly anti-Marshall. Judge Spencer Roane of Virginia issued a steady stream of newspaper-essay criticism of Marshall and his Court's decisions using different pseudonyms.[31] In the wake of the decision in *McCulloch v. Maryland* (1819), one critic argued that the Court's opinion was "not more binding or obligatory than the opinion of any other six intelligent members of the community," and another warned that the Court's decisions should not be received as "the law and the prophets."[32] Another newspaper described the *McCulloch v. Maryland* decision as a "monster of iniquity." Still another editorialized that the decision was "the most flimsy and false attempt at reasoning that can be found in the annals of any nation."[33]

The new institution, which was still establishing its role in the national government, as well as in the public mind, was the target not only of criticism of specific decisions but also of attempts to weaken the power of the Court. Between 1819 and 1827, eighteen bills were offered in Congress to limit judicial power. And after the *Cohens v. Virginia* decision in 1821, the editor of a popular Republican newspaper proposed that the Supreme Court simply be abolished.[34] Still another attempt to weaken the Court was through the threat of impeachment. A Republican paper, the *Philadelphia Aurora*, was so outraged by the Court ruling that the federal government was at war with France despite Congress' failure to declare war that it opined that "every Judge who asserted we were in a state of war, contrary to the rights of Congress to declare it, ought to be impeached."[35] Not surprisingly, both John Marshall and Joseph Story viewed the Court as under severe attack from anti-Federalist forces who sought to diminish the Court's political and legal influence.[36]

At times, the press criticism centered more on individual justices. Samuel Chase was the most common target of Republicans. He was accused of wearing a "party colored robe." In 1800, Chase instigated and then presided over the sedition trial of James Callender, a Republican editor, who was prosecuted under the controversial and short-lived Sedition Act of 1798. While in jail, Callender wrote essays against Chase in the Republican press. Furious, Chase threatened to beat Callender when he was released. Chase's partisanship was so intense that he encouraged grand juries to pursue Republican editors who opposed the Adams administration and charge them as violators of the Sedition Act.[37]

The Republican press was incensed by Chase's conduct while presiding over Callender's trial and his pursuit of Republican editors for criminal prosecution. They railed against Chase and, as early as 1800, proposed that he be impeached. The *Philadelphia Aurora* called Samuel Chase "this monster in politics."[38] Chase was impeached by the House of Representatives, although later acquitted by the Senate, even though Republican newspapers repeatedly called for the Republican-dominated Congress to take action to remove him from the bench.[39] However, the experience chastened the associate justice, and he avoided political statements from the bench thereafter. Describing an after-impeachment grand jury charge statement by Chase, one newspaper reported that "Justice Chase delivered a short and pertinent charge to the grand jury – his remarks were pointed, modest and well applied."[40]

Supreme Court justices were the subject of accusations that were both political and personal. As mentioned previously, Samuel Chase was viewed as a partisan judge because of his behavior at Callender's trial and other partisan statements in his grand jury charges. In the wake of a decision on the Cherokee cases in 1832, the *Niles Weekly Register* charged that Marshall and Story had collaborated with Daniel Webster and Henry Clay to decide the case on political grounds. The allegation incited opponents of the Court to consider impeachment proceedings against Marshall and Story.[41] One paper accused Chief Justice John Rutledge of moral outrages it could not repeat. Another accused Rutledge of "mounting a hogshead, haranguing a mob assembled purposely to reprobate the [Jay] treaty and insult the Executive of the United States."[42] Rutledge, who was serving in a recess appointment as chief justice, was subject to particularly virulent criticism because of his opposition to the Jay Treaty and ultimately was not confirmed for a permanent appointment. Distraught about the Senate's rejection of his nomination for a permanent position as chief justice, Rutledge reportedly attempted to drown himself in the Potomac. News accounts were not reticent about covering the chief justice's personal problems. One paper reported that "Judge Rutledge is so disordered in his intellect, as to render it necessary to have him constantly guarded, he having threatened and even attempted his own destruction."[43]

Interestingly, one of the instigators of public criticism was Thomas Jefferson, both while president and afterward. Jefferson was the leader of the Republican Party and promoted the view that Marshall, as well as the other Federalist appointees, sat on the Supreme Court primarily to thwart Republican Party objectives. Jefferson once charged Marshall with manipulating the law and argued that Marshall's opinions "show dexterously he can reconcile law to his personal biases."[44]

The press became a tool for critics of the Court to foment opposition to the Court's decisions. For instance, in 1815, the Virginia Court of Appeals unanimously refused to obey a ruling of the U.S. Supreme Court in the *Fairfax* case, which had overruled an earlier decision by the Virginia court. To assure that their opinions were widely publicized, the presiding judge of the Virginia court, Spencer Roane, had each Virginia judge's separate opinion in the case published in the Richmond *Enquirer*. Roane not only launched the series of essays against the *McCulloch* and *Cohens* decisions mentioned early but he also repeated the tactic in 1821.[45]

In the midst of this criticism, Marshall's efforts to reshape the image of the Court began to pay off. Gradually, Marshall began to win over the press and the public to the view that the Court was not a bulwark of partisanship and the justices were not bent on promulgating Federalist views. In 1809, a Republican paper praised one of the court's decisions and urged that "here is a point at which the independence of the Judiciary, in its strict and constitutional sense, exists and demands to be supported. . . ."[46] During the War of 1812, the Court's opinions were applauded even by Republican newspapers. The *National Intelligencer*, a prominent Republican paper, opined that the Court was "a branch of the Government which it is important to hold in due veneration, and whose decisions are entitled to the highest respect."[47] Again in 1826, the *Niles Weekly Register*, previously a virulent critic of the Court, concluded that "as there must be some power in every government having final effect, it could hardly be vested anywhere more safely than in the Supreme Court, as at present filled."[48]

AWARENESS OF PRESS COVERAGE

The criticism lodged at justices, whether decision related or personal, did not escape their notice. Newspaper reading was a habit of justices in that day, even though most of the political papers of the time were viewed as partisan organs designed to serve the interests of a particular party or politician.[49] The justices usually followed newspaper coverage of the Court and commented about it to each other and to others. For example, James Iredell wrote to his wife that he had just "this moment read in the newspaper, that Mr. Ellsworth is nominated our Chief Justice."[50]

As the chief justice, John Marshall in particular was a keen observer of press coverage. When a series of articles appeared in Virginia newspapers criticizing *McCulloch v. Maryland*, Marshall wrote to Bushrod Washington that "the storm which has been for some time threatening the Judges has at length burst on their heads, and a most serious hurricane it is." He also admitted, "I find myself more stimulated on this subject than on any other."[51]

The justices closely watched for news about themselves. Samuel Chase threatened to sue the author of a letter published in the *Richmond Examiner*. Chase wrote his own letter in response, charging that the anonymous writer had besmirched his integrity. Other Republican newspapers published both letters.[52] In 1828, John Marshall objected to a newspaper article that reported he was urging voters not to support Andrew Jackson for president.

The *Marylander* quoted Marshall as saying he needed to vote in the presidential election because "should Jackson be elected, I shall look upon the government as virtually dissolved."[53] Marshall denied he had used those words and complained about the newspaper quoting him as "using language which could be uttered only by an angry party man."[54] In an unusual move, he made a public declaration in a letter to the Richmond *Whig and Advertiser* that "he never did use the . . . expression ascribed to me."[55] He also publicly corrected a newspaper story that he was writing a history of the United States. Rather, he explained, he was revising his earlier biography of George Washington.[56]

The justices also were keenly interested in press reaction to their opinions. When commenting on press reaction to one case, Marshall revealed that he had been a close observer of press coverage of the Court: "The opinion of the Supreme Court in the Lottery case has been assaulted with a degree of virulence transcending what has appeared on any former occasion."[57] *Cohens v. Virginia* (1821) had been the object of attack in pseudonymous essays, and Marshall declared that "their coarseness and malignity would designate the author of them if he was not avowed."[58]

When *McCulloch v. Maryland* was issued in 1819, Marshall even knew in advance that a series of attacks on the Court would be published in Virginia newspapers. He wrote to Joseph Story that the *McCulloch* decision would be "attacked in the papers with some asperity, and as those who favor it never write for the publick, it will remain undefended."[59] Marshall worried about the effect of the press assaults on the Court. He wrote to Story that the press efforts were "a masked battery aimed at the government itself."[60]

Yet Marshall was also an early proponent of perpetuating a public image that the justices were distant from what was taking place in the broader political environment. He attempted to send the signal to others that he did not pay much attention to politics. During the 1808 election, Marshall wrote to Charles Cotesworth Pinckney, the Federalist candidate for president that year, that he "scarcely ever read a newspaper." He said he had made "attempts to produce an indifference to what was passing around me." However, he was unable to do so because the country was in danger. Then, contradicting his supposed indifference to and ignorance of political events, Marshall provided Pinckney with his assessment of how the Federalist Party would fare in Virginia and why Federalists were splitting their vote between Pinckney and James Monroe.

Obviously, Marshall's attempt to portray himself, and the Court generally, as separate from the political fray was intended to bolster the reputation of the Court as beyond partisan politics. This was a critical message for Marshall as chief justice to convey to the nation, particularly given the frequent attacks by the Republican press.[61] However, the idea that he, a former member of

Congress and cabinet member, did not read the newspapers much was not credible, as indicated by Marshall's own keen assessment of then-current Virginia politics.

SHAPING PRESS COVERAGE AND PUBLIC OPINION

As would be true of their successors, early justices felt they held a significant disadvantage in the shaping of the public's opinion about their decisions and even toward the institution itself. Although critics could condemn the Court's decisions in the press, the justices themselves were supposed to remain silent. John Marshall expressed this view to Justice Bushrod Washington in 1819 when he wrote that "we shall be denounced bitterly in the papers and, as not a word will be said on the other side, we shall undoubtedly be condemned as a pack of consolidating aristocrats."[62]

The justices of the early court were not as defenseless as Marshall implied. Actually, there were several avenues early justices used to make their points. The press constituted the most important forum. This was particularly true because the press was the main vehicle for disseminating the Court's decisions. Prior to the creation of the Government Printing Office in 1860, government documents were published in newspapers at the government's expense. Newspaper publication guaranteed a wide circulation for government documents.

The justices knew the press could be useful to them in circulating opinions and garnering public support for their decisions. They were well aware of the role the press had played in the Revolution and the constitutional ratification process. Some had even participated in that process. Samuel Chase had employed the press during the Revolution to oppose the British. One set of biographers concluded that "few contemporaries matched Chase's skillful use of the press...."[63] Because Supreme Court decisions were circulated through the press, Marshall urged Congress to remunerate an individual to be the Court reporter – that is, the individual who recorded the decisions and then distributed them to the press. Marshall was cognizant of the importance of the press in enhancing public support for the Court, and he knew the public needed accurate reporting of the decisions to understand what the Court was doing.[64]

The justices' use of the press also was related to the political circumstances of the day and their unique position for many years as the last bastion of Federalists. As mentioned, during the first quarter century of the Court's existence, most of the justices were Federalists appointed by Washington or Adams. However, the Federalist Party was dying as a viable political party. The last presidential election the party won occurred in 1796, and the party lost control of Congress by 1800. The public began voting against the party as early as the Adams administration and had turned it into a regional New England party. Justices on the Supreme Court like John Marshall and Samuel Chase viewed themselves as the last remnants of Federalist power. Some of them construed their role as critical in shifting public opinion away from the Republicans. When Andrew Jackson held a White House reception on Inauguration Day that led to the public pouring into the White House uncontrollably, Joseph Story called it "the reign of King 'Mob.'"[65]

That approach, although not necessarily blatant, enraged many Republicans who sought to undermine the Court to limit the influence of Federalist judges. The impeachment of Samuel Chase and possible impeachment of other Federalist justices, such as John Marshall and William Paterson, were extreme, and ultimately unsuccessful, efforts to curb the power of the Court. But there were other methods. Virginia state court justices used their position to ignore, rather than sustain, the rulings of the U.S. Supreme Court. The Virginia legislature passed resolutions expressing opposition to federal appellate jurisdiction over the states.[66]

True to his reputation, Samuel Chase used the press to fight his own impeachment. While the House of Representatives was considering an impeachment resolution against him, the embattled jurist wrote an open letter to newspaper editors defending his actions. In the letter, Chase accused Thomas Jefferson of instigating the impeachment campaign to create a vacancy to appoint Republican justices. Both Federalist and Republican papers published Chase's defense.[67]

At times, the press strategy was designed to protect not the justices' ideology, but the institution itself. In 1801, as the Republicans took over both the White House and the Congress, the Federalists were viewed by the Republican press as retreating into the safety of the judicial branch. John Marshall bemoaned this "strange revolution which has taken place in public opinion."[68] Federalist judges dominated the U.S. Supreme Court and, with life tenure, were likely to do so for years to come. However, Marshall knew that the Republicans would not long tolerate Federalist dominance over the judiciary, particularly if the Court actually fulfilled its role as a check on the other branches. He needed to protect the institution's power, and the role of public opinion would be important in that process.[69]

The justices also felt that they had few defenders within the press. As a consequence, the justices themselves concluded that they must provide a defense for individual decisions and the Court when both were under condemnation by opponents. However, that involvement had to be circumspect to avoid dragging the Court into a public debate. They had to find subtle ways to influence public opinion. The justices also knew they could not simply engage in the kind of public exchange common at the time among politicians. Joining the public debate on controversial issues would undermine the Court. Marshall admitted that the Court lacked "legitimate means of ingratiating itself with the people. . . . "[70]

Written Opinions

One vehicle for affecting public opinion about the Court was its written decisions. Unfortunately for the Court, in the first decade of its existence, the process of issuing decisions only reinforced the criticism of the institution. Prior to Marshall's tenure as chief justice, the justices each offered separate opinions on cases before them. Marshall convinced the associate justices to support a policy of per curiam opinions that failed to distinguish how the individual justices felt about the issue. Such opinions, Marshall believed, strengthened the power of the Court in handing down decisions to the public. The chief justice was remarkably successful in maintaining an image of Court unanimity. During three of Marshall's terms, all of the Supreme Court's decisions were unanimous. During many others, dissents were rare.[71]

Marshall would use dissenting opinions in his favor as well. When the Court ruled in *Cherokee Nation v. Georgia*, Marshall was unhappy with the result because he felt the current case was not the suitable format for expounding his views on the removal of native Americans. Thus, he urged two justices to read their dissents from the bench. One of those opinions included guidance on how another case, if brought before the Court, might receive a different outcome. Moreover, Marshall urged the court reporter to write a description of the case for public consumption that clearly sided with the native American tribes. He hoped that press coverage of the case would impel the tribes to bring forward another case. His tactic worked. The next year, the Court received a subsequent case that allowed Marshall to make another argument for national government supremacy.[72]

At a time when the chief justice urged per curiam opinions, Justice William Johnson preferred his own separate, though concurring, opinions so that, according to Johnson, he could "avoid having an ambiguous decision hereafter imputed to me, or an opinion which I would not wish to be understood to have given." Johnson's concern was directly connected to public opinion of his role on the Court. He explained that "in questions of great importance, and great delicacy, I feel my duty to the public best discharged by an effort to maintain my opinions in my own way."[73] Johnson was encouraged in that view by fellow Republicans who wanted to prove that the Court was more divided than Marshall's per curiam opinion policy suggested. Thomas Jefferson even urged Johnson to write separate opinions to weaken the power of the Federalists on the Court.[74]

Grand Jury Charges

Another tool for affecting press coverage and public opinion was the grand jury charge. In the early years of the Court, justices rode circuit and presided over grand jury trials. They charged the jury before it went into deliberations, and frequently those charges were published in the newspapers of the day because the justices used the charges to make political statements. As their charges became newsworthy, the justices adopted the process of charging a jury as a means to make remarks that would have potentially broad circulation locally, regionally, or even nationally.

Those charges tended to range much more broadly than a judge's jury charge would today. When the justices delivered their charges, they imagined an audience that included not just the grand jury in front of them but also the nation as a whole.[75] As a consequence, their charges often were written for the general public. One newspaper praised a charge by Jay as "expressed in the most plain and familiar style. . . . "[76] If the justices did not readily supply their written charges, newspapers often asked for a copy to print. On at least one occasion, the grand jury itself asked John Jay for his charge in order to deliver it to the newspapers so "that it may be more influential and impress the mind of our fellow citizens at large."[77] Justices sometimes went out of their way to ensure that their charges were reported accurately in the newspapers. When one of Chase's charges was incorrectly reported in the press, Chase delivered a copy of his charge to a Federalist newspaper, which then circulated it to other similarly minded papers.[78]

The press' interest in their charges provided Jay and the other justices with an opportunity to express their views on constitutional issues as they traveled from state to state. They used these grand jury charges as informal advisory opinions to the government and the public. Through these charges, justices could weigh in on contemporary issues. William Paterson used one charge to defend the recently passed Sedition Act of 1798 and urge the jury to indict a Republican editor charged under the controversial law. Federalist justices used their grand jury charges to defend Federalist administrations – those of George Washington and John Adams – and then, after 1801, to criticize Republican ones. The jury charges were not necessarily so much about the case at hand or even the law. John Jay used a grand jury charge to support a foreign neutrality proclamation issued by President Washington in 1793.[79]

Reaction to the charges varied by party. Federalist papers praised the practice of Federalist justices speaking out through the medium of grand jury charges. One newspaper account of a grand jury charge by William Paterson recorded that "politicks were set in their true light, by holding up the Jacobins, as the disorganizers of our happy Country. . . . "[80] Another paper praised Jay's charges to grand juries as "full of good sense and learning."[81] Predictably, Republican critics of the Court in turn condemned the practice. The impeachment of Samuel Chase was spurred by Chase's use of the grand jury charge to criticize the Jefferson administration and accuse it of undermining constitutional government. During the 1800 election between Jefferson and Adams, Chase employed his grand jury charges to praise Adams and attack Jefferson. Chase went even further; his charges included his views on pending legislation.[82]

Not only were the charges covered by the press but they also became the object of debate between Federalist and Republican papers both in terms of the substance of the judicial comments and their propriety. The public debate about the charges, as well as Chase's impeachment, ultimately made justices nervous about the publicity regarding their charges. John Marshall worried that the practices of some of the other justices would undermine his efforts to bolster the Court's image as above partisanship. He then attempted to set an example for other justices by keeping his grand jury charges uncontroversial and declining offers to publish them.[83] As justices gradually abandoned the use of the grand jury charge as a vehicle for expressing their political views, this tool disappeared as a means for shaping press coverage.

Pseudonymous Essays

Early Supreme Court justices were familiar with the rhetorical volleys, particularly in the partisan press, that characterized partisan politics in the first half century of the American government. As mentioned previously, many of them had joined the Court after political careers during which political leaders did not leave printed attacks unanswered but responded with their own essays. However, Supreme Court justices were expected to represent a judiciary that was separate from partisan politics. These early justices were conscious of the dilemma caused by their position. They understood that direct public conflict with opponents might undermine the authority and dignity of the Court. But that did not mean they could not respond at all.

Instead, they used a common tactic of the day: penning essays under a pseudonym. In the midst of the controversy about the Jay Treaty, William Paterson weighed in to defend the treaty in a series of essays published in

New Jersey newspapers. Writing as "Horatius," Paterson sparred with the treaty's critics in harsh terms that would have seemed unbecoming of an associate justice of the U.S. Supreme Court. Horatius reappeared in 1798 and again in 1800 to criticize the Jeffersonians and defend Federalist thought. Eventually, Paterson wrote forty-six newspaper essays under a pseudonym while serving on the Court. Paterson used the essays to address legal and political issues of the day, although he did not discuss pending cases before the Court.[84]

John Marshall also believed that negative press coverage was potentially harmful to the Court and was willing to take on opponents through the pseudonymous essay. In the wake of the *McCulloch* decision, he became alarmed when the *Richmond Enquirer* published essays denouncing the Court's ruling because the paper's essays were widely reprinted by other newspapers of the time. In response to these attacks on *McCulloch*, Marshall wrote two newspaper essays under the pseudonym "A Friend to the Union" and another nine essays using "A Friend of the Constitution." The essays appeared in Pennsylvania and Virginia newspapers. Marshall engaged in an ongoing yet anonymous debate with his critics as they wrote newspaper essays back and forth. He even circulated copies of his essays to the Virginia General Assembly to forestall legislative efforts to instruct the state's federal representatives to curtail the courts. Two years after the McCulloch decision, Marshall again sought to reply through the press to criticism in Virginia papers of *Cohens v. Virginia* (1821). This time, the Virginia press would not publish his essays.[85]

Public knowledge of a chief justice writing newspaper essays would have been damaging to the Court. Indeed, Marshall was concerned that his identity not be revealed and went to great lengths to assure that his secret was kept. He worked through an intermediary, Bushrod Washington, to publish the essays. He also instructed Washington to tell the printer to burn the manuscripts and send copies of the articles to Marshall's son, rather than directly to him, explaining: "I do not wish them to come to me lest some suspicion of the author should be created."[86]

Other justices participated in similar essay writing. Bushrod Washington also wrote essays while on the Court. James Iredell wrote an essay defending the administration's controversial excise tax on whiskey. In fact, the Court's first official reporter, Henry Wheaton, even published anonymous newspaper essays defending the Court.[87]

In one case, a chief justice wrote an essay openly. Yet the experience may have been a warning to his successors on the Court. John Jay attacked Edmond Genet, France's ambassador to the United States, in a letter to New York newspapers regarding Genet's threat to appeal to the American people to overturn presidential decisions that France opposed. Genet responded with an attack on Jay. Genet went even further by requesting that the U.S. attorney general prosecute Jay for libel. Jay then responded with another letter, again attacking Genet.[88]

Yet anonymity allowed the justices to write more freely. They could defend the Court's decisions without revealing that they were, in fact, the authors of those decisions. Nor did they want others to know that pseudonymous essayists actually were part of an institution that was supposed to be above such things. Ironically, in one of his pseudonymous essays, Marshall accused his critics of launching an attack on the Court because they knew the Court could not answer.[89]

Marshall also could become personal in his rebuttal of critics. He argued that his critics were "once more agitating the publick mind, and reviving those unfounded jealousies by whose blind aid ambition climbs the ladder of power."[90] He also called them "certain restless politicians of Virginia" who were members of a party "without the legitimate means of ingratiating itself with the people."[91]

Sometimes the justices used a variety of techniques to make their point. In May 1799, Chief Justice Oliver Ellsworth used a grand jury charge to blunt Republicans' criticisms of the doctrine of federal common-law crimes. Newspapers across the nation reprinted Ellsworth's statement.[92] But four months later, Ellsworth dealt with the issue in an opinion in the case of *United States v. Williams*. Once again, he pressed the point about federal common law in his opinion. Not surprisingly, the Republican press roundly condemned Ellsworth's opinion.[93]

Samuel Chase even took on the press itself. When the French ambassador to the United States launched a publicity campaign to woo the United States away from Britain and toward France, Chase responded in anger. However, Chase did not condemn merely the ambassador, but he also criticized the press that printed the ambassador's essays. Chase wrote that "the Printer ought to be indicted for a false and base Libel on our Government."[94] As mentioned earlier, Chase also was an active prosecutor of Republican papers, which he felt violated the Sedition Act. He traveled across various states urging grand juries to indict newspaper editors.[95]

Chase went a step further. He decided to start his own newspapers to have a vehicle for the dissemination of his views. He joined with Robert Goodloe Harper, a prominent Maryland Federalist, to found a newspaper intended to be supportive of Chase's views. The two invested $8,000 in the publishing enterprise. However, the effort was a failure; the paper lasted less than a year and had little influence during its existence.[96]

Newsworthy Events

Unlike today, Supreme Court justices served as trial judges when circuit courts sat as trial courts. When those trials became public spectacles, the justices received extensive press attention. Yet when a trial had national significance, newspapers across the country covered the trial itself and the role of the Supreme Court justice who was presiding. The most prominent example was the treason trial of former Vice President Aaron Burr in 1807. Burr was accused of plotting to raise a militia to capture southwestern areas of the United States. The trial was the sensation of the day. Newspapers across the country carried the trial's proceedings. The crowd gathered to hear the trial was so large that the hearings had to be moved to the Virginia House of Delegates.[97] The trial promised to be a battleground for the president's supporters in the prosecution and the Federalists defending Burr, many of whom viewed Jefferson as their prime enemy.

John Marshall personally served as the presiding judge at the trial because Burr was tried within Marshall's own circuit. In addition to extensive coverage of the trial itself, newspaper content also featured Marshall's role.[98] One Marshall biographer noted that "Marshall's every move was reported and scrutinized."[99] Hence, Marshall sat in a difficult position as one who had been connected to a Federalist administration and therefore should be a defender of Burr, but who also needed to reassure the public that he was unbiased in the execution of justice. In fact, Marshall may have agreed with Burr's defense team, particularly in their statements about Jefferson, but it was imperative that the presiding officer appear impartial. At times, that required him to limit the Federalists' use of the trial to criticize Jefferson.[100]

Marshall was aware of the public scrutiny of his conduct as the presiding judge and the effect that conduct would have on public opinion of him, but also on the Supreme Court generally. According to contemporary accounts, Marshall presided in a deliberate manner and kept his own temper throughout. He was also cognizant of the fact that public opinion favored Burr's conviction and that if that did not occur, the public, particularly the Republicans, would blame Marshall. When Burr received a light punishment from the jury following Marshall's opinion that Burr had not committed treason against the United States, Marshall's fears were realized. Republican newspapers condemned Marshall and some urged his impeachment. President Jefferson recommended that Congress approve a constitutional amendment allowing Supreme Court justices to be removed from office by the president, although the proposal went nowhere. Marshall was hung in effigy in Baltimore.[101] However, Marshall's approach to the trial resulted in general respect for the chief justice and ultimately did not undermine deference for the Court.

THE COMMUNICATION LEGACY OF THE EARLY YEARS

Justices in the early years of the Court were familiar with the role of the press in early American politics. They had served in political positions in which they interacted with partisan editors and correspondents. Some had written essays in the press and had participated in the debates of the day prior to coming to the Court. While on the Court, they continued to be consumers of press information. They tracked press coverage of themselves individually as well as of the Court as an institution. They were acutely aware of how the Court's decisions generally, and their own actions specifically, were being related in the press.

They believed the press was powerful in shaping public opinion. As evidence, some, such as William Paterson and Samuel Chase, had urged the indictment of Republican newspaper editors under the Sedition Act of 1798 to prevent those editors from mobilizing public opinion against the Adams administration. Their grand jury charges were published to sway public opinion on current issues. Press coverage also could harm them individually and institutionally. Attacks on their decisions by newspapers held the potential of undermining support for the Court as well as compliance with its decisions, thus emasculating the Court as a third branch of government. They also were aware that partisan attacks on the Court by newspapers likely had contributed to the Chase impeachment effort and the threat of more possible impeachments that would make the justices subordinate to the Congress and the president.

Therefore, they sought collectively to shape that press coverage for their own objectives. They needed to do so to protect the developing institution under their care. The fact that the Court was defining its own role in the new government, particularly in the Marshall Court years, and that the Court relied heavily on public opinion to withstand attacks by Thomas Jefferson and other Republican leaders, necessitated overt efforts to shape public opinion. They used the methods at their disposal to influence public views on public policy issues of the day. A couple of the methods they used, such as pseudonymous essays and grand jury charges, are not common today, but the use of opinions to influence press coverage and public opinion still is.

Their individual objectives dominated the first years of the Court. Some justices specifically promoted their Federalist ideology through their communications with the public. However, John Marshall directed their efforts toward institutional communication. Through per curiam opinions directed at the public and the use of consensus decisions reducing the prospect of dissent, Marshall played a critical role in sublimating the disparate individual objectives of the justices to the broader objective of institutional communication. That institutional communication was designed to promote public support for the Court and its respective decisions. Under Marshall's guidance, the effort worked. The Court effectively weathered opposition and established itself as a permanently important institution as a result of Marshall's efforts to garner public confidence through communication. The post-Marshall years through the rest of the nineteenth century, however, were a somewhat different story.

4

The Nineteenth Century

On July 6, 1835, John Marshall died in his bed, surrounded by his family. The passing of the third chief justice in the Court's history signaled the end of an era. In the nearly half century the Court had been in existence, no justice had served as long as Marshall. Even today, his thirty-four-year tenure as chief justice has yet to be surpassed by any of his successors. More importantly, Marshall had permanently shaped the institution over which he had presided for so long.

The press of the day recognized the significance of Marshall's passing.[1] The *Richmond Enquirer*, which had been no fan of Marshall, noted that "the city bells tolled yesterday nearly the whole day – guns were fired – and, perhaps no funeral procession, in this city, has ever been more extensive and solemn than the one which yesterday attended him to the grave."[2] The Richmond *Whig and Public Advertiser* opined that "no man has lived or died in this country, save its father George Washington alone, who united such a warmth of affection for his person, with so deep and unaffected a respect for his character, and admiration for his great abilities." The *Niles Register* noted that "a great man has fallen in Israel."[3]

At the time of Marshall's death, the Court had firmly established itself as a force in American government. Marshall's efforts had preserved the Court from attacks by opponents who repeatedly had sought to weaken the institution. As discussed in Chapter 3, many of those efforts had been undertaken through the press in the form of essays criticizing the decisions of the Court, the individuals who served on it, and even its role in American government.

As the Court neared the half-century mark of its existence, the justices' relations with the press remained, on the whole, consistent with the past. The Court continued to receive press coverage when significant decisions were announced, particularly as they touched on what had become the most salient issue of the day – slavery. And those decisions were condemned by opponents, whose statements occasionally were answered by the justices themselves. Some justices became enmeshed in current politics, including electoral campaigns. Justices sometimes sought to influence the press coverage of themselves and their institution in subtle and not-so-subtle means.

Yet the nineteenth century also would bring changes in the nature of that interaction. One change would be in justices' previous experience with the press. Like their predecessors in the early years, most nineteenth-century justices possessed political backgrounds. But, like many others in national government in that age, some also had press backgrounds as well, including past careers as editors, publishers, and even correspondents.

PRIOR INTERACTION WITH THE PRESS

One reason justices perpetuated their interaction with the press through the nineteenth century was the extent of the continuing influence of the press in politics. Newspapers were widely read, particularly as suffrage was extended and ordinary citizens increasingly voted and participated in political rallies and other events. Newspapers covered politics extensively as politics itself became a mass-oriented activity rather than one directed primarily at a social elite.

The press itself changed dramatically during the nineteenth century. This was a period when the partisan press began to fade and its replacement was a more autonomous entity in politics later known as the Penny Press. However, at the time of Marshall's death, the partisan press still dominated the news media.[4] This partisan press had largely appealed to segments of the population who constituted the literate, more affluent elite. Then, the Jacksonian era broadened interest in politics and made political communication via newspapers more possible. A new type of newspaper appeared as an alternative to partisan newspapers.[5]

Shortly before Marshall's death, *The Sun* appeared on the streets of New York City. This new newspaper appealed to a general audience, not just political elites, featured human interest stories and not just political essays and documents, and sold on the street for a penny rather than the annual subscription rate that only the well-to-do could afford. The rise of this "penny press" helped newspapers establish a financial independence from politicians that they previously had not enjoyed. Politicians had considered the partisan press to be their mouthpieces, and newspaper publishers had complied. The penny press, however, meant newspapers no longer had to rely on endorsements, government contracts, or even loans from key politicians or political parties to survive.

As a result of this independence, newspaper editors and publishers eventually became powerful forces in the community and the nation in their own right. Those who ran newspapers gained prominence in public life; they became influential in policy making and in presidential nominations and elections. Some entered politics themselves. Duff Green, editor of several newspapers in the 1800s, was an advisor to Andrew Jackson in the 1830s.[6] Indeed, Jackson appointed more newspaper editors to federal government positions than had any previous president.[7] Horace Greeley founded the *New York Tribune*, helped form the Republican Party, and then became an unsuccessful presidential candidate in 1868.[8] This was a period when many people in public life had some connection with the press. James G. Blaine ran the most influential newspaper in Maine before he was elected to the U.S. House of Representatives and then Speaker of the House and, ultimately, became a presidential candidate.[9]

Interestingly, the growing political independence of the press intertwined the careers of several future Supreme Court justices. Unlike their predecessors, who had been lawyers or politicians from an early age, these justices began their careers as editors or writers for newspapers of the day. These early experiences must have helped them gain insights into the workings of the press, a knowledge that would not have been discarded once they joined the Court. Justice John McLean bought a printing office in Lebanon, Ohio, and published the weekly Lebanon Ohio *Western Star* before commencing his law career. In 1822, McLean also was a regular pseudonymous essayist in Ohio, writing articles supporting the presidential candidacy of John C. Calhoun. Seven years later, he was appointed to the Court by President Andrew Jackson.[10] Justice Stanley Matthews, who came to the Court in 1881, was an editor of the *Cincinnati Herald* during the 1840s. While serving as editor, Matthews published an essay criticizing the current justices for their pro-slavery views.[11] Similarly, while a young man, Chief Justice Melville Fuller was the editor of a Democratic newspaper in Augusta, Maine, called *The Augusta Age*.[12] Later, Fuller worked as a correspondent for the *New York Herald*.[13] During the Civil War, future Associate Justice Lucius Q. C. Lamar was a representative of the Confederacy and wrote articles on behalf of the South that appeared in British newspapers.[14]

The justice who was most integrated into the world of the press, and one of the most politically oriented justices in history, was Chief Justice Salmon Chase. Chase once related that his interest in politics actually began when he found a collection of old Federalist newspapers in the attic of his schoolmaster's home. Chase read the papers thoroughly. However, he admitted he did so despite his mother's warning that newspapers "were not to be implicitly relied on for the truth."[15]

Chase's fascination with the press continued throughout his life. He wrote editorials for the *Cincinnati American*. He also edited a quarterly periodical called the *Western Review*.[16] In addition, he attempted to start an antislavery newspaper in Washington and gave financial support to antislavery papers such as William Lloyd Garrison's *The Liberator* and a Washington newspaper called *The National Era*.[17] Also, using his own funds, Chase successfully founded a Free Soil paper in Columbus, Ohio.[18]

Chase's press background helped him deal with the press during his tenure as governor of Ohio. He cultivated editors and reporters while in office, even inviting them to his home for Thanksgiving dinner.[19] Three of Chase's closest aides throughout his political career were newspaper editors in Ohio.[20] He also became good friends with Horace Greeley, the publisher of the *New York Tribune*.[21] As Chase moved to national politics, he continued to utilize the press to help him gain public office and shape policy. In 1854, Chase, along with others, published essays in newspapers across the nation designed to influence Democrats in Congress to oppose the Nebraska Bill that was headed for a vote.[22] Six years later, Chase also sought to gain press support for a Republican Party presidential bid in 1860. Four years after that, he tried for the presidency again and attempted to mobilize press endorsements for his bid.[23]

JUSTICES AND POLITICS

Even for those justices without press backgrounds, a political background was more common than a judicial one. Like justices in the early Court, those who joined the Court during the nineteenth century often came to the highest bench after at least some involvement in national or state politics. Many years prior to his appointment, Melville Fuller was an activist in the Democratic Party. He campaigned for presidential candidate Stephen Douglas and served in the Illinois state legislature.[24] Salmon Chase was a U.S. senator, governor of Ohio, and a member of the president's cabinet prior to his appointment as chief justice in 1864. Chief Justice Roger Taney had been a close advisor to Andrew Jackson and served as Jackson's secretary of the treasury and attorney general before his appointment to the Court. Justice Philip Barbour was a member of Congress. Justice John McKinley was a U.S. senator from Alabama, and Justice John Marshall Harlan ran for governor of Kentucky in 1871.[25]

One of the most direct connections of this age between a politician and a justice was the relationship between Abraham Lincoln and Justice David

Davis. In 1860, Davis served in Lincoln's presidential campaign. Lincoln, in turn, appointed Davis to the Court in October 1862. Donald Grier Stephenson, Jr. noted that "as Davis would almost certainly never have been placed on the Supreme Court without Lincoln, it is highly probable that Lincoln would never have been elected president without Davis."[26]

In fact, for justices in the nineteenth century, political office was a more common stepping-stone to the Court than judicial service. Of the justices who were appointed to the Court from Roger Taney in 1837 to the end of the century, more had previously served in elective or appointive political office than had been judges. Of the thirty-five Supreme Court justices appointed during this period, ten had served previously as state judges and seven had been federal judges. However, nineteen had served as a state legislator; a state-elected official, such as governor or lieutenant governor; or as a member of the U.S. House or Senate. Just six justices had only judicial experience prior to their appointments to the Court. One example of the presence of former elected and appointed political officials among the justices was the Court headed by Chief Justice Morrison Waite. During a four-year period (1877–1881) of the Waite Court, six of the justices had been elected to the state legislature or had run for state office, two were former members of Congress, and one was a former U.S. attorney general. Only four of the justices had previously been a judge.[27]

Even though previous political experience was the norm, there was a growing expectation that the justices should be above the political fray. When they were not, they were subject to press criticism. The press was particularly suspicious of partisan politicians who suddenly took on the role of neutral judges supposedly acting as though they were above politics. Newspaper editors criticized Salmon Chase for his political background and continued involvement in politics even while he served as chief justice. One newspaper called him "more a politician than a lawyer." Another said they could not imagine previous chief justices "on the balcony of a hotel, bidding for the cheers of a crowd."[28] Even his successor, Morrison Waite, later criticized Chase, saying that Chase "detracted from his name by permitting himself to think he wanted the presidency."[29] Indeed, Chase was a perpetual candidate for the presidency, both before and during his chief justiceship. Chase also did more than just run for president. While chief justice, he continued to lobby senators and the White House on various policy issues. He advised President Andrew Johnson on conditions in the South following the Civil War and was a public proponent of more lenience in the reconstruction of the war-torn region.[30]

Ironically, at the same time, many newspapers of the day also served as the chief proponents for justices to become involved in politics. Throughout the nineteenth century, newspaper editorials touted various justices as possible presidential candidates. Some of those justices fueled press speculation because of their presidential ambitions, whereas others made no effort to fan the flames and sometimes tried their best to end the rumors of a presidential bid. For example, Morrison Waite was prominently mentioned as a presidential candidate for the 1876 election. Newspapers across the East and Midwest suggested Waite as a presidential candidate. Waite used the press to respond by writing a letter to an editor declaring that he was not running for office, and he even suggested that the Constitution should prohibit the chief justice from being a presidential candidate.[31] Similarly, Salmon Chase's candidacy was urged by several newspapers around the country. The *New York Sun* urged that Chase be nominated by the Democrats, and the *New York Herald* suggested the formation of a third party with Chase as the presidential nominee. The paper editorialized that "Chief Justice Chase stands prominently before the country today as the people's candidate for the Presidency."[32]

It was difficult for justices to resist the importuning to become more politically involved, particularly because most of them had had political careers prior to joining the Court. Moreover, many of the justices did not abandon their interest in politics once on the bench. As the nineteenth century ended, Chicago newspaper columnist Finley Peter Dunne's fictional Mr. Dooley remarked that "the Supreme Court follows the election returns.'

Mr. Dooley was right. The justices literally were following the election returns. Shortly after the presidential election in 1888, Melville Fuller wrote to a Mr. Grannis: "The election returns depress me. The country parts for four years with one of its purest and ablest servants."[33] Fuller's disappointment over Grover Cleveland's failure to win reelection, particularly after Cleveland had appointed Fuller as chief justice, was typical of several justices' close observance of, and partisan reaction to, elections. Morrison Waite wrote a letter to Rutherford B. Hayes when Hayes received the Republican nomination for Ohio governor: "I am delighted at your nomination. . . . How I wish I could give you a helping hand on the stump, as well as elsewhere."[34] When James Garfield won the presidency in 1880, Waite wrote to a friend: 'Hasn't the election come out gloriously . . . ?"[35]

Justices in the 1800s not only followed the election returns but also at times attempted to affect them. For example, Melville Fuller encouraged Cleveland to run again for president in 1892, which Cleveland eventually did. Fuller counseled Cleveland to accept an invitation to speak to the National Press Club, terming the occasion "a new political opportunity that might be availed of," and declared that "you are the only possible nominee absolutely certain of success. . . . "[36]

But some justices went further by becoming candidates for president themselves. Salmon Chase already had been bitten by the presidential bug. He was strongly encouraged to run for president in 1868, even though he was already sitting on the Court as chief justice. The New York *Herald* urged his nomination for months before the national nominating conventions.[37] The publicity placed Chase in an awkward position because of changing modes of electoral candidacies. Whereas during the first decade of the Court, John Jay had gone on to be elected governor of New York and Oliver Ellsworth had been a presidential candidate, the expectations of judicial involvement in politics had changed since that time.

The difference lay in the role of campaigning. In earlier days, drafts to be a candidate were common. Supreme Court justices could "run" for office in such a political climate because running did not imply actual campaigning. Jay eschewed campaigning for governor but was still elected. As long as justices in that earlier era did not explicitly reject the efforts by others to nominate them for office, but merely made themselves available for a draft, they could act as candidates for office.

That model had become less prevalent by the middle of the nineteenth century. Candidates were expected to play a greater role in effecting their own elections. Campaign biographies, speeches to various groups across the country (although not billed as "active campaigning), and meetings with political leaders increasingly became the norm for presidential candidates. Even if they were not publicly campaigning, presidential candidates increasingly were expected to work actively behind the scenes on their own behalf.

This change in the nature of campaigning made the effort more difficult for Supreme Court justices, who were viewed as nonpartisan jurists rather than candidates. They could not become more overt campaigners, as had become expected for presidential candidates. It is true that it was not until 1896 that a presidential candidate campaigned in a manner similar to today's presidential campaigns. Yet by the mid- to late 1800s, candidates for a major party nomination certainly had to meet with party leaders, create a campaign organization to lobby convention delegates, publish literature about themselves, and orchestrate press coverage to convey momentum and public support. Supreme Court justices could not do all that without attracting criticism that they were partisan candidates rather than independent jurists.

Despite those obstacles, some Supreme Court justices still harbored political ambitions, particularly relative to the presidency. They attempted to navigate the new environment in a way that allowed them to launch a presidential bid while preserving their Supreme Court status. Despite repeated failure throughout the nineteenth century by Supreme Court justices to wage a successful presidential campaign, the presidential itch continued to affect them. Salmon Chase is a classic example of such judicial tightrope walking. Chase desperately wanted to be president. He had already run for president in 1860 and 1864, and despite his position as chief justice, he was ready to run again in 1868 regardless of criticism from others that he was too ambitious. David Davis called Chase "the most ambitious man, except Douglas, that I ever knew personally," and Justice Samuel Miller related that Chase was "warped, perverted, shriveled by the selfishness generated by ambition.[38] Moreover, Chase was bored with his job as chief justice. He wrote once that he was "working from morning till midnight and no result, except that John Smith owned this parcel or land or other property instead of Jacob Robinson; I caring nothing, and nobody caring much more, about the matter."[39]

Despite his frustration with his job, Chase did not want to simply leave it. He wanted to run for president while serving as chief justice. Yet being chief justice hampered his ability to become a full-fledged candidate; it severely limited his ability to engage in overt strategizing and organizing that had become the expectation for presidential races and certainly characterized other candidates' campaigns.

Chase's dilemma became public in the spring of 1868 after an encounter with a newspaper editor. The editor of the *Independent* had interviewed the chief justice at Chase's house and subsequently wrote an article titled "A Folded Banner." The article stated Chase's views on the upcoming presidential nomination process, including the chief justice's negative assessment of his own position as a possible Republican presidential candidate. He had told the editor he did not think he could win the Republican nomination. However, the editor reported that Chase had admitted he would accept the Democratic Party presidential nomination. The interview indicated how serious Chase was about running for president and that he was eager to accept a party nomination if he could secure it. Moreover, he was willing to encourage others to assist him in his attempt to secure a nomination without having to actively campaign for it. Chase wrote privately to others that he was "not indifferent" to the talk of a possible presidential candidacy and that he would "not be at liberty to refuse the use of my name."[40]

However, Chase was mortified by the article. He feared that his frank views on his own possible candidacy would harm his chances for a nomination. The article had revealed publicly what Chase wanted to withhold – that is, that he wanted to be drafted for either party's nomination. He did not want to make that known publicly for fear of criticism about using the chief justiceship to win the White House. On the one hand, a public effort to attain a party nomination, along with the accompanying criticism from the opposition, would undermine the image of partisan detachment he sought to display. On the other hand, he worried that once the article had appeared describing his views toward the two parties, both sets of partisans would be offended to the point that neither would allow his nomination as their presidential candidate.

Characteristically, the chief justice used the press to regain his position as a candidate for either party. In response to the article, he wrote a letter to the editor saying that he and the editor had visited at Chase's house and that Chase had not realized he was "on trial before an editor." Chase said that he had not anticipated that the conversation would result in the article and admitted that he should have "observed a prudent silence." He then tried to explain that the Republicans had moved away from his views and that there were "new shibboleths of Republican faith" that he "could not frame my lips to pronounce." However, he did make clear that he agreed with most Republican positions. He also denied he had said he would accept the Democratic nomination. "It would be ridiculous in me to say that I would not accept what had not been offered, and was not likely to be." Chase asserted that he "wanted no nomination at all."[41]

The letter to the editor of the *Independent* was part of a press-oriented strategy to suggest he was above partisan politics and a paragon of disinterest in presidential nominations while still disseminating his views to the public and keeping his name available as a nominee. At the same time the letter to the *Independent* was published, Chase also wrote to the editor of the *Cincinnati Commercial*. In that letter, Chase said that he was uninterested in the presidential nomination and had "neither the ambition nor the vanity which some unambitious and very modest gentlemen are pleased continually to ascribe to me."[42] Chase then gave an interview to the editor of the *New York World* explaining his political views, particularly urging better relations between the North and the South. Although Chase requested that the editor not publish his views, the interview subsequently was published. He also issued a press statement promising to support the Democratic nominee yet attempted to stop publication because he was afraid it would harm his chances of getting a nomination. Like a presidential candidate, the chief justice announced his fifteen-point platform to the public and moderated his views on suffrage to make them more palatable to southern Democrats.[43]

As the nominating conventions of the two major parties neared, Chase became desperate and therefore more open about his ambitions. On June 19, 1868, he wrote a letter to William G. Bryant, editor of the *New York Evening Post*, about a possible presidential run. Chase concluded that many northern Democrats would accept him as a candidate because "they have been led to defeat" during the previous ten years and that the southern Democrats would favor him because of his "ideas of restoration, on the basis of universal suffrage and universal amnesty. . . . " He admitted that there were forces in the Democratic Party that would oppose him as a nominee, and he assured Bryant that even though "the movement for my nomination has taken me entirely by surprise," he did not think the convention would nominate him. Regardless, he spelled out what he would want in a party platform if he were to be a presidential candidate.[44]

Chase's letters were not merely defensive. They were designed to signal his continued interest in the nomination while he still declared that he did not think a nomination was really forthcoming. What Chief Justice Chase did not do, which after a lifetime of politics would have been uncharacteristic, was keep silent. He had likely concluded that such a strategy would not have furthered his prospects. Instead, he attempted to walk the fine line between active campaigning, which would have damaged his credibility as chief justice, and his Supreme Court position, which he used to promote his own candidacy.

Chase's efforts failed, but he was hardly alone as a sitting justice of the U.S. Supreme Court in furthering his political ambitions. Several justices were mentioned as possible presidential candidates during the nineteenth century. John McLean sought the first Republican presidential nomination in 1856.[45] McLean's presidential ambition dated back to the late 1820s, when he thought he could succeed Andrew Jackson as early as 1832. During his thirty-two years on the Court, McLean was frequently mentioned as a possible presidential nominee for the Democratic, Anti-Mason, Whig, and Republican Parties. McLean even quietly pushed his own presidential candidacy with key politicians around the nation while he was riding circuit. As a result, newspapers frequently promoted McLean as a presidential prospect.[46] McLean and his supporters even attempted to establish McLean-owned newspapers in Ohio to publicize his candidacy.[47] The 1856 nomination from the newly created Republican Party seemed particularly attainable to McLean because his antislavery views had become popular with Republicans.

McLean was accused of using his Supreme Court opinions for campaign purposes. One example was the pending Dred Scott decision on the constitutionality of slavery. McLean may have had his own written dissenting opinion on the case ready as early as 1856. Supporters of his presidential prospects urged that the decision be released so that McLean's views, via his own written opinion, could receive publicity prior to the Republican Party nominating convention. However, the other justices worried about the case's impact on the 1856 election. One theory was that the Dred Scott case was delayed for a year – until after the 1856 presidential election – specifically to prevent McLean from using it in a campaign bid.[48]

McLean may not have been able to get his views on the Dred Scott case out through an opinion during the campaign, but he found another way to separate himself from the Court's majority who upheld slavery. He wrote essays in the press, particularly in northern newspapers, to publicize his views against slavery.[49] Unlike his predecessors during the early Court, McLean's essays were signed. That effort signaled to Republican voters that McLean shared their antislavery views.

McLean failed in his presidential bid, but four years later, another justice became the object of a draft movement for the presidency. John Campbell was suggested by several newspaper editorials as a possible compromise candidate for president in the 1860 presidential election. Campbell was a southern-born justice who opposed secession. However, unlike McLean and later Chase, Campbell made no effort to encourage the effort, and he was not nominated by any party.[50]

In 1872, however, another justice did become an active presidential candidate. One year earlier, David Davis, who had been Lincoln's campaign manager during his successful 1860 presidential campaign, had been approached by a group of Illinois legislators seeking a candidate for president. Davis turned them down but admitted that "after they left, I had not walked six blocks before I had my entire cabinet picket out."[51] Davis encouraged two friends to become his campaign managers. They lobbied newspapers sympathetic to the Democratic Party to tout Davis. As a result, newspapers began to endorse Davis as a possible presidential candidate. Simultaneously, a group of Republicans who were unhappy with the administration of President Ulysses S. Grant called for their own "Liberal Republican" convention, where Davis was considered a strong candidate for the nomination of the new group. At the same time, a new minor party called Labor Reform met in a convention and gave Davis their nomination. The party expected that Davis would be nominated as well by the Liberal Republicans and the Democrats. However, the Labor Reform platform of a paper currency not grounded in metal was largely unpopular. Davis, not wanting to foreclose the possibility of a nomination by the other parties, refused to either explicitly accept or decline the nomination.[52]

Davis was the likely nominee of the Liberal Republican Party until four leading newspaper editors met the day before the convention and collaborated to kill Davis' chances. One of the editors reported the cabal: "Seated at the same table, each of us indited a leading editorial for his paper, to be wired to its destination and printed next morning, striking D. Davis at a prearranged and varying angle." The papers, which included the *Chicago Tribune* and the *New York Tribune*, covered themes against Davis such as the amount of money the Davis campaign had spent to secure the nomination, the campaign's use of hired men to outshout their opponents at the convention, and the inappropriateness of a justice running for president. All of the editorials were reprinted in the *Cincinnati Commercial*, the main paper in the convention city of Cincinnati.[53] The ploy worked. The delegates moved away from Davis and eventually nominated Horace Greeley, editor of the *New York Tribune*. Davis then discouraged the Democrats from nominating him and declined the Labor Reform nomination as well.[54]

Like Chase and Davis, Justice Stephen Field actively sought a presidential nomination.[55] Again, the press was an important element in Field's strategy of running while not admitting he was running. Field had been appointed to the Court by Abraham Lincoln, even though he was well known as an ardent Democrat. During his first thirteen years on the bench, Field distanced himself from active political involvement. In 1876, Field told a San Francisco newspaper reporter that he had no comment on the nomination of Samuel Tilden as Democratic presidential nominee. "My present office is foreign to politics and forbids my canvassing the merits or demerits of the gentlemen who are now striving for the chief magistracy."[56]

However, that was before the 1877 electoral commission. Field served on that commission as one of two Democratic justices on the Court. Despite Field's efforts to encourage the commission to recommend Tilden's election, the commission tipped to the Republicans and sided with Rutherford B. Hayes. Field was so disturbed by the outcome that he decided to enter partisan politics in the next presidential election.[57]

Not long after Hayes' inauguration, Field began to take steps to run for president. In 1877, he wrote a memoir that looked much like a campaign biography. In 1880, in the midst of the presidential campaign that year, the biography was shortened to a pamphlet for broad distribution. Field also used his opinions to clearly articulate his views about states' rights. Also, in a decision popular with southern Democrats, Field wrote a dissenting opinion saying that states could ban blacks from jury duty. Field was absent from the Democratic national convention in Cincinnati that year, but so were other presidential candidates. As was the case with other candidates, Field's supporters shepherded his campaign at the convention. They met with delegates and distributed thousands of copies of the pamphlet-biography.

However, Field's candidacy was undermined by events at the convention. Field was nominated by a California delegate, but the speech was declared by the press as "a decided failure."[58] Moreover, the California delegation, which should have favored Field as a favorite son, was divided over possible candidates.[59] Also, Democratic Party leaders did not expect to win western states and were not interested in a candidate from the West. They wanted to concentrate on voters in the Northeast and Midwest and nominated General Winfield S. Hancock from Pennsylvania for president and William H. English of Indiana for vice president. Moreover, some of Field's previous decisions from before he had decided to run for president hurt him with the delegates. As a Supreme Court justice, Field had ruled in favor of Chinese immigrants fighting discriminatory California state laws, which rankled many voters in his home state. And as a presiding judge in a district course case, Field had thrown out an ordinance requiring that Chinese prisoners' pigtails be cut off. With strong anti-Chinese sentiment among Californians, Field's decision was highly unpopular.

By the second ballot, Field had won only sixty-five-and-a-half votes, which was his high point in the balloting. The result of the initial balloting was disappointing for Field. He had expected to get 250 votes.[60] After losing badly, Field did not send a congratulatory letter to General Hancock. He was interviewed by a reporter after the convention and said that his loss was due to lack of support in California and that he would have nothing to do with politics in the future.[61]

Despite his promise to the reporter, Field did not discourage others from promoting him as a possible presidential nominee four years later. Field's possible presidential candidacy in 1884 was debated in the California press. He was criticized by some newspapers, such as the San Francisco *Chronicle*, but praised by two other San Francisco newspapers – the *Argonaut* and the *Evening Post*.[62] An anonymous letter sent to California Democrats suggested that Field be considered as a presidential candidate at the convention and receive the support of the California delegation. Like Salmon Chase during an earlier campaign, Field was placed in an awkward position by the letter. He wrote to the editor of the San Francisco *Alta* saying that he had not sponsored the campaign to promote him. But, acting like a presidential candidate, Field also used the opportunity to launch a defense of the opinions that had engendered public opposition. He predicted that "one of these days our good people will see their error, and then they will do me full justice."[63]

During the campaign, a group of Democrats from Missouri visited with Field and urged him to allow them to promote his presidential candidacy. They asked him if he would accept the nomination if it were offered. He replied that he would. However, the prospect of his candidacy so infuriated many California Democrats that the state party convention in 1884 met and passed an unusual resolution repudiating his possible presidential candidacy and pledging not to support any national convention delegate who endorsed Field.[64] With the express opposition of his own state delegation, Field's candidacy was impossible.

McLean, Chase, Campbell, and Field were not the only justices who were promoted as possible presidential candidates. Indeed, most presidential elections during the nineteenth century included efforts to recruit a Supreme Court justice to run that year. Some Democrats sought to obtain the Democratic presidential nomination for Justice James Wayne in 1860.[65] Similar efforts were made in 1892 in behalf of Melville Fuller while he was chief justice. However, as mentioned earlier, Fuller was a proponent of Grover Cleveland's renomination.

Presidential ambition was not uncommon, because the Supreme Court still was not viewed generally as the culmination of a public service career. Nor was the presidency the only allure for justices who might have been interested in using the Court as a stepping-stone. Presidents repeatedly sought to lure justices away to fill posts within their administrations. John Tyler offered leadership of the War Department to John McLean in 1841.[66] Following his reelection in 1892, Grover Cleveland offered Melville Fuller the post of secretary of state in his second administration.

Alternately, some justices sought to change the image of the Court as a stepping-stone to other office. For instance, in response to Cleveland's offer, Fuller sought to persuade Cleveland that the Court was a pinnacle of public service. In a letter to Cleveland, he responded that the "surrender of the highest judicial office in the world for a political position, even though so eminent, would tend to detract from the dignity and weight of the tribunal."[67] That image, which Fuller was determined to establish, would only begin to take hold later in the twentieth century.

The difficulty of a justice moving to another office, particularly an elective office, was indicated in an exchange between newspaper publisher Duff Green and John McLean, who was contemplating a run for the presidency. In 1829, Green wrote in the *Cincinnati Gazette* that it would corrupt the bench for a judge to have to run for political office. He was referring to attempts to position John McLean for a presidential run if Andrew Jackson, at age sixty-five, decided not to run again.[68] McLean responded with a letter to Green disputing his view of judicial advancement to political office. McLean argued that in the past, there had been no objection to judges becoming candidates for governor or senator. He also pointed out that he was disadvantaged as a possible candidate because he had no patronage to give out. In fact, McLean noted, if anything, he was severely disadvantaged; his decisions were bound to make enemies. McLean complained that Martin Van Buren, the Secretary of State at the time, had far more opportunity to campaign than he did. "The Secretary has his agents and his presses in this state and in western states ... approaching to the object [Van Buren's nomination] with a step that never tires and an eye that never winks."[69] In another letter, McLean complained that Jackson, whom he sought to replace in the White House, had so much influence over the Democratic-leaning press that if he "should call out a regiment and drive the Senate or perhaps the House of Representatives into the Potomac, the act would be eulogized by the great mass of his editors. . . . "[70]

McLean's letters are prescient descriptions of the problems Supreme Court justices faced when they attempted to run for president through the nineteenth and twentieth centuries. Justices did not possess the political tools available to other candidates, including patronage or the ability to campaign actively. Moreover, the cases they took, which they were required to accept at that time, could lead to unpopular opinions that might place any presidential candidacy in jeopardy. The letters also are remarkable admissions of McLean's own political ambition and his serious consideration of the advantages and disadvantages of running for office, including the critical role of the press in obtaining that objective.

Even when justices were not running for office, some were involved in political issues beyond the Court. James Wayne publicly opposed the U.S. role in European affairs in 1852.[71] As southern states seceded from the Union, Wayne, Campbell, and Justice Samuel Nelson tried to mediate between the South and the federal government.[72] Nelson did say publicly that he felt the South was correct in seceding and that he would have gone with the South had he lived there.[73]

Even when justices wanted to separate themselves from political activities, it became difficult to do so. When David Davis came to the Court in 1862, he vowed to avoid being "mixed up in politics." However, because he retained his interest in Republican Party affairs, knew and regularly associated with many Washington politicians, and was a close friend of the president, Davis ultimately found his vow difficult to keep.[74]

Whereas previous justices had been state candidates, the presidential ambitions of later justices suggested that as the national government's power was increasing, the federal government, not the state, seemed the appropriate next step for Supreme Court justices. Also, it indicated that Supreme Court justices as individuals had acquired a national status that they believed could be translated into national electoral support, although none of the nineteenth-century justices had been able to accomplish this.

THE COURT, AND THE JUSTICES, IN THE PUBLIC EYE

Like their colleagues in the twentieth century, Supreme Court nominees received press attention at the time of their appointments. Newspapers were quick to praise nominees they believed would represent their views. The

Richmond Whig wrote that Lucius Q. C. Lamar, a former Confederate official, possessed a "maturity of his intellect . . . with a ripe experience in law and in public service that cannot fail to place him among the most distinguished jurists that ever graced the Bench of the Supreme Court.'[75] However, the *New York Evening Post* accused Lamar of unethical conduct while in office and immoral activity. The paper wrote that Lamar had been having an affair with a woman in Mississippi and had given her government jobs.[76]

Once on the Court, individual justices also became the object of press attention when they delivered opinions of interest to the public. Occasionally, newspapers praised justices when their opinions were agreeable to them. A news story for the *Boston Post* in February 1846 opined about newly appointed Levi Woodbury, a New Hampshire native. The newspaper described Woodbury's opinions as "distinguished for ability, clearness and sound law which have elicited warm commendations from all quarters." Regarding Woodbury himself, the correspondent said that he was "holding fast to the integrity of his original principles."[77]

Justices also were criticized, typically again for the quality of their opinions. Like the politicians of the day, justices occasionally were compared with their predecessors on the Court who had loomed large in American history. After comparison with earlier justices such as John Jay, Oliver Ellsworth, or John Marshall, the *New York Commercial Advertiser* concluded that newly appointed chief justice Roger Taney did not measure up to his predecessors. The paper concluded that the wisdom of the early justices "is to be set at naught by such small lights as have been recently placed on the bench." Similarly, the New York *Review* declared at the same time regarding Taney's appointment that "a gathering gloom is cast over the future."[78]

The Court and the justices were criticized at a personal level that is unusual today, particularly during the fractious pre–Civil War era. The *New York Independent* wrote that the Court was acting "at the will and instigation of the Slave Oligarchy."[79] The *New York Tribune* called Justice Benjamin Curtis "a slave-catching Judge, appointed to office as a reward for his professional support given to the Fugitive Slave Bill."[80] Other papers attacked Roger Taney as no more than a political hack because of his close relations with Andrew Jackson. One paper offered that Taney was "inferior in talents and learning, and especially in legal reputation" and that "he does not enjoy the confidence of a very large portion of the community."[81]

The growing polarization in the nation in the 1850s affected press treatment of the justices. The chief justice was described as "the unscrupulous Taney," and the Court itself was called "scandalously sectional, grossly partial, a mockery of the Constitution, a serf of the slave power, and a disgrace to the country."[82] After the Merryman case in 1861, in which Taney ruled that the writ of habeas corpus could not be suspended by the president, the *New York Tribune* opined that Taney "takes sides with traitors." The *New York Times* concluded that the chief justice "uses the powers of his office to serve the cause of the traitors," and another newspaper wrote that if the trend of the Court continued, "treason will find a place of refuge, and its abettors encouragement and sympathy, in the Supreme Court."[83] Newspapers reflected the general disregard for the Court that characterized the period. Opinions of the Court sometimes were characterized as irrelevant. One paper called James Wayne's decisions "no more than opinion, supported by no proofs or reasons, and to be taken only for what it is worth."[84]

The justices were assumed by the press to be first and foremost regional partisans. In northern newspapers, southern justices were denounced as spies. A couple of weeks after Fort Sumter was attacked, John Campbell, an Alabama native, resigned to return to his home state. However, the *New York Evening Post* accused Campbell of staying too long in the capital and charged that the former justice was a "convenient spy for the Montgomery mutineers."[85] Northern newspapers praised James Wayne, a Georgia native, for staying loyal to the Union and attending the August 1861 session of the Court. But a Georgia newspaper declared, "Georgia does not claim him, and he is no more of us."[86]

The Reconstruction period was no better for the justices. As Radical Republicans sought to limit the Court's power, the press joined in. While Massachusetts Representative Thaddeus Stevens proposed remodeling the Court and the Congress voted to limit the appellate jurisdiction of the Court and eliminate one justice position, the press frequently joined the general attack on the Court's role and the integrity of the individual justices. In the wake of the Milligan case in 1866, in which the Court declared that military tribunals were unconstitutional where a civilian court was in operation, Republican newspapers condemned the justices. The *Washington Chronicle* opined that "the hearts of traitors will be glad," and the *Independent* sniffed that the opinion was "a sorry attempt of five not very distinguished persons to exhibit themselves as profound jurists."[87]

Even after the Civil War, individual justices became the subject of personal vituperation launched by some newspapers. The *Cincinnati Gazette* concluded that James Wayne had "passed beyond the age allotted to man, and with his tottering and shattered frame his intellect is crumbling too." Justice Robert C. Grier was described as "the fossil which he is."[88] David Davis was linked to Jefferson Davis by *The Philadelphia North American* when an editorial charged that Lincoln had "made a mistake in appointing a Judge of the fatal name of Davis." Given the viciousness of the attacks on the Court as an institution and the individual members, it may not have been surprising at the time for one paper, the *New York Herald*, to even recommend abolishing the Supreme Court.[89]

Dred Scott

Coverage of the Court was sparked by key events during the nineteenth century, most importantly the Dred Scott case. Interestingly, the case initially elicited limited attention from the press. With the exception of a few abolitionist newspapers in the North, the press largely ignored the oral arguments made in the case.[90] After the Dred Scott decision appeared, however, the press devoted extensive coverage and commentary to it. The decision clearly divided the nation, as indicated by each region's response to it. Northern newspapers saw the decision as purely political.[91] The *New York Tribune* opined that "the court has rushed into politics" to serve the "cause of slavery." The newspaper called the Court majority in the case "five slaveholders and two doughfaces."[92] Even a less vitriolic response was still highly critical; the Springfield (Mass.) *Republican* opined that "the majority of the Court therefore rushed needlessly to their conclusions and are justly open to the suspicion of being induced to pronounce them by partisan or sectional influences."[93] Not surprisingly, southern papers praised the decision. The *Richmond Enquirer* termed the Court "a tribunal of jurists, as learned, impartial and unprejudiced as perhaps the world has ever seen."[94]

Because the decision came from a deeply fractured Court with multiple opinions, press attention was devoted to individual justices' opinions. The *New York Independent* termed Taney's opinion "a stump speech spoken for political effect" and called for opposition to the decision, writing that it was "the utter subjugation and extermination of all that remained of the protesting voice of liberty."[95] The *Cleveland Herald* called Taney's opinion "monstrous," while the paper praised McLean as "a fearless, intelligent, and brilliant intellect."[96]

The 1876 Election Controversy

Another high mark for press coverage of the justices during this period was the controversy regarding the 1876 presidential election and the subsequent 1877 electoral commission.[97] Democratic presidential nominee Samuel Tilden won the popular vote in the centennial year presidential election and initially had a twenty-vote electoral college margin over his Republican opponent, Rutherford B. Hayes. However, electoral college votes in Florida, South Carolina, and Louisiana were disputed by both sides amidst charges of electoral fraud.

In January 1877, Congress met to open the electoral ballots. When the ballots from the three southern states in question were disputed, Congress referred the matter to a fifteen-member bipartisan electoral commission to resolve the electoral college vote controversy. Five of the commissioners were Democratic members of Congress, whereas another five were Republican members. The remaining five were Supreme Court justices. At first, two of the justices on the commission were Republicans and the other two were Democrats. Those four were charged with selecting a fifth justice, who would be the fifteenth member of the commission.

Initially, the four justices chose David Davis, a political independent on the Court. Although Davis had been Lincoln's campaign manager during the 1860 presidential election and ostensibly a Republican, his attempt to gain the nomination from the Liberal Republican Party placed him apart from traditional Republicans. Moreover, early in 1877, the Illinois state legislature, dominated by the Democrats, elected Davis to be a U.S. senator. Davis surprised observers by accepting and resigning from the Court. Because he was no longer on the Court, he could not serve as the fifth, supposedly independent, member of the commission. That left the justices with a dilemma. Only two justices were Democrats and already served on the commission. The remaining six were Republicans. The two Democrats – Field and Nathan Clifford – agreed to the appointment of Joseph Bradley, who was viewed as the weakest Republican of the justices.

The connection to the Court did not end there. The Supreme Court chambers became the meeting place for the new ad hoc commission. The commissioners sat at a table in front of the Supreme Court bench, although the justices did not wear their robes when they sat with the other members of the commission. Like Supreme Court justices, the electoral commission heard arguments from both the Democrats and the Republicans. The surroundings and the proceedings made it seem like this was yet another case the Court was deciding, although most of the participants were members of Congress. The press sat in the press gallery, as they did during a Supreme Court session. According to a reporter for the *New York World*, an officer of the Court reminded the members of the press that they couldn't smoke.[98]

Much like an election 124 years later, the justices, particularly Bradley, became crucial in the determination of who won the election. The commission deliberated in secret after hearing testimony from both sides and, with the inauguration date (March 4) approaching, they finally voted. Bradley, who was undecided until the end, was subjected to intense lobbying by both the Democrats and the Republicans. Ultimately, he voted with the Republicans to certify the Republican electors from the disputed states.[99]

Despite their agreement to participate in the commission, the justices who did so were well aware of the political nature of the activity they were engaged in and the fact that, in a closely divided nation, one-half of the electorate would be unhappy with the outcome. The justices expected that the unhappy party would take its wrath out on those who had decided the outcome, including the justices of the Supreme Court. Justice William Strong told another commission member who was not on the Court that "all the judges except one were very sorry to be called to the commission."[100] Strong and the other justices were correct in their assessment of who would be blamed. Around the nation, Republicans cheered the decision, but many Democrats were bitter. They vilified the Republican justices – Bradley, Miller, and Strong. In Monticello, New York, an angry crowd hung the three in effigy.[101]

Worse, internal deliberations on the commission, particularly those involving Bradley, became well known in the press. Stephen Field reportedly circulated a rumor that Bradley initially had been willing to grant Florida's electors to Tilden but changed his mind after a secret nighttime session with Republican leaders. The accusation went public. Bradley decided he needed to explain his actions to the nation and used the press to do so. He wrote a letter to the editor of the Newark *Advertiser* to blunt the accusations that he had caved to pressure from Republicans. He acknowledged that he had vacillated on the Florida case at first but argued that he believed he had come to the right decision eventually.[102] In response to the published letter, Field wrote to Samuel Tilden: "The language of the letter justifies some of the comments of the press upon the change of views which the judge experienced shortly before the vote was taken. . . ."[103]

The criticism of some of the justices continued even after the new president was inaugurated. Field and Clifford were so unhappy with the result that they boycotted Hayes' inauguration. Republican-leaning newspapers noted that the two Democratic justices who had been on the electoral commission were absent from Hayes' inauguration and commented on it. Republican papers accused the two of "an act of discourtesy as discreditable and unworthy as it was uncalled for and undignified." The paper asserted: "[N]ot being able to forget that they were Democrats, they were unable to remember that they were justices."[104]

The Impeachment of Andrew Johnson

Another dramatic incident bringing press attention to the Court, or at least to Salmon Chase, was the impeachment trial of President Andrew Johnson. The trial was the first in the history of the nation, and the image of the chief justice presiding over a trial of a president also was a first. To date, only one other chief justice, William Rehnquist, has had a similar experience, 130 years later.

Johnson's impeachment trial, which lasted from March 30 to May 16, 1868, was occurring while rumors were circulating about Chase's presidential ambitions. Because Chase had been a presidential candidate eight years earlier, had attempted to wrest the nomination from Lincoln in 1864, and was publicly toying with the idea of running in 1868, it was easy to believe that Chase had a stake in Johnson's removal from office. Chase was accused by some critics of lobbying senators to acquit Johnson. Chase protested that his role as the presiding officer was nonpolitical. He wrote that he did not understand how presiding over a trial would be considered political. Chase wrote: "I suppose there is no man in the country who had less personal interest in the result than myself."[105]

As a result of the rumors about Chase's efforts to affect the outcome, the press covered Chase more thoroughly than they had any previous chief justice. Much like the paparazzi of later days, journalists followed Chase around Washington during the trial to observe what he did and with whom he spoke. Newspapers gave accounts of seemingly his every activity in relation to the trial. Newspaper stories reported Chase talking with wavering senators during a carriage ride, in a street conversation, and over dinner.[106] Accusations of Chase actually affecting the outcome were not proven, and coverage of Chase returned to more normal levels after the trial ended.

PAYING ATTENTION TO PRESS COVERAGE

The justices were hardly uninformed about what the press said about them. In fact, like their predecessors in the early years, they tracked closely what the press reported about specific decisions as well as about the Court generally. On April 19, 1839, Joseph Story wrote to Roger Taney, following the corporation cases, that "your opinion in the corporation cases has given very general satisfaction to the public...."[107] Morrison Waite kept news clippings of numerous Supreme Court decisions during his tenure, particularly about press coverage of high-profile decisions. He also tracked stories of speeches by other justices as well as news about the presidential candidacy of Stephen Field, including editorial commentary urging Field to run. The justices also noted how the institution of the Court generally was being treated in the press. In the midst of congressional battles with the Supreme Court about Reconstruction, David Davis wrote to his wife in 1868 that "you will see by the papers that the Supreme Court is in bad repute with Congress."[108]

Naturally, they seemed most interested in press coverage of themselves. As just mentioned, some of them were inveterate news clippers. Not surprisingly, Salmon Chase kept a large file of newspaper clippings about himself while he was chief justice. Actually, Chase was continuing a practice he had started forty years earlier.[109] Morrison Waite also maintained an extensive clipping file that even included news coverage of his daughter. One clip described her as "having marked personal beauty of the Portia type, intellect, and vivacity."[110]

Their news consumption was not always a pleasant experience, however. Lucius Q. C. Lamar reportedly was so disturbed by a newspaper story reporting his failing health that he "stood under his chandelier, and, leaping up straight, kicked it, being then about sixty years of age and weighing two hundred pounds."[111] David Davis was wounded deeply by newspaper attacks on him. In the wake of criticism of the Milligan case, Davis remarked that "newspapers can't write down Magna Carta."[112] Morrison Waite chafed over Charleston, South Carolina, newspapers that suggested the chief justice was ill-treated by local citizens during his visit there and complained about it. Waite wrote to an editor of an Ohio newspaper to correct the rumor of ill treatment and that he had been unhappy with his reception.[113] Samuel Miller, in particular, thought considerably about the press, and his thoughts were rarely positive. Once he charged that "the newspaper tyranny is the most oppressive now in existence, and the gravest problem of the age is to determine where relief shall come from." Miller opined that the press had "respected the Courts longer than anything else, and lately they have combined to bring the Courts and the administration of justice under their control. . . ."[114] He also wrote to a friend that newspapers were becoming corporate enterprises governed by dividends and that "honor, religion, morals, political principles are only to be referred to and thought of as cards in [the] game for dividends."[115] Samuel Miller admitted to a friend that he was "not very thick skinned about newspaper stories."[116]

Nor was Miller alone in bemoaning how justices were treated by the press. Roger Taney expressed his views about the press to the court reporter after being criticized for a decision.

The daily press, from the nature of things, can never be the "field of fame" for judges; and I am so sensible that it is the last place that we should voluntarily select for our decisions, that, on more occasions than one, when I have seen my opinions at Circuit incorrectly stated, I have declined publishing the opinion really delivered, because I did not think it proper for a Judge of the Supreme Court to go into the newspapers to discuss legal questions.[117]

JUSTICES' EXTERNAL STRATEGIES

The justices were not just observing press coverage; they were attempting to shape it. Perhaps even more so than today, justices felt compelled to respond to press coverage. They even urged each other to affect their own press coverage. During Melville Fuller's confirmation process for chief justice, John Marshall Harlan, who was already on the Court, wrote to Fuller urging him to respond to newspaper criticism of Fuller's war record. "This is not an occasion for too much dignity. You and your friends should not stand still and allow you to be put down or hurt by misrepresentation."[118]

Some of the methods for influencing coverage had changed since the early years. For the most part, the justices had abandoned the use of grand jury charges to score political points. Yet, occasionally such charges sparked attention. In the late 1850s, Justice John Campbell was criticized for grand jury charges condemning the slave trade and urging juries to act firmly against offenders.[119] Pseudonymous essay writing also declined. One notable exception was John McLean. McLean took exception to an article in the *Washington Globe*, the Jackson administration's paper. The paper opposed the Court's actions in the Cherokee Nation cases. Lewis Cass, Jackson's secretary of war, had written a response that was approved by Jackson and published in the paper. McLean decided to reply in print as well. He wrote an essay that was given to Joseph Gales, the editor of the *National Intelligencer*. But McLean didn't want his name to be attached. He asked Gales to publish it under the pseudonym "A Member of Congress." However, the letter was never published.[120]

In the late 1840s, McLean again was incensed by press criticism of the Court. In this case, the criticism came from the *Cincinnati Herald* and was penned by Stanley Matthews. The future justice published an editorial in the *Cincinnati Herald* that censured the Court for its 1847 *Jones v. VanZandt* decision. It involved the case of an Ohio farmer who had given a ride in his wagon to slaves who had escaped from Kentucky. McLean replied in a letter to the editor. He called himself "A Subscriber." He took Matthews to task for the criticism, pointing out that the Court was not deciding cases all in one direction. He pointed to the Amistad case of six years earlier in which the Court had ruled in favor of liberating an African slave.[121] However, McLean's pseudonymous essay writing was less the rule and more the exception by the 1840s and 1850s.

In fact, McLean himself abandoned the pseudonymous essay when he sought the presidency in 1848. After an invitation to express his views on national issues more fully, McLean provided a statement of his positions to a supporter with the expectation that it would be printed in newspapers with his name attached. The *Gazette*, the *National Intelligencer*, and the *Washington Union* all printed the statement expressing McLean's views on the Mexican War, Treasury notes, and direct taxation. McLean's use of the press to further his political ambitions even provoked an attack from the floor of the U.S. Senate. In a speech, Mississippi Senator Henry S. Foote denounced McLean as "a political letter-writer." Perhaps not surprisingly, McLean replied in the newspapers to assert he had a right to express his views in the public papers. He wrote: "As a citizen, I claim the right and shall exercise it, of forming and expressing my opinion on public measures."[122]

Written opinions remained a vehicle for justices seeking to affect press coverage and public opinion. Today, opinions delivered from the bench in the courtroom are immediately released by the Public Information Office. However, in the nineteenth century, opinions were read from the bench but were not printed and released until some time later. In the Dred Scott case, the time difference became important. Two dissenters, John McLean and Benjamin R. Curtis, released their opinions to the press before the Court's opinion, written by the chief justice, was made available.[123] In response to the reaction to his opinion, Taney added several pages after the announcement but before its printing.[124] As mentioned earlier, some justices used their opinions for their own political ends – McLean to win over Republican voters on the slavery issue and Field to court states rights' voters. Both expected that such decisions would be widely published in the press.

Justices also used another tactic – providing additional, and sometimes confidential, information to reporters writing about the Court. During the early years of the Court, newspapers were filled with partisan essays, often written by politicians. After the press became more independent of political control, journalism as we know it today emerged. That included the practice of reporters seeking scoops, as suggested by the pursuit of Salmon Chase by reporters while he was presiding over the impeachment trial. In contrast, the Court's deliberations typically have been characterized by intense secrecy. The secrecy of the Court seemed to attract the interest of nineteenth-century journalists who were anxious to acquire inside information about the Court's deliberations. Indeed, with the assistance of some of the justices, occasionally journalists were able to penetrate the Court's inner sanctum to glean confidential information. Shortly after Melville Fuller took office as chief justice in 1888, the *Chicago Tribune* ran a story with detailed information about Fuller. These included personal trivia such as Fuller's dislike of having to wear a robe, the fact that he eschewed socializing, and his penchant for reading novels in his spare time. The story was so personal that the unnamed source had to be Fuller or someone who was very close to the new chief justice.[125]

On several occasions, the justices' private decision-making processes became public. One example was news coverage of the Dred Scott case. In
early 1857, President-elect James Buchanan asked Justice John Catron when
the Dred Scott decision would be made available. Catron replied that the
chief justice was sensitive about the release of this information to anyone
because the New York *Tribune* seemed to know what was going on concerning the case inside the Court.[126] Indeed, James S. Pike, one of the *Tribune's*
Washington reporters, wrote accounts of the justices' likely positions on the
case before the decision was announced. Taney concluded that Pike's information could have come only from one of the justices. A Taney biographer
concluded John McLean was the likely source because McLean sympathized
with the paper's leanings and had been angling for the Republican Party presidential nomination.[127] Pike seemed to know how each justice would rule
and what he would say when the decision was announced. He predicted that
McLean, Curtis, and Grier would dissent and that Nelson would join the
majority. Even though the Court seemed likely to deliver its opinion on the
case in 1856, Pike knew that the decision would not be forthcoming that year
but would be held for reargument during the next term.[128]

Another case of a leak from inside the justices' conference room came
in 1895 as the Court was on the verge of announcing its decision on the
constitutionality of a federal income tax. Two days before the decision was to
be announced, the *Chicago Tribune* announced what the decision would be.
The story, which appeared on April 6, 1895, detailed how each justice would
vote on the case and exactly how the Court would rule on specific provisions of
the law. The story was distributed by wire associations to newspapers across the
nation. The *Tribune*, along with other papers, also reported that one justice,
George Shiras, had switched his vote on the case, although Shiras later denied
it. [129] The leaking continued even after the initial story appeared. The *Nashville
American* published a report from a Washington correspondent that "one of
the justices of the Supreme Court practically admitted, after consultation
Saturday [April 6], that the abstract of the decision in the income tax case
printed in the Tribune was absolutely correct. . . . "[130]

The opportunity to leak to a reporter was readily available to the justices. As
reporters became common fixtures as observers of life, society, and politics, justices found them to be a regular presence surrounding them as well. Reporters
were eager to interview justices, who found they could use such interviews to
attempt to shape public opinion. However, they also were concerned about
that very perception that they were seeking to influence the public. For example, Lucius Q. C. Lamar gave an interview in February 1889 to a reporter for
the *Baltimore Sun*. During the course of the interview, Lamar delivered his

personal views about the current administration of Grover Cleveland (in its last days), the federal government policies toward the South, and the incoming president, Benjamin Harrison. Lamar praised the outgoing administration of Grover Cleveland, who had appointed him. He said that previous administrations had treated Southerners with hostility and mistrust and that they were viewed as "a community apart." However, after Lamar reviewed the transcript of the interview, he concluded that it lacked propriety and refused to allow publication. The interview was not published until after Lamar's death.[131]

Other justices, though, were not so circumspect. Immediately after the Civil War, Salmon Chase made a lengthy tour of the South. While traveling, Chase frequently wrote to Andrew Johnson about his observations. But Chase also wanted the public to be aware of his southern mission and his reaction to what he saw. He brought along newspaper editor Whitelaw Reid, who gave the Associated Press a series of articles about Chase's visit and his views on Reconstruction.[132]

Indeed, the justices were more readily accessible to the press than they are today. Whereas justices today park in an underground parking garage and are unlikely to be casually approached by a reporter on the street, the nineteenth century was significantly different. Justices walked to the Supreme Court building from their homes. Reporters easily could approach them and talk. One Washington correspondent once walked Morrison Waite from the Court to his home. Upon arriving, Waite invited the reporter into his house.[133] Shortly after Lucius Q. C. Lamar was confirmed, a reporter from the *New York World* called on Lamar at his home and reported that he was ushered in and joined a party of friends of Lamar extending his congratulations.[134]

The ease with which justices could be informally approached on a regular basis led the justices to make statements to the press that would be more difficult to obtain today. On December 11, 1876, Samuel Miller was quoted in the *Chicago Times* on current politics, including derogatory remarks he made about the Democrats and their presidential candidate, Samuel Tilden. Miller reportedly said that Tilden's past "indicates that he would resort to anything to carry his point and attain his ambition."[135] Miller claimed he never gave the interview but had only met the man in the street and talked with him after the man started a conversation about the electoral vote controversy, although Miller admitted he knew the man was a reporter.[136]

NINETEENTH-CENTURY JUSTICE-PRESS RELATIONS

Justices of the nineteenth century held political backgrounds that made them familiar with the press prior to their Court service. Moreover, some even had worked in the press as reporters or editors prior to pursuing legal careers culminating in their positions on the Court. The press acquired a new standing in political life as largely autonomous players no longer bound by explicit ties to individual politicians or political parties. Although the press continued to be partisan, journalists held independent positions rather than as mouthpieces that were at least partly financially dependent on their patrons.

Journalists became more like reporters are today. As such, they covered the Court differently than partisan editors had during its early years. Justices were news, much like other players in government. Nor were they above criticism. Editors were quick to disparage justices' opinions of which they disapproved and to censure particular justices with whom they disagreed.

Justices of the day often interacted with reporters in a variety of ways. Many justices thought about the press, followed what the press said, and, like others in national government, used the press to understand what was going on in the larger political environment. At times, they also attempted to influence what the press said about them. Some, such as John McLean, Salmon Chase, and Stephen Field, did so to further political ambitions. They viewed the press as a vehicle for wooing delegates and voters.

Even those not running for president still sought to shape their images in the press. Occasionally, their written opinions served that purpose. In the case of Dred Scott, the justices knew that their opinions would be thoroughly examined by the press. Therefore, those opinions served as opportunities to articulate their views on slavery and influence the direction of public opinion on the most important public policy issue of the day. Yet press coverage of controversial opinions did not necessarily engender public support, as Field learned. Nor could an individual justice control when a Court opinion appeared in order to further his political ambition, as McLean discovered.

But their opinions were not the only method of communication justices employed to reach the press and the public. They wrote essays – sometimes pseudonymous and sometimes not – to present their views to the public. They also used letters to the editor. They gave off-the-record or background interviews about the Court's internal deliberations. Some even sat for on-the-record interviews with reporters.

Nineteenth-century justices engaged in press relations to a greater extent than their predecessors had. Perhaps this was due to the larger number of justices with explicit presidential ambitions during this period or the fact that there were more former politicians who sat on the Court. Or perhaps the previous experience some had as members of the press influenced their relations with the fourth branch of government. Moreover, some of the justices engaged in highly individualistic external strategies, particularly related to presidential ambition. This individualistic approach to the press also may have been the result of the loss of a strong chief justice like John Marshall. Marshall had kept the justices unified for most of his tenure, particularly through the use of seriatim opinions that hid the individual justices' views and personalities behind a combined opinion. No subsequent chief justice was so successful at directing the justices toward institutional rather than individually oriented communication with the press and the public.

As Chapter 5 shows, as the twentieth century dawned, significant challenges to the Court as an institution, and the reputations of individual justices, would occur. The Court would face pressures from the new broadcast media and changes in the role of journalism that would challenge the justices' ability to interact with the press while maintaining the image of distance from the press and the public. Additionally, the Court would experience public fissures among the justices, high-profile cases that attracted press and public notice, and a changed judicial selection process. Finally, the first (and so far only) resignation of a justice under media pressure over ethics would occur in the twentieth century. But the first issue for the Court would come when one of the justices did what none of the eighteenth- or nineteenth-century justices could – that is, actually win a major party presidential nomination.

5

The Twentieth Century

On June 10, 1916, Associate Justice Charles Evans Hughes was nominated at the Republican National Convention as the party's presidential candidate. The primary reason for Hughes' nomination was not his service on the Court. In fact, Hughes was still a relatively new justice with only six years on the bench. Rather, it was Hughes' political background that attracted the Republicans. He had been governor of New York for two terms before being appointed to the Court by William Howard Taft in 1910. He also had been Taft's choice for vice-presidential running mate in 1912, although Hughes had declined the offer.[1]

Hughes' move from Supreme Court bench to presidential candidate marked a high (or low, depending on the perspective) of an individual justice's involvement with electoral politics. Never before had a sitting Supreme Court justice received a major party nomination. Nor had one left the bench to run for president. Remarkably, this event came after more than a century of efforts by some of his predecessors to reinforce the notion that what Hughes was doing was something justices simply did not do – that is, use the Court as a stepping-stone to higher office or even possess much of an interest in or involvement with the electoral process. Hughes' candidacy in 1916 was the most visible contrary evidence to that message in the history of the Court. It clearly indicated that justices did not abandon interest in national politics because they sat on the Court and that partisan politics and political appointments could and indeed did beckon U.S. Supreme Court justices. Like justices in an earlier day, the justices in the twentieth century still followed the election returns, as Mr. Dooley had proclaimed.

Like their nineteenth-century counterparts, twentieth-century justices literally did follow the election returns. In 1928, Republican presidential candidate Herbert Hoover and his wife invited close friends to his house to watch the presidential election returns that ultimately made Hoover president. Among those friends were then–Associate Justice Harlan Stone and his wife.[2]

More typically, following the election returns was done privately, but no less intently. For example, Justice Harold H. Burton, a former Republican U.S. Senator from Ohio, wrote in his diary in 1952: "Today is the N.H. Primary.... I am looking for Eisenhower to win the Republican preference and most or all of the Rep. delegates." The next day, he wrote, "Eisenhower and Kefauver made clean sweeps in the N.H. primary. A healthy sign & most encouraging in the Republican result."[3] Similarly, after the 1948 presidential election when President Harry Truman won reelection and Democrats regained control of both houses of Congress, Justice Hugo L. Black, a former Democratic U.S. senator from Alabama, wrote to Justice Sherman Minton, another former Democratic U.S. senator from Indiana, that the election seemed to have improved Minton's health. Black added in jest that "[o]f course, as a political eunuch I can have no political thoughts, but I must say that the election results did no injury to my health."[4]

Other justices similarly had "no political thoughts" as they routinely discussed politics, particularly during electoral campaigns. Several of the justices speculated on electoral outcomes together. Just before the 1952 presidential election, Burton wrote in his diary: "We guessed at the electoral vote: C. J.: Stevenson 232, Reed – reserved his guess, Minton: Stevenson 324, Clark: Stevenson 312, Burton: Eisenhower 300."[5] Burton, the former Republican senator and the only Republican in the group, won because he was the sole justice predicting an Eisenhower win.

Some of the justices seemed almost obsessed with elections and politics in general. William Howard Taft, at that time chief justice, wrote to Justice George Sutherland, a former Republican U.S. senator from Utah, about Washington politics and, in one letter, related to Sutherland that when he couldn't sleep, he would name and count the individual senators to determine how many would support the Coolidge administration's policies. In another letter, he analyzed how various states were reacting to the nomination of Al Smith as the Democratic presidential candidate.[6]

This interest was not merely benign. Occasionally, justices even sought to influence certain electoral outcomes. In December 1910, Justice Horace Lurton, who had been on the Court for only a year and still was involved in Tennessee politics, wrote to Horace Van Deventer, a Knoxville attorney, to urge him to work with the various parties in Tennessee to help a local politician secure enough votes to become a U.S. senator. Lurton directed Van Deventer: "If it should turn out, as seems to be most probable, that McMillin cannot get votes enough and that the Regulars shall have to resort to a compromise man,

it has occurred to me that Dickinson would make an admirable selection."
Lurton added that he was "writing you of course confidentially."[7]

CHANGES IN DIRECT ELECTORAL INVOLVEMENT

Despite the continued interest in politics, and perhaps even occasional intervention, the climate for the involvement of justices in electoral politics had changed by the time of Hughes' candidacy. Prior to the Hughes' nomination, there was a certain ambivalence among the justices about direct political involvement. With the encouragement of some nineteenth-century justices mentioned earlier, that concern about propriety had increased over the years. For example, after Hughes was confirmed as an associate justice in 1910, but before he actually took his seat, President Taft asked Hughes to make a campaign speech in Ohio for the Republicans. Unlike some of his predecessors in the early years of the Court, Hughes demurred with the response that it would be inappropriate for him to do so, even if he was not yet officially a justice.[8]

In contrast to some of his predecessors, such as John McLean, Salmon Chase, and Stephen J. Field, Hughes did not make any effort to secure the nomination for the presidency. Indeed, there is strong evidence that at first he attempted to discourage it. In 1912, when Hughes initially had been approached, he made it clear he would not accept a nomination even if it were proffered. He said he was worried that a campaign would bring the Court into politics.[9]

The pressure on Hughes continued with the onset of the 1916 presidential campaign. When a former governor of New York wrote to encourage him to run for president, he requested that "no steps be taken to bring my name before the convention."[10] Additionally, Hughes refused appointments with people he thought might encourage him to run. He even threatened court proceedings to keep his name out of a presidential preference primary. But others took matters into their own hands. Then former President (and still future Chief Justice) Taft wrote to Hughes pleading with him to allow his name to be put before the Republican convention. Meanwhile, Taft's 1908 campaign managers organized support for Hughes within the Republican Party.[11]

Hughes closely followed the convention proceedings while they were taking place. However, neither during the convention nor in the days preceding it did he indicate publicly whether or not he would be willing to be the nominee. Regardless, Hughes was nominated on the third ballot. This occurred despite the fact that the delegates did not know whether Hughes would even accept.[12] However, Hughes had already decided that if the nomination were extended, he would accept it. Rather than even wait for the formal notification by a committee designated by the convention, Hughes telegraphed his acceptance immediately and tendered his resignation as a justice at the same time.

When Hughes did accept the presidential nomination, the response by others suggested the extent to which public expectations of Supreme Court justices' political involvement had changed. Editorials in the press opined that the Supreme Court had become a body expected to be above politics and its members uninterested in moving from the Court to electoral campaigns. Hughes' nomination and subsequent acceptance undermined that perception of aloofness and diminished the Court as a whole, they argued. The *New York World* editors wrote that "the nation has grown to think of its highest judicial tribune as something stable and permanent, wherein men sat as with a final dignity befitting ultimate honor. This new view is something of a shock." And the *New York Times* urged Hughes' defeat at least partly because his election would set "a precedent too dangerous for following."[13]

Nor were his fellow justices pleased with Hughes' action and how it reflected on the Court. It had been more than thirty years since a justice had been a presidential candidate, and the justices may have concluded that the Court had permanently achieved an image of distance from presidential politics. Hughes' run had undermined that image. Chief Justice Edward G. White confided to a friend that Hughes' acceptance was "a very great blunder and one from which we will be years in recovering."[14]

However, Hughes had a refined air that caused people to view him as destined for high office, even the presidency. When Taft was president, he confided in a letter that, regarding the man he had placed on the Supreme Court, he felt Hughes might challenge him for president in 1912 and that Taft would "always think of Hughes as President."[15] Moreover, the image of moral rectitude Hughes had cultivated as an attorney, governor, and Supreme Court justice may have made the transition from justice to presidential candidate more acceptable to the public. In fact, it is unlikely that his move from the Court actually had hurt him that much with the voters. Hughes lost by only 3 percent of the popular vote to an incumbent president.

Yet the actual fact of a Supreme Court justice leaving the Court to become a presidential candidate altered the culture of judicial involvement. Some nineteenth-century justices had campaigned for the presidency, but none had gained a major party nomination. Interestingly, an actual win by a justice led to a nearly hundred-year period since during which no justice has publicly sought the presidency or left the Court for elective office. Although some future justices – Fred Vinson, William O. Douglas, Earl Warren, and Sandra Day O'Connor – would be mentioned for president or vice president and, in the case of Douglas, would take some steps toward it, none would receive a nomination and none would actively campaign, as had Field, Chase, and McLean.

That does not mean that vigorous efforts were not made throughout the twentieth century to draft Supreme Court justices for elective office. A "draft Harlan Stone" movement emerged in the 1930s in response to Franklin D. Roosevelt's electoral victories. The *Detroit News* touted Stone as "the logical candidate." The chair of the New York Republicans urged Stone's candidacy, as did William Allen White, the nationally known newspaper publisher and editor.[16] Stone made no efforts to encourage the draft movement. Later, it was Roosevelt who appointed Stone as chief justice.

Similarly, Justice William O. Douglas, former chairman of the Securities and Exchange Commission, was mentioned repeatedly in the 1940s as a possible presidential or vice-presidential candidate. News stories reported "Douglas for President" clubs springing up in various cities during the spring of 1948, when many Democrats feared that President Harry Truman would lose his bid for reelection. Reportedly, the support for Douglas was so strong that Truman's advisors feared Democratic convention delegates would choose Douglas over Truman.[17]

Douglas' own response to the presidential boomlet was mixed. On the one hand, Douglas did not actively campaign for the position, as had previous justices in the nineteenth century. Indeed, Douglas told his colleagues on the Court and others that he had no interest in running for office. He wrote to one friend: "I do not think it would comport with judicial standards for one on the Court to nurture political ambitions." He wrote to another that it would be a disservice to the Court for a justice to run for office while he was on the Court.[18] On the other hand, Douglas engaged in behavior suggesting he clearly was interested. He gave speeches in the late 1940s and early 1950s to various important constituent groups that reinforced the idea he wanted to be politically active. He authored an autobiography that appeared in 1950, portrayed him as an heroic, rugged man of the West, and, with its fictional account of how he overcame polio, characterized Douglas as the heir to Franklin D. Roosevelt. The book was a best-seller and heightened his high profile, which was unusual for a Supreme Court justice but not for a presidential candidate.[19]

With the exception of Hughes, Douglas was the only justice who came close to actually becoming a candidate on a major party ticket. In 1948, Truman offered Douglas the vice-presidential nomination, which may well have established Douglas as the likely presidential nominee four years later. Truman's proposal may have been an attempt to forestall a Douglas challenge to Truman's renomination bid. Regardless of Truman's motive, Douglas declined the offer because he did not think Truman could win the election that year.[20]

The other justices were aware that a Douglas candidacy would affect the public's perception of the Court. Some justices, including Felix Frankfurter, closely followed the talk of Douglas' candidacy, as indicated by the newspaper clippings they kept.[21] Nor were they necessarily pleased by the prospect and the potential effect on the Court. Justice Robert Jackson jokingly suggested at a conference in 1947 that the Court should adjourn until after the presidential election.[22] Two of the justices accused Douglas in his concurrence in the *Hirabayashi* case of using his opinion for political purposes. Felix Frankfurter called Douglas' opinion a "spread eagle speech" designed to help Douglas' presidential prospects, and Frank Murphy considered it "a regular soap-box speech."[23]

Four years later, a Supreme Court justice once again became the subject of a draft movement. When Truman decided not to run for reelection, Chief Justice Fred Vinson, a former secretary of the treasury and member of Congress from Kentucky, was widely mentioned as a possible successor. Vinson dismissed the talk by saying he could "dispose of that possibility any Monday afternoon." He meant that on any decision day for the Court, which at the time was Mondays, he could issue an unpopular opinion that would squelch any interest in having him run for president. Nevertheless, the *New York Times* called him "the strongest, if most reluctant, candidate for the Democratic nomination."[24] Truman himself favored Vinson as the next Democratic presidential nominee. On several occasions between 1949 and 1951, Truman met with Vinson to convince him to run for president in 1952. However, Vinson finally persuaded Truman that "he did not think he should use the Court as a steppingstone to the presidency."[25]

Vinson's successor, Earl Warren, also was considered as a possible presidential candidate. In the next election cycle, Warren, who had been chief justice for three years, was mentioned as a possible Republican presidential candidate if President Dwight Eisenhower did not run for reelection. In a Gallup Poll, Warren was the choice of 29 percent of voters, which was higher than the support for any other potential candidate, including Vice President Richard Nixon.[26]

One justice did not wait for a draft movement to attempt to run for national office. In 1940, Hugo Black wrote a letter to President Franklin D. Roosevelt offering to resign from the Court to help Roosevelt win a third term that November.[27] In other words, Black was suggesting that Roosevelt choose him as his running mate. Roosevelt apparently did not seriously consider Black's offer. This may have been because it had been only three years since Black had admitted that, at one time, he had been a member of the Ku Klux Klan.

Moreover, the presidency was not the only office beyond the Court that justices were considering through much of the twentieth century. Presidents occasionally sought to lure justices away from the Court for high positions in their administrations. In 1929, President Herbert Hoover urged Harlan Stone to leave his associate justice post and become Hoover's secretary of state. Stone seriously considered accepting. He even wrote to a friend that "my instinct and inclination are against it, although I know that the possibilities of public service and my readiness to tackle a new and difficult job argue for it."[28] Stone ultimately declined.

Harry Truman attempted to lure two justices away from the Court. In 1947, he offered William O. Douglas the post of Secretary of the Interior. Douglas told Truman that he might leave to become Secretary of State, but not head of Interior. Truman did not offer the State job. Similarly, Fred Vinson may have come close to leaving the Court in 1950 to become Truman's Secretary of State. In the midst of rumors about a possible appointment to succeed Dean Acheson, Vinson told his colleagues that he had not asked to be Secretary of State, nor did he want to be, but that he might accept Truman's offer. When one of the other justices questioned the wisdom of the move and brought up the Hughes precedent of 1916, Vinson replied that he "thought resigning to become Secretary of State might be better understood and accepted than doing it to run for the presidency." Yet Vinson, like Stone, ultimately stayed put.[29]

In one case, a president's effort to shift a justice off the Court actually worked. In the mid-1960s, Lyndon Johnson attempted to persuade Justice Arthur Goldberg, a former Kennedy cabinet member, to become U.S. attorney general or Secretary of Health, Education, and Welfare. Goldberg initially demurred. However, Johnson finally succeeded when he offered Goldberg the UN ambassador position, which Goldberg was willing to accept.[30]

Not all resignations were politically motivated. Some justices in the twentieth century left because they disliked the work and believed they could be useful elsewhere. James Byrnes, a former U.S. representative and U.S. senator, served on the Court for only one year and admitted he was thoroughly unhappy as a justice. William O. Douglas termed Byrnes "a man for the hustings." When Franklin D. Roosevelt offered him a position in his administration, Byrnes jumped at the chance to leave the Court.[31] Similarly, John H. Clarke left the Court after only six years of service so he could lobby for U.S. involvement in the League of Nations. Upon leaving, Clarke wrote to Justice Louis Brandeis that he felt it was far more important for him to devote his time to promoting the League of Nations than "determining whether a drunken Indian had been deprived of his land before he died or whether the digging of a ditch in Iowa was constitutional or not."[32]

The potential of the revolving door of political involvement and judicial work in the nineteenth century was enhanced by the continued appointment of justices with political backgrounds. That trend carried through the first half of the twentieth century. Former politicians were prominent on the Court. In addition to those already mentioned, such as Vinson, Black, Byrnes, Sutherland, and Taft, other justices also were drawn from the ranks of legislative or executive branch office holders. Several justices, including William Henry Moody, James McReynolds, Harlan Stone, Robert Jackson, Frank Murphy, and Tom C. Clark, were serving as U.S. attorney general at the time of their appointment to the Court. Both Edward Sanford and Willis Van Devanter worked as assistant attorney general in Theodore Roosevelt's administration. William R. Day previously had served as Secretary of State.

Several others had held elective office. Mahlon Pitney had been a member of Congress from New Jersey, and William Henry Moody had represented Massachusetts. Joseph Lamar had been elected to the Georgia legislature. John H. Clarke had never served in political office, but he was familiar with electoral politics. Twice, Clarke ran for and lost races for the U.S. Senate from Ohio. Indeed, some presidents seemed to favor justices with political experience. Four of six justices appointed by William Howard Taft had previously served in elective office, and one was a sub-cabinet official. All of Harry Truman's appointments were men who had previously served in Congress or in the cabinet.

It is important to note that even justices without experience in political office were hardly politically naïve. As previously mentioned, Horace Lurton had never served in public office, but he was willing to assess an electoral opportunity and attempt to influence others to seize it. Louis Brandeis, another justice with no formal political experience, was one of the shrewdest politicians on the Court. He served as an advisor to Presidents Woodrow Wilson and Franklin D. Roosevelt. Brandeis even criticized Wilson for not understanding the politics of the Treaty of Versailles that Wilson had negotiated at the end of World War I.[33] Felix Frankfurter was appointed while a professor at Harvard Law School. However, Frankfurter described himself as "not a cloistered scholar," and he was an active advisor to Franklin D. Roosevelt before (and after) joining the Court.[34] Similarly, Abe Fortas had little direct office-holding experience, and even that was twenty years in his past by the time he joined the Court. However, Fortas was viewed as more of a politician than a jurist. One former clerk for another justice related that Fortas' clerks disliked his pragmatism and what they perceived as his obsession with making deals rather than following legal principles.[35] Another politician within the Court was William Brennan. A Brennan biographer concluded that "Brennan was a politician, an operator who conceived of his role in a completely different fashion from that of most judges. He worked the justices the way Lyndon Johnson worked the floor of the Senate."[36]

JUDICIAL, NOT POLITICAL, BACKGROUNDS

A dramatic change occurred in judicial backgrounds and political involvement during the last half of the twentieth century. Suddenly, Court appointees no longer had held elective office. The last member of Congress to come directly from elective office was Harold Burton, who was appointed in 1945 and served for thirteen years. The last elected official to serve was Earl Warren, who was appointed in 1953. Warren was governor of California at the time of his appointment and had been the vice presidential candidate on the Republican ticket in 1948.

This change in the backgrounds of the justices is demonstrated by the fact that although none of the chief justices since Earl Warren (Burger, Rehnquist, and Roberts) had held elective office prior to their appointments, all but one of the chief justices appointed in the twentieth century prior to Warren had. Fred Vinson was a member of Congress from Kentucky. Charles Evan Hughes served as governor of New York before he was appointed an associate justice and later served as Secretary of State before rejoining the Court as chief justice. William Howard Taft was president, and his predecessor, Edward Douglass White, was a Louisiana state senator. The exception was Harlan Stone, who never held elective office but was U.S. Attorney General in the Coolidge administration.

The same is true for associate justices. Only one of the associate justices appointed in the last half of the twentieth century (Sandra Day O'Connor) had held elective office previously. O'Connor was elected as an Arizona state senator and even served as the body's majority leader. Only one justice, Arthur Goldberg, was a cabinet member, although Abe Fortas had been a sub-cabinet member. Clarence Thomas was a political appointee as head of the Office of Equal Employment Opportunity in the Reagan administration.

None of the justices since Justice Tom C. Clark have been attorney generals prior to their appointment. (Clark was appointed by Truman in 1949.) Three served in lower levels in the Justice Department. Byron White was deputy attorney general under John F. Kennedy, and William Rehnquist and Antonin Scalia served as assistant attorney generals in the Nixon and Ford administrations, respectively. Elena Kagan was solicitor general in the Obama administration.

Even those more limited political backgrounds of justices appointed in the 1950s through O'Connor in 1981 were not shared by subsequent appointees. After O'Connor, none of the ten justices appointed to the Court during the 1980s, 1990s, and early 2000s had previously held an elective office. None, except Kagan, had served in a cabinet or in a sub-cabinet position. Instead, they had judicial backgrounds. All, except Kagan, were members of federal appellate courts immediately prior to their service on the Court.

As mentioned earlier, political experience, particularly elective office, likely familiarizes an individual with the press more than does strictly judicial experience stemming from service on a state or federal lower-level court. Elected or even appointed office holders understand and utilize press relations and have extensive experience with press releases, press conferences, and interviews with reporters. They are more likely than those without such experience to appreciate the imperatives of journalism and to understand how to utilize that knowledge to manage a positive public image via the press.

DISTANCING FROM POLITICAL INSTITUTIONS AND POLITICIANS?

Yet some of the most political justices – Brandeis, Frankfurter, and Fortas – had never held elective office. (Interestingly, none of the three had been a judge before, either.) They did have a common thread; they were not interested in maintaining a distance between themselves and "political" branches. They served as advisors to presidential administrations as well as to presidents directly.

The most common source of advice was on judicial appointments. William Howard Taft, as chief justice, advised Calvin Coolidge on appointments. Taft even claimed that he had "rather forced the President into the appointment" of Harlan Fiske Stone in 1925.[37] During the Hoover administration, Harlan Stone became a key advisor to the president on judicial appointments. Stone urged Hoover to appoint New York Judge Benjamin Cardozo, and when Hoover replied that there were too many Easterners on the Supreme Court, Stone even offered to resign to facilitate Cardozo's appointment.[38]

Felix Frankfurter advised Franklin D. Roosevelt on filling Court vacancies and, in one case, heavily lobbied Roosevelt to appoint Judge Learned Hand of the New York State Court of Appeals. Frankfurter informed Roosevelt that Hand was in the same league as previous luminaries such as Cardozo, Brandeis, and Holmes. However, Frankfurter also viewed Hand as a potential ally on the Court. The effort backfired when Frankfurter pushed too hard.

Roosevelt was so annoyed by Frankfurter's aggressive lobbying that he refused to appoint Hand and instead appointed Justice Wiley Rutledge, who became an opponent rather than an ally of Frankfurter.[39]

The advisory roles by justices continued into the Nixon administration. Chief Justice Warren Burger advised the president on Supreme Court appointments. After two of Nixon's nominations – Clement Haynsworth and G. Harold Carswell – were rejected, Burger suggested his old Minnesota friend, Harry Blackmun. Nixon went along, and Blackmun was easily confirmed. Burger also sought to discourage Nixon from appointing a woman.[40]

However, justices' roles in personnel matters often did not stop with judicial appointments. They became advisors in other personnel appointments for both legal and nonlegal posts. Louis Brandeis was solicited for advice by both Woodrow Wilson and Franklin D. Roosevelt on various cabinet posts in their respective administrations. Wilson even visited Brandeis at his house to ask his advice about a Cabinet secretary. Wilson came to Brandeis because he concluded it was inappropriate to invite a Supreme Court justice to the White House for advice on a political matter.[41]

Some justices did not wait to be asked; they simply volunteered to advise the president. For example, soon after Hoover was elected in 1928, Harlan Stone wrote to him and offered to assist in personnel appointments, telling Hoover that "if it is agreeable to you, I should like at some appropriate time to bring to your attention the names of some men who are worthy of consideration for a position in your Cabinet."[42] Stone was consulted by Hoover on various appointments, including Cabinet appointments unrelated to legal issues. Stone's friendship with Hoover led him to a role of advising the president in areas beyond appointments, such as presidential messages and the texts of speeches. Later, William O. Douglas made occasional recommendations to Robert Kennedy regarding appointments to Kennedy administration positions, including assistant attorney general and, in accordance with Douglas' environmental interests, under-secretary of the Interior.[43]

Judicial advising also expanded beyond personnel appointments. James Byrnes spent much of his brief tenure as a justice working directly with the president on current legislation.[44] Felix Frankfurter was a frequent policy advisor to Franklin D. Roosevelt prior to and during his time on the Court.[45] The perception of Frankfurter's influence even extended into the Truman administration and prompted Frank Murphy, who wanted an ambassadorial appointment, to confide in Frankfurter while both were sitting on the bench hearing an argument. According to Frankfurter, Murphy said: "I just want you to know that if I were asked to go to Paris I would go at once and I think I could be of great help to the President. I thought you ought to know that in view of your relations to Dean Acheson [then Secretary of State]."[46]

Some advising by justices even transcended policy and moved into the area of electoral politics. Fred Vinson met occasionally with Truman to discuss politics. In early 1952, Vinson, while chief justice, participated in election strategy meetings with Truman and others regarding the 1952 presidential election. The participants weighed possible presidential candidates to succeed Truman, who was not planning to run again. At these meetings, Vinson even attempted to convince Truman to reconsider his decision not to run.[47]

The justice who may have had the closest advisory relationship to a president was Abe Fortas. Fortas had a long personal association with Lyndon Johnson dating back to Johnson's days as a member of Congress. When Johnson appointed Fortas to the Court, he never gave Fortas a chance to refuse. According to Fortas, Johnson invited him to come to the White House just before Johnson was going to hold a televised press conference. As Johnson was walking down the hall toward the press conference, he mentioned to Fortas that he was appointing him to the Supreme Court. "To the best of my knowledge," Fortas later recounted, "I never said yes."[48]

From the day of Kennedy's assassination, Fortas was an informal advisor to Johnson. His appointment on the Supreme Court two years later did not curtail his advisor role. Fortas helped write presidential speeches, drafted presidential signing statements, gave legal advice, made recommendations on personnel appointments, and counseled Johnson on Vietnam policy.[49] The White House installed a private phone line in Fortas' Supreme Court office and gave the number to Johnson so he could reach Fortas at any time. Despite his position on the Court, Fortas had no intention of ending his advisory role. When he moved to the Court, he wrote Johnson that "I can only hope that you will continue to see me and to call upon me for anything that I can do to help."[50]

At first, Johnson distanced himself from Fortas in keeping with the expectation that Fortas, as a Supreme Court justice, would cease his advisory role and be aloof from presidential politics. Yet eventually, Johnson's contact with Fortas resumed. In one month alone, Fortas had sixteen phone conversations with Johnson, four private meetings, and four other meetings where Johnson was present. *Time* magazine suggested that no one really knew how many times Fortas had gone through the White House's back door, but "any figure would probably be too low."[51] Fortas' work for Johnson sometimes even extended to foreign affairs. Johnson asked Fortas to help him handle the Dominican Republic conflict in 1965 and specifically to meet with Juan Bosch in Puerto Rico. Fortas secretly traveled to Puerto Rico, met with former Dominican Republic President Juan Bosch, and then reported back to Johnson.[52]

Several justices during the twentieth century accepted formal extrajudicial roles assigned to them by presidents. In 1914, Justice Joseph Lamar served as a U.S. representative to a peace conference to resolve U.S.-Mexican hostilities.

Subsequently, Lamar was asked by Wilson to represent the United States at a Pan-American conference in Chile, although Lamar declined that role. Justice Owen Roberts was appointed by Franklin Roosevelt to serve on a commission studying Pearl Harbor.[53] Justice Robert Jackson became a prosecutor at the Nuremberg trials in Germany following World War II. He left the Court for a year while he assisted in the trials of Nazi war criminals. Jackson confessed that he took the job to get away from the Court, particularly the internecine environment among the justices at that time. He felt that serving on the Court at that time was like "being in a back eddy with important things going on in the world." He also admitted that he might not have taken the Nuremberg assignment "if internal matters at the Court had been pleasant and agreeable."[54]

The highest-profile involvement by a justice was the chairmanship of the Warren Commission by Earl Warren, then chief justice. The commission, which investigated the assassination of John F. Kennedy, was the brainchild of Lyndon Johnson, and Warren was Johnson's first choice to head the commission that would subsequently be identified with him. Warren did not want to serve on the commission. He believed the chief justice should not take on such a strenuous and public responsibility outside the Court. However, Johnson persuaded him that the commission was of such importance that it should be headed by the highest judicial officer, and Warren acquiesced.[55]

Extrajudicial service or advisory roles to presidents or other policy makers drew justices closer to either direct interaction with the press through specific off-the-bench roles or, at the least, to a greater degree of awareness about the role of the press and the importance of shaping press coverage while advising policy makers. Even if justices had no incentive to interact with the press and the public in their on-the-bench roles (which was not the case), their other roles would have given them sufficient reasons to do so to carry out extrajudicial service or to assist an administration in winning over public opinion.

Political Actors/Public Strategies

The frequency of political backgrounds prior to joining the Court and political involvement for some while on the Court suggests that many justices were involved in the political environment in which they operated, both before and during their tenures on the Court. These justices were hardly the image of monastic individuals divorced from the political realities of their day. For many with backgrounds of political involvement before serving on the Court, from Congress to the executive branch to state office, involvement with the press in some form was a given. They understood the press' role as a political actor germane to their own external strategies of shaping elite and mass opinion. Others, such as Brandeis, Frankfurter, and Fortas, were similarly cognizant of the role of the press as they served as advisors to presidents seeking to affect public opinion.

Their political backgrounds prior to their service on the Court and their political involvement while on the Court affected their approach to external relations as justices. This appreciation of external relations became particularly important when the Court itself acquired a higher-than-normal profile at key points during the twentieth century. This spark in public attention occurred during the following type of events – judicial selection, external attacks on the Court, scandals involving justices, and announcement of key decisions.

SUPREME COURT NOMINATIONS

One set of events that significantly marked the public profile of twentieth-century Supreme Court justices was the process of judicial selection. The Bork nomination in 1987 was a signal event in the extent of media strategy used by opponents to a nomination.[56] Broad-based interest group coalitions, print and television advertisements, and rallies all were features of a process that looked more like an electoral campaign than a traditional judicial confirmation process.

Yet the Bork nomination was one of a succession of controversial and newsworthy confirmations during the twentieth century. A biographer of Louis Brandeis noted that when a Court vacancy occurred in 1916, which Brandeis subsequently would fill, "newspapers overflowed with conflicting advice for [President Woodrow] Wilson."[57] Obviously, like the Bork nomination, some nominations were the source of controversy involving larger issues than the actual confirmation of the nominee. Those confirmation processes received extensive press notice and possessed the potential of affecting the public's image of the Court itself. One particular type was the confirmation of a chief justice.

The Special Case of the Chief Justice

The appointment of a chief justice determines the shape of an era. Even though the chief justice carries only one vote and may be overshadowed by other personalities on the Court, chief justices tend to be the definers of an era. In the past half century, the Warren Court, Burger Court, Rehnquist Court, and now the Roberts Court each have been labeled according to the individual serving as the chief justice during that era. Their names become associated with certain trends on the Court. Hence, the chief justice nomination takes on a special significance.

At times, a retiring chief justice, with the cooperation of an administration, has circumvented the debate about the selection of a new chief justice. This occurs when the chief justice offers a president the opportunity to make the selection process private. This happened in 1986 when Warren Burger quietly informed President Ronald Reagan that he was retiring and a successor should be appointed. Only when Reagan held a news conference and announced Burger's retirement, William Rehnquist's nomination as chief, and Justice Antonin Scalia's nomination as Rehnquist's successor did the press realize a judicial selection process was taking place within the White House. True to Burger's enmity toward the press, he had facilitated a process that excluded the press from any role in the presidential selection stage of judicial nominations. Burger's move was uncommon, but not unique. Typically, chief justices in the twentieth century either died in office (such as Fuller, White, Vinson, and Stone) or publicly announced their retirements (Hughes and Warren). Another exception, however, was Taft. As Burger would do fifty-six years later, Taft quietly informed the White House that he would resign upon the appointment of his successor. Herbert Hoover revealed a successor the same day Taft's retirement announcement was made public in order to avoid, in Hoover's words, "all the political pulling and hauling that takes place over an open vacancy."[58]

A public vacancy, the more usual occurrence, can affect the Court beyond the prospect of a new leader. The vacancy, or even the potential vacancy, of the chief justice position can cause friction within the Court. Some associate justices may feel that, given their experience on the Court, they should be appointed, as opposed to someone who is not a current member. Press coverage of various possible candidates invariably occurs, particularly when the presidential decision stage continues for days, weeks, or even months. When speculation ensues, associate justices may see their names bandied about in the press as possible nominees for chief. For example, in 1910, a *Washington Post* story declared that Charles Evans Hughes would be the next chief justice. Hughes was the most junior member of the Court, having served for only a few months. But several more senior justices desired the post. Another newspaper, the *New York Sun*, reported that two of the other justices were lobbying against Hughes' appointment.[59]

Again in 1969, news reports circulated that Potter Stewart was on Richard Nixon's short list for chief justice. Stewart gave an on-the-record interview with Fred Graham of the *New York Times* to announce he had read his name in the newspapers as a possible chief justice appointment and subsequently visited with Nixon to ask that he not be considered. According to the *New York Times*, Stewart was concerned about how Abe Fortas would feel because Fortas and Stewart had a tense relationship, and there were rumors within the Court that Fortas would resign if Stewart became chief justice.[60]

The chief justice appointment stirring the most controversy, and publicity, in the twentieth century was Lyndon Johnson's selection of Abe Fortas, a current associate justice. Even the manner of the retirement that caused the vacancy was criticized. Earl Warren submitted his retirement letter to Lyndon Johnson to become effective when a successor was confirmed. Under other circumstances, that statement might have seemed innocuous. However, Johnson was already a lame duck president, and Republicans were expecting to take back the White House in the November election. Warren's wording carried the potential that he would withdraw his nomination if Johnson could not get a replacement before the end of his term and one of Warren's arch California political enemies, Richard Nixon, became president. The *Washington* Post urged Warren to reword his letter to be more definite about the time he would leave office.[61]

Fortas was the second-most-junior member of the Court at the time, having served only three years before Johnson's attempt to elevate him to chief justice. However, it was not Fortas' junior status that was the problem; rather, it was Johnson. Fortas was criticized for his role as Johnson's close friend and advisor. As previously discussed, Fortas was known to spend much of his time at the White House counseling the president, writing speeches, and even engaging in diplomacy on behalf of Johnson. Yet the issue was not that Fortas would continue his association with Johnson, because Johnson would end his presidency shortly after Fortas would take office as chief. Rather, it was the perception of cronyism.[62] Moreover, Johnson's lame-duck status weakened his ability to secure Fortas' appointment. His power had ebbed by the summer of 1968, and the Congress was not willing to acquiesce to Johnson as it had earlier in his administration. Republicans, who sought to delay a confirmation in order to allow a Republican president to choose the new chief justice, and southern Democrats, who were angry about the decisions of the Warren Court, combined to deny Johnson the ability to name a chief justice in the waning days of his presidency.[63]

The Court itself was on trial during Fortas' confirmation hearing. Although Fortas was only one of nine justices and had served as an associate justice for only three of the fifteen years of the Warren Court, he became the available symbol of a Court criticized by conservatives as too activist. Fortas was painted as being pro-pornography because of Warren Court free-speech decisions. Indeed, Fortas' confirmation hearings became a venue for some Republicans and southern Democrats to use their question time to rail against the decisions of the Court.[64] After confirmation opponents were able to sustain a filibuster of the nomination, Fortas withdrew. He remained on the Court as an associate justice. But the high visibility for the Court during this failed confirmation did illuminate one justice's extrajudicial activities, as well as provide a venue for those who sought to discredit the Court in the public eye.

A similar case was the confirmation of William Rehnquist as chief justice in 1986. Like Fortas, Rehnquist had already been an associate justice. His extrajudicial activities were not at issue, as Fortas' had been, but Rehnquist's service on the Court to that point, which was eleven years longer than Fortas', was a factor. Senator Edward Kennedy used his question time as a member of the Senate Judiciary Committee to point to Rehnquist's record and accuse him of being "too extreme on race, too extreme on women's rights, too extreme on freedom of speech, too extreme on separation of church and state, too extreme to be Chief Justice."[65] The thirty-three Senate votes cast against Rehnquist's nomination constituted the largest number against a successful nominee in history to date. Once again, an associate justice became a target for opposition to the Court generally.

Several associate justice appointments also sparked controversy and drew press attention to the Court during the twentieth century. The first controversial nomination was Louis Brandeis' in 1916. Brandeis was a Boston lawyer famous for taking on corporations, and his selection came as a surprise and a shock to many. Former President Taft called Brandeis "a muckracker, an emotionalist for his own purpose, a socialist."[66] Press reaction was, at best, mixed. One newspaper called Brandeis "utterly and even ridiculously unfit." Another termed the appointment "an insult to members of the Supreme Court." However, some were more laudatory, calling Brandeis a "great force for progressive thought," and another called him a "noted jurist."[67]

Brandeis himself kept a low profile during the nomination, which was part of his confirmation strategy. When asked by a reporter from the *New York Sun* to comment, he replied: "I have nothing to say about anything, and that goes for all time and to all newspapers, including both the *Sun* and the moon." Yet Brandeis did work with Norman Hapgood, editor of *Harper's Weekly*, to plot his strategy for winning over public opinion and, indirectly, a majority of senators. He also collaborated with Felix Frankfurter, who issued an unsigned editorial in *The New Republic* urging Brandeis' confirmation. Brandeis also aided columnist Walter Lippmann in boosting support for his own nomination in the press. And when his opponents, particularly William Howard Taft and former American Bar Association presidents, issued a press statement opposing his confirmation, Brandeis responded with a request to

Hapgood to launch a press campaign countering Taft's efforts.[68] The efforts of Brandeis and his supporters, including those among the press, resulted in his successful confirmation and, ultimately, twenty-three years of service on the Court. However, there would be another effect: Brandeis' interaction with the press continued during his tenure as a justice as he attempted to shape press content and public opinion.

Fourteen years later, another controversial nomination would become a subject for press coverage. U.S. Appellate Judge John J. Parker was nominated by Herbert Hoover to serve on the Court. Parker's nomination was an important landmark for the Republican Party. He had run three times as a Republican candidate in North Carolina. Although Parker had lost in each bid, including his last one for governor, he had done far better than any Republican to date. Moreover, Parker represented a new Republican Party in the South dedicated to winning white votes rather than being associated with the party of Lincoln. Parker used his speeches in his gubernatorial campaign to repudiate Republican support for African Americans. The National Association for the Advancement of Colored People (NAACP) announced its opposition to Parker and used the Negro press of the day to promote that opposition. That press became important in engendering opposition to Parker among northern senators.[69]

Parker's nomination was the only unsuccessful confirmation vote of the century until 1969. Following the failed Fortas nomination for chief justice in 1968, Richard Nixon was able to appoint Warren Burger as chief justice. But the Fortas nomination left a bitter taste in the mouths of Democrats who felt that Fortas had been unfairly treated. That hostility was not manifested in opposition to Burger, who sailed through the confirmation process.[70] It may well have surfaced with the subsequent nominations of Clement Haynsworth and then G. Harrold Carswell.

Clement Haynsworth was nominated to replace Abe Fortas on August 18, 1969, three months after Fortas' resignation. Haynsworth was on his way to confirmation when several problems occurred. Haynsworth was opposed by civil rights leaders because his decisions consistently opposed their positions. In addition, Haynsworth was a proponent of South Carolina's "right to work" law, which earned him the opposition of labor leaders. Next, reports arose of potential ethical conflict of interest issues involving Haynsworth. The opposition of the civil rights and labor movements weakened the nomination, but the conflict of interest charges became too much for Democratic senators. In the wake of the Fortas resignation under similar circumstances, the Senate rejected Haynsworth's nomination.[71]

Nixon then nominated Carswell, a U.S. appellate judge from Florida. Carswell initially was considered certain to win confirmation because he recently had been confirmed by the Senate as an appellate judge. However, Carswell had significant problems that emerged in the course of the confirmation process. One was a racist past. While running for the state legislature in Georgia, Carswell had given a speech supporting white supremacy.[72] The news about the speech came out two days after Nixon's announcement of the nomination. Another problem was the slender nature of Carswell's qualifications for the Supreme Court. Whereas Haynsworth had served as an appellate judge for twelve years, Carswell had been on the appellate bench for only six months. Moreover, Carswell's opinions were not well respected by higher courts. His decisions had been reversed more than 60 percent of the time.

The Senate floor manager for the debate on Carswell's confirmation attempted to come to Carswell's defense. Senator Roman Hruska of Nebraska argued that even if Carswell was mediocre, "there are a lot of mediocre judges and people and lawyers. They are entitled to a little representation, aren't they, and a little chance? We can't have all Brandeises, Cardozos, and Frankfurters, and stuff like that there." Senator Russell Long went even further in maligning the Court when he said: "Does it not seem . . . that we have had enough of those upside down, corkscrew thinkers."[73]

The debate about Carswell was not limited to the floor of the U.S. Senate. The press and the public also joined in. The press contributed to the discussion of who belonged on the Supreme Court and what the Supreme Court stood for as an institution. The *New York Times* editorialized that Carswell was "so totally lacking in professional distinction, so wholly unknown for cogent opinions or learned writings, that the appointment is a shock. It almost suggests an intention to reduce the significance of the Court by lowering the caliber of its membership."[74] The Carswell nomination and his ultimate rejection by the Senate raised the question of who should be allowed to serve on the Supreme Court. Were the justices "upside down, corkscrew thinkers" who needed to be balanced by mediocre judges who deserved some representation? Had the Court become out of touch with society? Was the Court too distant from the public?

In the wake of the Warren Court, clearly the justices were facing negative public perceptions about their function in American public life. In 1968, according to the Gallup Poll, 44 percent of Americans said their view of the Supreme Court had changed in recent years, and two-thirds of that sentiment was negative. But the nomination process involving Abe Fortas may well have affected public views, along with Richard Nixon's theme about the need to restore "law and order" during his 1968 presidential campaign, which indirectly targeted the Warren Court. All of this news about the Court as well as dramatic societal change, including student protests, racial riots, and tragic assassinations, may have become linked in the public's mind with the decisions of the Supreme Court. Public support for the Court fell during this period. According to the Gallup Poll, public approval of the Court dropped from 43 percent rating the Court as good or excellent in 1967 to 31 percent in 1969.[75]

Bork and Thomas

The two nominations that sparked the most press coverage in the twentieth century were those of Robert Bork in 1987 and Clarence Thomas in 1991. Both nominations, and their effects on the society at large, have been widely discussed by journalists and academics.[76] The two nominations appeared to alter the nomination process by involving public opinion, interest groups, and the press to a degree unheard of in previous nominations. Both nominations acquired high levels of media coverage. The second round of the confirmation hearings in the Thomas nomination received saturation coverage in the press as Thomas and Anita Hill competed for the public's trust.

Nominations affect the Court when the nominee loses as well because the confirmation process again revolves around the issue of who belongs on the Supreme Court. The cases discussed earlier demonstrate this point. The discussion about Brandeis centered on whether an individual known as "the people's lawyer" and a Jew belonged on the Supreme Court. Should the Court's membership go beyond traditionalists supported by the legal establishment? A similar argument arose during the nominations at the end of the twentieth century. At that point, the question was whether a justice needed to fall within the mainstream of American legal thought. One of the charges against Bork was that he was, like Rehnquist the year before, too extreme to sit on the Supreme Court. It was assumed that there existed a widely acknowledged mainstream of thought to which justices needed to ascribe. Liberal opponents of Bork, Thomas, and Souter attempted to portray them as too extreme to sit on the Court. Similarly, conservative opponents, in turn, made the same argument about Ruth Bader Ginsburg.

The accusation, which was not merely a twentieth-century phenomenon but certainly dominated nominations during this period, became a potent tool not so much for shaping senators' opinions but for affecting press coverage of and public opinion toward the nominee. Each new nomination process pointed to what a justice should be like, as well as what he or she should do. The battle over nominees affected not just those who were nominated but also the image of those who already sat on the Court.

ATTACKING THE COURT

As shown previously, the justices' images also are affected by other players, such as presidents, Congress, interest groups, and the press. These can take the form of assaults designed to alter the direction of Court decisions. One of the most significant of these in the twentieth century was Franklin D. Roosevelt's 1937 Court-packing plan. The plan specifically addressed the size of the Court, but also was part of a larger public-oriented strategy by Roosevelt to bend the Court to his will, particularly in relation to the constitutionality of New Deal legislation.

Early in his second term, Roosevelt used a national radio address to announce his plan to increase the size of the Supreme Court, allowing him to appoint up to six new justices and switch the Court's majority from an anti–New Deal stance. Roosevelt had become increasingly frustrated with the Court's decisions declaring his New Deal programs unconstitutional.[77] During a two-year period, the Court had invalidated the National Industrial Recovery Act (NIRA), the Frazier-Lemke Act, and the Railway Pension Act. Adding to Roosevelt's frustration was his landslide reelection in 1936, accompanied by the continuance of hefty majorities for the Democratic Party in both houses of Congress. In his address, Roosevelt asserted that the Court had not been a team player with Congress and the White House in a three-horse team driven by the people. The Court was not pulling "in unison with the other two." He also argued that new blood was necessary to speed up the execution of justice and that new individuals would be able to understand the immediate pressing social and economic problems of the country in a way that the current justices, particularly those who had served for many years, could not.[78]

The president's plan was not an impulsive decision. Roosevelt had been laying the groundwork for some time. When the Court was considering the Gold Clause cases, which addressed whether Congress had the power to regulate the currency in the midst of the Depression, Roosevelt was prepared to deliver a national radio address directly criticizing the Court for contributing to a deepening of the economic crisis. Following the Schechter decision overturning the NIRA, Roosevelt used the forum of his regular press conference to accuse the Court of relegating interstate commerce to a "horse-and-buggy definition." However, Roosevelt's general approach was to let the Court become less and less popular on its own.

Simultaneously, the mystique of the Court was challenged. In the period immediately preceding Roosevelt's announcement, the justices were subject to increasing examination and even disparagement. The debate about the plan itself led to heightened press and public analysis of the justices. The Court itself became the center of attention. According to *Newsweek* magazine, "state legislators, public officials, editors, and millions of plain John Does had joined in a furious debate."[79]

During this period of scrutiny, the press generally continued to refer to the Court in ways that were deferential to the Court's image as a nonpolitical, elitist institution. However, there were attempts to dispel that image. The *Literary Digest*, a popular magazine of the day, published an article in April 1934 emphasizing that the justices were mortal men and concluding that "the public should know as much about these nine men as about any others in the Government."[80] Two years later, Drew Pearson and Robert Allen, prominent Washington newspaper columnists, authored a best-seller titled *The Nine Old Men*. The book was strongly critical of individual justices. The columnists assigned less-than-deferential titles to most of the justices. Harlan Fiske Stone was termed "Hoover's Pal," Benjamin Cardozo became the "Hermit Philosopher," and James McReynolds was labeled "Scrooge."[81] Pierce Butler, called "mediocre" by Pearson and Allen, was accused of working zealously to "promote the power and glory of the Holy Roman Church" and big business. Willis Van Devanter was called "a fanatical reactionary" and described as having "literary constipation."[82]

However, neither increased attention to the Court as a result of Roosevelt's Court-packing plan nor the popularity of Pearson and Allen's book translated into majority public support for the plan. A spate of newspaper editorials, even from Democratic-leaning newspapers, opined against the plan. At no time did a majority of the public favor limiting the Court's power to declare congressional acts unconstitutional or enlarging the Court membership to give Roosevelt the opportunity to appoint new justices. Regardless, the Court's image was affected by the debate. According to Gallup, in 1936, 53 percent of Americans felt the Court should be "more liberal in reviewing New Deal measures," and, a few months later, after the announcement of the Court-packing plan, even though a majority did not approve of Roosevelt's plan, 53 percent favored some kind of change regarding the Supreme Court.[83]

While the furor over the Court-packing plan was occurring in the nation, the Court itself was hardly oblivious to what was going on. The justices closely followed the press' coverage of the Court-packing plan and the public's reaction. They worried about the image of the Court. Stone wrote that "we are certainly getting a thorough airing and if we can come through all this discussion without serious loss of the prestige of the Court the result may be good."[84]

The justices were uniformly hostile to the plan but could not "go public" in direct opposition. Charles Evans Hughes, then chief justice, suggested that he and another justice appear before the Senate Judiciary Committee as it was deliberating on the president's bill. However, Louis Brandeis, Hughes' choice to accompany him, opposed the justices' appearance. Instead, Hughes communicated to the committee that he would answer in writing any questions it had. The committee agreed, and Hughes, along with Brandeis and Van Devanter, crafted a letter for the committee.[85]

Through the letter, Hughes attempted to diminish support for the Court reform bill by attacking Roosevelt's central claim that the justices were incapable of performing their constitutional duties. He argued that increasing the number of justices actually would have the opposite effect; the change would impair the Court's efficiency by adding more complexity to the decision-making process. Hughes stressed that the current Court was of sufficient size to handle the workload before it. He asserted that "the Supreme Court is fully abreast of its work."[86] The publication of the letter by the committee undercut the president's arguments for Court reform. One of the president's supporters acknowledged that Hughes' letter "did more than any one thing to turn the tide in the Court struggle."[87]

It is unlikely that Hughes' public relations effort was sufficient in shaping the Senate and the public's image of Roosevelt's plan; the Court's change in direction regarding the constitutionality of Roosevelt's approach to economic change was likely the more powerful cause. Two months after Roosevelt's radio address, the Court announced a decision made earlier in the year that sided with Roosevelt's views on the economic regulatory power of government. Hughes held back the decision for a while to avoid appearing to cave to Roosevelt. Additionally, the retirement of one of the anti–New Deal legislation majority, Willis Van Devanter, offered Roosevelt the appointment opportunity he had been seeking for four years. Yet Hughes' letter, and the subsequent publicity, played its part in blunting Roosevelt's efforts to pack the Court.[88]

A second example occurred in the 1960s and early 1970s when Richard Nixon criticized the Warren Court for a series of decisions he portrayed as "soft on crime." Nixon was not alone in his censure of the Court. Rather, he was articulating criticism that had been building throughout the 1950s and 1960s among conservatives, particularly those in the South. Many Southerners had openly defied the Court's racial desegregation decisions. Conservative groups opposed a variety of decisions related to school prayer, free speech, and rights of the accused. "Impeach Earl Warren" signs dotted the South. However, given his platform as president, Nixon's criticisms, coupled with those of Vice President Spiro Agnew, generated the greatest press attention. Moreover, as mentioned earlier, Nixon was in a position to shape the Court's personnel through judicial selection. Not only did Nixon's "law and order" theme target the justices but he also used appointments to undermine the legitimacy of the Court. On the whole, his short lists seemed intended to demean the Court. Not surprisingly, the candidates on his short list did not receive high marks from the American Bar Association. In fact, Nixon even once sent signals that he would appoint Senator Robert Byrd, a former member of the Ku Klux Klan, to the Court. Byrd had no experience as a judge or even as a lawyer; he had never practiced law.[89]

Hugo Black and the Ku Klux Klan

To replace Van Devanter, Roosevelt nominated Alabama Senator Hugo Black. A strong proponent of the New Deal, Black would be a certain vote on the Court to support any future challenges to the constitutionality of Roosevelt's economic programs. Moreover, Black was only fifty-one and promised to serve for a long time, which he ultimately did.

Although Black had almost no judicial experience, he had extensive political experience, which led to strong criticism of the appointment. Additionally, Black was accused of being a racist and suspected of having once belonged to the Ku Klux Klan. A *Newsweek* columnist opined that "there have been worse appointments to high judicial offices but . . . I can't remember where or when."[90]

Black was confirmed, but the controversy was only beginning for Black and the Court. After the Senate confirmation vote, the *Pittsburgh Post-Gazette* ran a series of articles providing specific evidence of Black's previous membership in the KKK. The newspaper's stories immediately led to a public outcry against Black. Several senators who had voted for Black's confirmation announced they would have voted against him had they known about his KKK affiliation. Newspapers editorialized against Black. The *New York Times* predicted that Black's presence on the Court will be "a living symbol of the fact that here the cause of liberalism was unwittingly betrayed."[91]

Initially, Black responded by telling reporters that he had nothing to say about the controversy. Immediately after his confirmation vote, Black had taken a vacation to Europe prior to the Court's fall opening session. While in Europe, he attempted to stay out of sight of reporters to avoid talking about the allegations. However, pressure quickly intensified from the press for the new associate justice to respond to the charges. On September 22, 1937, *New York Times* columnist Arthur Krock urged Black to offer an explanation to the American people. However, other newspapers, such as the *Los Angeles Times* and the *Philadelphia Record*, called for his resignation.[92] When Black returned to the United States on a cruise liner, fifty reporters met the ship at the dock. NBC radio network offered Black radio facilities at the dock in

Norfolk, Virginia, so he could comment on the controversy as soon as he left the ship.[93] However, Black declined NBC's initial offer and once again avoided discussing the controversy.

Nevertheless, Black was not immune to the pressure placed on him by the press. He was following closely what the press said about him. Even though Black was in Europe for part of this controversy, he kept extensive news clippings files on the press' coverage of his nomination, as well as on the controversy surrounding his KKK membership.[94] That pressure from the press and others finally convinced Black that he had to speak out. In an historic first for a justice, Black appeared on a national radio broadcast to answer press allegations. In his speech, he admitted he had belonged to the KKK but insisted he had long since left the organization He also repudiated the KKK.

The speech was effective. Black stayed on the Court, and the furor eventually died down. Black refused to discuss the incident again, which helped to tamp down the story. However, the incident was significant in the role of the press in raising charges against a Supreme Court justice, compelling him to respond to public accusations, and becoming the medium used to convey the justice's message and, as a tool to aid him, in diffusing public calls for his resignation.

SCANDAL

Another type of event raising the profile of the Court was scandal. Obviously, scandal alone is newsworthy, but one involving a justice is doubly so. The justices' aloof position magnifies the news interest, but scandal news is rare at least partly because the justices are so successful in shielding themselves from such coverage. There were several highly newsworthy scandals involving ethical behavior of the justices in the twentieth century. One involved a justice violating the norms of the Court and creating the scandal by using the press to accuse a colleague of unethical behavior. In another case, the justices' own personal behavior attracted press attention. And in two others, the press was the instigator of scandal coverage.

Public Feuding – Hugo Black and Robert Jackson

Hugo Black and Robert Jackson became the subject of news coverage in 1946 when their long-simmering personal feud broke out in public. The resulting news coverage offered one of the uncommon glimpses into the private relations among justices. The feud received so much publicity that the *New York Times* editorialized on it, urging both justices to stop their public attacks and restore the dignity of the Court. And congressional leaders even began talking about conducting an investigation into whether Congress should pass legislation limiting justices' involvement in possible conflict of interest cases, the issue that sparked public visibility of the feud.[95]

Feuding among the justices was frequent in this time period. The late 1930s and early 1940s brought to the Court several strong personalities, including Hugo Black and William O. Douglas in one camp and Felix Frankfurter and Robert Jackson in another. The tension on the Court at the time is indicated in the tone of a letter Frankfurter wrote to Wiley Rutledge: "Since we are not corner grocers pursuing cut-throat competition, but are engaged in a common enterprise – that of trying to analyze and solve complicated intellectual problems by joint endeavor – I want to enlist your help in the Oklahoma liquor case."[96] A year later, Frankfurter told Rutledge that he felt that there was "an increasing tendency on the part of the members of this Court to behave like little school boys and throw spitballs at one another."[97] Frankfurter himself was blamed by other justices as the cause of the intense battles occurring among the justices. In an interview with Professor Walter F. Murphy, Douglas said that Frankfurter "spent his time going up and down the halls putting poison in everybody's spring... trying to set one Justice against another...."[98]

The Black-Jackson feud was not the first among the justices involving Hugo Black. Press accounts two years earlier had suggested that Black, along with William O. Douglas, was fighting with Justice Owen Roberts. Roberts accused Black and Douglas of waffling on important issues and preventing the Court from providing a consistent message about constitutional issues. Black responded by refusing to sign a letter at Roberts' retirement that expressed the justices' regret that he was leaving, although Black admitted that if he did not sign, "this information is certain to be adroitly passed to the public, with invidious implications."[99]

The factional feuding stayed private for the most part. However, the justices occasionally carried their animosities into the public, particularly through biting dissents. In 1944, an article in *The New Republic* by Alexander H. Pekelis recounted the concern in the legal community that the justices were too divided and issued too many dissents. Particular attention was given to the public differences between Felix Frankfurter and Hugo Black as indicated by their dissents. Although Pekelis argued that such divisions were not unusual, the article's apologetic tone suggested that the criticism of the Court's public divisions was real, even before they came to a head with the public Jackson-Black feud.[100]

The Jackson-Black feud erupted into the open when Robert Jackson used a dissent to question whether Hugo Black should have participated in a case that involved a union that Black had once represented. Because Black provided the crucial fifth vote in the case, the issue affected the case's outcome. Jackson's dissent was atypical in its accusation of a conflict of interest implied by a fellow justice's decision not to recuse himself from a case. Not surprisingly, the dissent became news. And the press reaction to the dissent may have been directed by the justices themselves. Some commentators criticized Jackson for his use of an opinion to question the ethics of his colleague. They may well have been encouraged by Douglas, who had good relations with reporters. In return, Jackson's supporters, likely including Felix Frankfurter, retaliated by telling the press that Black had threatened to publicize Owen Roberts' conflicts of interest after Roberts sided with Jackson in the feud. Drew Pearson interviewed a justice (again, likely Douglas) who indirectly supported Black by relating to Pearson similar cases from which justices had not recused themselves.[101] One story even reported conference deliberations about the case, which could only have come from a justice.[102]

The feud also stemmed from the ambition of both Jackson and Black to be chief justice. After the death of Harlan Stone in April 1946, both men had lobbied Harry Truman not to appoint the other as chief justice. Rumors spread that an appointment of Jackson by Truman would lead to Black's resignation from the Court in protest. In the midst of this controversy, Black, or those close to him, may have been working the press to shape his own positive coverage of the dispute. Doris Fleeson of the *Washington Star* wrote an article that not only favored Black in the dispute but also contained insider information that would have been known only by the justices.[103]

Under the circumstances, Truman could not choose either Black or Jackson as chief justice. The negative publicity had tied his hands. Rather, he was forced to choose someone who would be perceived as a mediator by both Black and Jackson and who could lower the temperature among the justices. His choice was an outsider to the Court – Secretary of the Treasury Fred Vinson.[104]

Jackson was incensed that he was not picked and was angry about the news accounts that Black had scuttled his nomination. He responded with his own press statement about Black's role in stopping Jackson's nomination. At the same time he was releasing his statement, Jackson defended his actions to Truman, who had urged him to keep the whole matter quiet. Jackson told Truman he had concluded that "I could not accept your conclusion that this matter should not be made public. I think no good can come from further suppression of the facts that are favorable to me since part of the facts have been peddled."[105]

Personal Lives of Justices

Although most of the justices attempted to remain anonymous on a personal level, their personal lives occasionally attracted press attention. Notable birthdays for older justices produced newspaper tributes. The press noticed Louis Brandeis' seventy-fifth birthday in 1931. The *New York Times* noted that Brandeis' "stature as a Judge has increased. He has come to be regarded with general respect and affection such as surrounds his elder brother, Mr. Justice Holmes."[106] Five years later, the *New York Times Magazine* featured a lengthy article on Brandeis as he turned eighty.[107] Similarly, *The New Republic* featured a glowing article on Oliver Wendell Holmes on the occasion of his eighty-fifth birthday. The author, Elizabeth Shipley Sergeant, termed Holmes "a Yankee, strayed from Olympus."[108]

William O. Douglas received press attention when he traveled across the globe. Yet that notice was not coincidental; Douglas courted the press. When he traveled to the Soviet Union in 1955 to gain a better understanding of America's competitor in the Cold War, he arranged with *Look* magazine to write several articles about his trip in return for the magazine's financial support for Douglas' travel. Douglas even arranged for a journalistic photographer to accompany him.[109]

When a bullet was shot into the window of Harry Blackmun's apartment in 1985, the incident sparked news coverage of Blackmun. The justice was uninjured, but the incident led to press coverage of the justices' security as well as speculation as to whether it was an assassination attempt, perhaps in connection with the *Roe* case. In a speech years later, Sandra Day O'Connor even linked the incident to death threats against Blackmun. However, the police concluded that the bullet came from a random gunshot.[110]

Generally, the justices shied away from coverage of their personal lives. They did little to encourage such coverage, with the exception of Douglas, and sometimes went to great lengths not to publicize personal matters. For example, the justices did not announce marriages. Sometimes they did not even tell their colleagues they were getting married. For the vast majority of justices, the names, or even existence, of spouses and children, where they lived in Washington, and the birthdays they celebrated did not become public knowledge.

The notable exception was William O. Douglas. Until the early 1950s, no Supreme Court justice had ever been divorced. William O. Douglas became the first justice not only to divorce but also to remarry. In fact, during a fifteen-year period, Douglas divorced and also was married three times. Douglas' marital problems became a subject of interest in the press. His divorces were duly covered, as was his penchant for marrying women considerably younger than he. *The New York Daily News* headline, for example, read "Justice Douglas Wants Divorce to Wed; She's 30ish," and the article noted that "this personal scandal has touched the highest court of the land."[111] Press

coverage of his troubled marriages also included accusations of domestic violence on the part of Douglas.[112] The press coverage of Douglas' personal life
did not seriously jeopardize his position on the Court, but it did raise eye-
brows among the justices. It also led to criticism of Douglas's moral character
by members of Congress, as well as the first of two efforts to impeach him in
the 1960s and early 1970s.[113] Other justices kept clippings of news coverage of
Douglas' divorces and marriages. His marital problems also raised his profile
in the press to the extent that reporters began to examine other facets of his life.

Ethics and Justices

In 1966, Douglas was criticized by the *Los Angeles Times* for accepting an
annual stipend as president of the Parvin Foundation. However, Douglas
responded that his taking the money was not a violation of judicial ethics.
The newspaper urged congressional action if the Court did not adopt rules
prohibiting such activity.[114] Although the Parvin Foundation issue reemerged
when then-Representative Gerald Ford sponsored an impeachment resolution
against Douglas four years later, Douglas' position on the Court was not
affected by the press coverage, and the issue temporarily was dropped.

Ethics issues resurfaced two years later, this time centering on another
justice – Abe Fortas. At that time, Fortas had just withdrawn from the confirmation process for chief justice. Also, because Johnson was leaving the White
House, his advisory role had diminished. In October 1968, William Lambert,
a reporter for *Life* magazine, received a tip to investigate Fortas' relationship
with Louis Wolfson, a financier who was a client of Fortas before he joined
the Court. After Fortas became a justice in 1965, Wolfson and Fortas agreed
that the justice would receive twenty thousand dollars a year for life to serve
as a consultant to Wolfson's foundation. However, Wolfson soon was facing
criminal prosecution for securities violations. Fortas later resigned from Wolfson's foundation and eventually returned the money Wolfson had already paid
him. The story about Fortas' connection to Wolfson did not appear that fall.

However, Lambert did not let go of it, either. To shake Lambert off the
story, one of Fortas' former law partners met with Lambert and attempted to
downplay the relationship between Fortas and Wolfson. Instead, the reporter
became more interested in pursuing the story. The reporter sat on the information until the Supreme Court ruled in April 1969 that Fortas had recused
himself in a case involving Wolfson. With the help of a Justice Department
official in the Nixon administration, the reporter was able to complete the article, and the magazine published it on May 4, 1969, under the heading "Fortas
of the Supreme Court: A Question of Ethics." The article then prompted the
Justice Department to complete its own investigation of Wolfson and Fortas.[115]

Fortas admitted later to a reporter that he handled the story badly; he should have issued a detailed public statement explaining his relations with Wolfson. Instead, he had provided a brief public statement that raised more questions than answers.[116] He had denied that he had been given any payment by Wolfson, although he had suggested a fee had been tendered but returned. The eleven-month difference between the tendering and the returning had not been not mentioned by Fortas, nor had his long-term relationship with Wolfson been explained.

The press response was critical. The *New York Times* focused on the contradiction between Fortas' statement that he had received no fee and the fact that he had been given a fee by Wolfson. The *Washington Post* urged Fortas to provide a detailed accounting of his relationship to Wolfson or to step down. The *Los Angeles Times* went further and suggested Fortas resign immediately. Other major newspapers soon followed the latter's lead. Fortas' resignation, only six months after his withdrawal as a Supreme Court nominee, was the first by a justice under an ethical cloud.[117]

A Fortas biographer accused the press of "hounding" Fortas. Indeed, it appeared that Fortas was treated not like a Supreme Court justice; rather, he was considered to be similar to any other political figure hit by a scandal. Broadcast news teams set up cameras in front of Fortas' house. Journalists followed him as he gave speeches. One reporter posed as an audience member and, while shaking Fortas' hand, began asking him questions.[118]

The Nixon administration helped the press "get" Fortas. The Justice Department's press officer contacted reporters prior to the *Life* magazine article to alert them it was coming. And shortly after Attorney General John Mitchell met with Earl Warren to inform him of the evidence against Fortas, *Newsweek* magazine detailed the supposedly private visit. The source for the article likely was not Warren, but the Justice Department.[119]

The Fortas incident affected the justices and the press corps for some time. Earl Warren commented that Fortas' actions had left "a blot on the image of the Warren Court."[120] The effect on the individual justices was more specific; Fortas' resignation led to calls for greater disclosure of Supreme Court justices' finances. News organizations, including the *Wall Street Journal* and the Associated Press, directly requested all the justices to disclose their income sources.[121] The *Los Angeles Times* sent a letter to each justice asking him to comment on judicial policy on ethics issues, particularly outside income. Justice John Harlan replied that "it would be quite inappropriate for me as a sitting member of this Court to accord you the requested interview. . . . " Harlan sent a copy of the letter to each of the other justices. Black, however, did respond to the *Los Angeles Times* and answered each of its questions.[122]

Fortas' resignation also emboldened the Nixon administration to wage additional campaigns against justices. Getting rid of Abe Fortas had been easier for the Nixon administration than it had imagined. The president had begun his term with one upcoming Supreme Court appointment (Earl Warren's replacement), and with Fortas' vacancy only four months into his term he had two. The administration then set its sights on a third.

The next target was William O. Douglas. Nixon aide John Ehrlichman related that removing Douglas was a priority because the justice "was the liberal ideologue who personified everything that was wrong with the Warren Court".[123] To accomplish its ends, the administration audited Douglas' tax returns and began compiling information about his relations with Albert Parvin. The FBI also tapped Douglas' phone.[124] Part of the vulnerability of Douglas was his already high profile as a Supreme Court justice. Douglas clearly was one of the most visible members of the Court, if not the most visible, even after presidential speculation about him had died out. In addition to his marital problems, Douglas was a prolific, but controversial writer. In 1969, he authored *Points of Rebellion*, a call for young people to resist the establishment. The book included a provocative statement that, in the face of societal problems and the inattention of those in power, "violence may be the only effective response."[125] A *Life* magazine commentary concluded that Douglas's concern for civil liberties "has now been translated into a near-paranoiac insistence that we have already lost our basic freedoms to an omnipotent and malevolent Establishment."[126] And his chosen venues were just as controversial. *Points of Rebellion* was serialized in *Evergreen*, an erotic magazine. Douglas also wrote articles for *Playboy* magazine. A columnist suggested that the men's magazine published Douglas' articles to win favor with the Supreme Court justice.[127]

Douglas also had become an environmental activist and wrote on conservation issues in environmental publications.[128] He was particularly known in the Washington metropolitan area for his interest in the Chesapeake and Ohio Canal located in Maryland. Douglas hiked the trail and received press coverage doing so, particularly as he led others in an annual trek designed to call attention to the need to preserve the canal. In January 1954, the *Washington Post* wrote an editorial endorsing the construction of a highway along the canal. Douglas was incensed and wrote a letter to the editor explaining the beauty of the area for hiking and camping. In his letter, he challenged the editorial writer to walk with him along the canal trail to understand the environmental effects of the proposed highway.[129]

In what appeared to be a coordinated effort with the White House, Gerald Ford initiated an impeachment resolution against Douglas. Because of Douglas' growing unpopularity, Ford was able to convince ninety-nine other members of Congress to join him. The Republican leader charged that Douglas was unfit to serve on the Court because he had written in 'a pornographic magazine with a portfolio of obscene photographs on one side of it and a literary admonition to get a gun and start shooting at the first white face you see on the other."[130] The impeachment effort failed in its objective of removing Douglas or even securing impeachment in the House of Representatives.

The impeachment effort may have achieved other goals, though. Douglas was scared about what might happen during the impeachment process. As a result, he held off on publishing writings that might inflame the situation. The episode did succeed in placing Douglas in an unfavorable light. He was criticized in the press for some time because of his former ties to Albert Parvin and for his writings. It was not until he came close to retirement that Douglas again received plaudits from the press.[131]

Key Decisions

Inevitably, when the justices announced controversial decisions, they attracted attention from the press. These included New Deal legislation cases in the 1930s, the Flag Salute Cases (*Gobitis* and *Barnette*), *Youngstown* (steel seizure case), the racial desegregation cases, school prayer, and abortion, as well as others. Not only would controversial cases provoke reaction but they would also stimulate further cases designed to overturn or diminish the previous cases. This was particularly true of issues like racial discrimination, affirmative action, and abortion, which spawned several cases during the latter half of the twentieth century. Each case, in turn, then fed press and public attention to the topic and the Court, as a possibility arose for the Court to shift direction, particularly in the wake of an intervening personnel change on the Court. The prospect of another controversial decision then resulted in expanded coverage of the decision to accept a case, the oral arguments, speculation on possible outcomes, the decision announcement itself, and then reaction from the press, interest groups, and public opinion.

Moreover, the cases would produce newspaper editorials inveighing on the wisdom of the justices' decisions. In the wake of one New Deal–era decision, the *New York Daily News* editorialized: "We do not see how old judicial gentlemen . . . can forever be permitted to override the will of the people as expressed through the people's own elected Legislatures, Congress and President."[132] After the cases requiring reapportionment of state legislatures, *Newsweek* opined that "the only kind of democracy that is to be tolerated in the present dispensation is Supreme Court democracy."[133]

The involvement of other high-profile players, such as the president or Congress, enhanced the likelihood of coverage because the decision would affect the news coverage of other institutions as well. *United States v. Nixon* was an example of an extensively discussed case because of its ramifications for the resolution of the Watergate case. Yet the fate of New Deal legislation, the steel seizure case, states' rights, and the Paula Jones suit were other examples of cases that drew attention because they brought the Court in potential conflict with the president and/or Congress.

FOLLOWING AND SHAPING PRESS COVERAGE

These twentieth-century events attracted attention to the Court. Some of them, such as the decision to take and decide cases related to high-profile issues, were Court initiated. Others, such as the ethics scandals and conflicts with presidents, were initiated externally. In these cases of externally driven conflict, the justices were faced with the dilemma of how to affect coverage in a way that preserved their institutional legitimacy or, in some cases, just an individual justice's own role on the Court.

The following section addresses judicial following and shaping of press coverage of themselves. Specifically, it addresses how closely the justices paid attention to press coverage of these events, whether they were affected by that coverage, and whether they were attempting to shape coverage of themselves. Additionally, it discusses the means for shaping press coverage and how the Court institutionally, and the justices individually, availed themselves of such means in order to engage in image shaping.

Following Press Coverage

Like their predecessors in earlier centuries, twentieth-century justices were consumers of media about themselves. Occasionally, a justice defended that practice. Abe Fortas argued for maintaining contact with the outside world: "You can't possibly make such judicial decisions unless you're aware of what's going on in the world."[134] However, that is not the same as saying that they read newspapers every day, which they did not publicly admit to doing. An important aspect of the image of aloofness includes perpetuating the myth that Supreme Court justices do not read newspapers or watch television news. Generally, as the myth went, justices would not seem to care what was written or said about them. The seeming insularity of justices from public opinion – no elections, no constituency – reinforced that message.

This myth often has been perpetuated by the justices themselves. Publicly and privately, they did that frequently in the twentieth century. In 1933, George Sutherland thanked a Mr. Glenn Frank for sending a copy of an article from the *Century Magazine*. Sutherland told Frank that the "Century Magazine steadily improves and this is one of its best numbers. Unfortunately, how-ever, I have little time for this sort of reading."[135] Interestingly, Sutherland acknowledged he had enough familiarity with the magazine to know its edito-rial content was improving but didn't want to leave the impression he actually read the magazine much. In a letter he wrote in 1946, Wiley Rutledge told a correspondent that "... much of the time we do not know whether our positions on specific matters are generally received one way or the other."[136] Former CBS news correspondent Rita Braver, who covered the Court in the 1980s and 1990s, once related that when she talked to the justices socially, "some claim not to watch television at all. Some of them say after meeting me that they will try to watch CBS so they can see me."[137]

Journalists knew the myth was not true, even though justices attempted to convince them of it. Richard Carelli, Associated Press reporter at the Court dur-ing the 1980s and 1990s, called the mythology a "sweet fabrication" and once recounted that even late-twentieth-century justices propagated the mythology: "I remember one time talking to Justice [Lewis] Powell on a Tuesday and he said he very rarely read the popular media. On the following day he was in the Court cafeteria reading *Newsweek* magazine."[138]

The reality is that justices as a group always have been highly interested in press coverage. With the extensive record keeping of justices and the avail-ability of those papers, scholars now can view the extent to which justices in the twentieth century paid attention to the press. An examination of many of their papers reveals that the justices in the twentieth century were watch-ing quite closely the press' reporting on the Court and its individual justices. One indication of the level of attention to the press is the extensive number of newspaper clippings justices kept in their files. The papers of the justices show that they routinely collected clippings from Washington newspapers, the *New York Times*, and newspapers throughout the nation as well as in their home states. Many clippings were forwarded by correspondents across the nation, as indicated by letters the justices received. However, clippings from the local Washington newspapers and the *New York Times* likely were clipped by the justices or their secretaries. During certain periods, the justices also received copies of clips from the Division of Press Intelligence in the Office of Government Reports.

Their media consumption habits included not only newspapers but also opinion magazines. Harlan Stone was an avid reader of *The New Republic* and the *Nation*. Holmes and Brandeis followed *The New Republic* closely. Holmes even lamented in a letter to Harold Laski that "I have been so busy that I haven't opened even last week's *New Republic*".[139]

Another piece of evidence of their interest in press coverage was the fact they routinely passed on to each other what they read in the press about other justices, pending cases, or general topics the Court had dealt with or might deal with in the future. Those notes usually included attachments of newspaper clippings.[140] For instance, Wiley Rutledge sent Hugo Black a copy of an editorial from the *St. Louis Star-Times* and added, "thought you might be interested in reading it."[141] Louis Brandeis passed on to Oliver Wendell Holmes clippings about Holmes' health and speculation about his possible retirement. Felix Frankfurter was one of the most frequent distributors of information to justices prior to and during his time on the Court. Before joining the Court himself, he would regularly send news clippings to Holmes and Brandeis.[142]

The justices sometimes were such avid followers of the press that they even debated how a Court action would be covered by the press. In a letter to a fellow justice, Frankfurter wrote "You win! The denial of certiorari in the F.B.I. case is on the front page of the Washington Post." Frankfurter then went on to defend himself in his own prediction. "But then, like most old New Yorkers, I am provincial in my outlook. In my confidence that the denial would not be a front-page story I was forecasting the significance of the story in the make-up of the New York Times. It is on page 22 of this morning's Times."[143]

At times, they admitted their media habits to each other or others outside the Court. Justice Stanley Reed, who served on the Court from 1938 to 1957, confessed in a note to Felix Frankfurter that he was a frequent reader of the *Washington Post* and the *New York Herald-Tribune*. Some were regular readers of their hometown newspapers. For example, even though he had lived in Washington for some time, Harold H. Burton kept clippings from newspapers in and around Ohio, where he had lived for most of his life. Their correspondence with others beyond the Court also suggested they were keeping in touch with press coverage of themselves as well as of issues related to immediately pending cases. In response to a letter from a woman writing about the upcoming segregation cases in 1953, Robert Jackson referred the woman to a recent *New York Times Magazine* article on segregation. Tom C. Clark corresponded with David Sarnoff, president of NBC, and commented on NBC news and public affairs programs he had seen.[144]

For some, the interest in the press was even stronger. Harry Blackmun kept a copy of the code of ethics for the American Society of Newspaper Editors in his files and even personally marked certain canons as if to emphasize his view that journalists were not abiding by them. One was the canon that "by every consideration of good faith a newspaper is constrained to be truthful," and another provision Blackmun highlighted advised that "it is the privilege as it is the duty, of a newspaper to make prompt and complete correction of its own serious mistakes of fact or opinion, whatever their origin."[145] Warren

Burger gave a speech on the press and the judiciary in the 1970s, and Antonin Scalia did the same twenty years later.[146] In his speech, Scalia criticized the press for using a results-oriented standard for judging decisions. Scalia warned the public not to rely on the press to understand the Court's decisions because of that results-oriented emphasis.[147]

Some justices were highly concerned about the quality of the press' coverage of the decisions of the Court. Felix Frankfurter was one justice who was particularly troubled about the Court's press portrayal and sought to convince his colleagues to do something about it. When the Associated Press suggested that the justices give off-the-record interpretations of decisions for reporters to help them understand and analyze the justices' opinions, Frankfurter circulated to the other justices a suggestion by a former clerk that the Court employ a competent lawyer familiar with the briefs who could "write an intelligent newspaper story on them within a short time after they have been announced."[148] However, the other justices declined to follow Frankfurter's advice. The failure to appoint a lawyer may have been due to a reluctance to be seen as catering to the press, or it could have been a fear that the lawyer's interpretation, not the written opinions, would become the news.

Interestingly, the justices' reliance on the press partly stems from the lack of regular interaction with others outside the Court that would offer them other gauges of public sentiment besides those they see in the press. Whereas members of Congress hold town meetings and interact with constituents back in their districts, justices do not possess such a mechanism. Their lack of direct information was suggested by a conversation Felix Frankfurter had with an old law school classmate from South Carolina. Frankfurter recorded in his diary that the first thing he asked his friend was "what the people of South Carolina are thinking about these days, what are their hopes and fears, etc.?"[149]

The habit of following press coverage became particularly important at election time when the justices gambled on the election outcomes across the country. Like their counterparts at the time of Mr. Dooley, the twentieth-century justices literally followed the election returns to win the Court's betting pool. William Rehnquist organized regular betting pools during presidential electoral campaigns to wager on how a presidential election would turn out. Rehnquist and Sandra Day O'Connor usually won. Antonin Scalia said he participated at first, but later declined when he saw how seriously Rehnquist and O'Connor were studying the various races in order to win.[150]

Following Press Coverage of Themselves

The justices' interest in the press was not abstract. They were highly interested in the press' coverage of individual justices and the cases they considered. Hugo

Black once wrote to William O. Douglas in response to Douglas' sending him a clipping from the *St. Louis Post-Dispatch*, noting that the *St. Louis Star-Times* also had covered the opinion, but that, "[s]o far as I know, these are the only papers that have yet discovered the *Adamson* case."[151] When writing to a correspondent discussing two World War II–related Japanese atrocity cases, Wiley Rutledge confessed that "nowhere since Monday have I seen anything other than the briefest comment in the press that Homma's petitions had been denied because they presented the same issues as Yamashita's."[152]

They also kept up with what the press said about them personally. Harry Blackmun maintained a large file of clippings of news coverage of his public activities, including speeches he gave around the country, as well as of his press interviews.[153] Tom C. Clark also had his own extensive clipping file, which covered his whole professional career, including his eighteen years on the Court.[154] Thurgood Marshall considered himself a strong advocate of the freedom of the press, but he was also sensitive about what the press said about him. He told Carl Rowan that "when they [the press] publish stories that I'm dead, or dying, or terribly ill, or something like that . . . I wonder how much free press I'm for."[155] Douglas once wrote a memo to his colleagues knocking down a rumor on the Drew Pearson radio broadcast that he was resigning to head the Ford Foundation.[156] Abe Fortas wrote an angry letter to *Life* magazine after it criticized him as a man who, "in the considered judgment of the U.S. Congress, condoned dirty movies, accepted extravagant fees, and befriended you-know-who [Lyndon Johnson]. . . ." In his letter, which he never mailed, Fortas accused the magazine of conducting a "brutal and savage assault" against a "defenseless subject."[157]

The justices regularly commented on press coverage of their opinions to each other and even to others. Sometimes they did so to complain, such as in the case of Wiley Rutledge, who wrote to a correspondent that "some of our most responsible papers have not fully stated the true facts either before or after the opinions came down."[158] But Harlan Stone once wrote to his sons about a decision to tell them "what most of the papers seem to have missed."[159] They also noted to each other how truthful to the facts certain press coverage was. Felix Frankfurter once responded to Sherman Minton about a *Saturday Evening Post* article Minton had told Frankfurter about. Frankfurter replied that he had read the article and thought it was accurate in discussing a particular Supreme Court case. In other situations, justices expressed appreciation for positive coverage of their particular opinions. One example was Harlan Stone, who had dissented in the first Flag Salute case. The dissent put Stone in the minority on the Court but won him the favor of the press. More than one hundred and seventy newspapers criticized the Court's decision, whereas only a few approved of it. Stone was gratified about the support for his position and commented to others about the press' endorsement.[160]

Following Press Coverage of Each Other

Justices also followed what the press was saying about other justices. In June 1947, Drew Pearson wrote that Harold H. Burton did not write as much as a Supreme Court justice should and that Burton seemed to "think that being on the Supreme Court is not for the purpose of handing down opinions but to enjoy a continued round of parties." In response, Felix Frankfurter and William O. Douglas sent notes to Burton to reassure him that they believed he was a hard worker. On the same day the column appeared, Douglas wrote to Burton "that was a most unfair below the belt article by Pearson this morning." Burton also noted in his diary that, in addition to the notes he received from Douglas and Frankfurter, four other fellow justices spoke to him personally to refute the Pearson charge.

Douglas' extrajudicial activities were of particular interest to the other justices on the Warren Court. Along with several other justices, Hugo Black kept clippings about Douglas' personal life, including his marriages, divorces, and remarriages, as well as controversies regarding Douglas such as ethical issues, controversial writings, and personal causes.[161] Douglas also kept track of what the press said about Earl Warren. Douglas, who initially disliked Earl Warren, once called him a "cheap politico" and wrote to Sherman Minton, who was retired: "The Washington press is, I think, now laying in wait for the old boy to pop off once more."[162]

In 1991, Clarence Thomas' confirmation process in 1990 attracted the particular attention of Harry Blackmun. As indicated by the extent of press clippings of the Thomas nomination found in his papers, Blackmun was keenly interested in what was being said about a potential colleague. Interestingly, the clippings he kept were mostly negative articles, editorials, and cartoons about Thomas. The press coverage may have affected Blackmun's assessment of Thomas as a colleague, because Blackmun held a low opinion of Thomas that carried on throughout their brief tenure together on the Court.[163]

Following Press Coverage of Current and Possible Cases

Justices also followed press coverage of issues that were pending before the Court. Blackmun kept editorials and news stories about abortion while he was working on his majority opinion on *Roe*. Robert Jackson kept extensive news clippings on the pending segregation cases in 1953 that eventually led to *Brown v. Board of Education*. Some of these clippings speculated on possible reaction to the decision by Southerners.[164]

Justices also followed the press' coverage of a case as it progressed through the judicial process. Robert Jackson tracked news coverage of the Steel Seizure issue involving Harry Truman's seizure of the nation's steel mills in 1952 to avoid a strike by steelworkers. Jackson's files included articles about lower court rulings as the case progressed to the Court. Harry Blackmun kept clippings of press attention to the Court's handling of various cases, particularly abortion. This included press coverage of Warren Burger shifting his position on abortion.[165]

Blackmun not only followed the abortion cases during consideration of *Roe* and its direct aftermath but he also continued to observe abortion developments as reported in the press during the next twenty years. He kept news clippings about how Norma McCorvey, the original plaintiff in *Roe*, had become an opponent of abortion, how NARAL Pro-Choice America was running ads discussing candidates' abortion stances, the way abortion was being treated by the courts in other nations, and the efforts of various states to create test cases to overturn *Roe*.[166]

Justices particularly noted press coverage of high-profile decisions. Harlan Stone wrote to Louis Brandeis that "the comments on the Minimum Wage Case continue to come in."[167] Jackson wrote to a correspondent after the *Barnette* case, the second of the Flag Salute cases in the 1940s, that "[a]lthough I expected that the opinion would be the object of a good deal of criticism, it does not seem to have been." In fact, on this reversal of the earlier Flag Salute case, Jackson kept thirty-two newspaper clippings in his files, including news coverage of, and editorial reaction to, the decision.[168] Jackson also read and clipped news coverage of the Steel Seizure decision from, among many other newspapers, the *New York Herald Tribune*, the *New York World-Telegram*, the *Washington Times Herald*, and the *Dallas Morning News*.[169] Hugo Black also kept clippings on the high-profile cases during his tenure, including the school prayer case, the reapportionment cases, and the segregation cases. He read and filed away editorials, news stories, and newspaper columns.[170] Robert Jackson kept a clipping from an editorial in the *Sacramento Bee* shortly after the *Barnette* case that included a line reading, "One thing can be said with certainty – former Chief Justice Charles E. Hughes was speaking truly when he said that the Constitution is what the Supreme Court says it is."[171]

Being Shaped by Press Coverage

The twentieth-century justices followed press coverage, but did that observation of what the press said about them make any difference in their attitudes or behavior? In her own testimony at her confirmation hearings, Ruth Bader

Ginsburg said that a judge should take account of "the climate of the era, yes, but not the weather of the day, not what the newspaper is reporting."[172] Ginsburg implied that "what the newspaper is reporting" did not affect a judge. But William Rehnquist once admitted that that reporting did. In a speech he gave shortly after becoming chief justice, Rehnquist admitted that:

> Judges, so long as they are relatively normal human beings, can no more escape being influenced by public opinion in the long run than can people working at other jobs. And if a judge on coming to the bench were to decide to hermetically seal himself off from all manifestations of public opinion, he would accomplish very little; he would not be influenced by current public opinion, but instead by the state of public opinion at the time that he came onto the bench.[173]

There is strong evidence that at least some of the justices were influenced by what news media sources said about them and their decisions. According to Holmes biographer G. Edward White, Holmes was affected by *The New Republic*'s editorials criticizing him for his position upholding the conviction of former Socialist Party presidential candidate Eugene Debs for opposing World War I. Holmes switched sides in the next case. He and Brandeis issued dissents in the subsequent Abrams case that reinforced his "clear and present danger" approach to government suppression of speech.[174] In the wake of strong criticism of the Court's decision in the *Gobitis* case in 1940 upholding a state law compelling Jehovah's Witnesses to salute the flag, Felix Frankfurter noted a conversation he had had with William O. Douglas. Douglas had begun the conversation by telling Frankfurter, who wrote the Court's opinion in the case, that Hugo Black had switched his position on the issue. Frankfurter had asked: "Has Hugo been re-reading the Constitution during the summer." Douglas had answered: "No – he has been reading the papers."[175]

The effect may not have been limited to opinions. In one case, it may have extended to the hiring of a clerk. When William Brennan offered to hire a clerk who had been involved in left-wing student groups, he was criticized by newspaper editorials questioning the wisdom of Brennan's choice and speculating on how the clerk might affect the Court's decisions. Earl Warren sent clippings of these editorials to Brennan, suggesting that the chief justice was concerned about public opinion in the matter. Ultimately, Brennan revoked the job offer to the clerk.[176]

Paying attention to public opinion even became a point of contention among the justices. Felix Frankfurter, who was no stranger to concern for public opinion, wrote in his diary on December 30, 1947, about his fear that some of his fellow justices were preoccupied with the opinions of outside commentators. Frankfurter wrote that three of the justices – Murphy, Black, and Douglas – were keeping their ears to the ground. This behavior, according to Frankfurter, was "part and parcel of the Court's failure to be aloof from the contentions of the day and unconcerned about either praise or blame from commentators, especially the popular press."[177] Given Frankfurter's own repeated statements about helping the press cover the Court, the other justices probably would have been amused at Frankfurter's hypocritical diary entry.

Concerns about the Perception of Following Public Opinion

The very tendency of justices to be attuned to public opinion, and the potential public awareness of that fact, worried the justices. For example, after the *Gobitis* case and the Court's pending announcement of its reversal of that view only three years later in *Barnette*, Harlan Stone, as chief justice, was concerned about the image of the Court as a body shaped by public criticism. Stone was concerned that the Court's opinion in *Barnette* might suggest that the Court had reversed itself under public pressure. After Stone saw the draft of the Court's opinion by Robert Jackson, he expressed a concern that Jackson's draft was too candid:

> I have had considerable doubt about the wisdom of some of the footnotes. Some of them seem to me rather too journalistic for a judicial opinion, notably those on pages 5 and 6. That on page 14 might well give the impression that our judgment of the legal question was affected by disorders which had followed the Gobitis decision. If the decision had gone the other way, it is quite possible that the Legion and other similar minded organizations would have produced similar disorders. But that, I think, should not affect our judgment, and if it doesn't affect our judgment is it worth repeating (?)[178]

The "disorders" Stone referred to represented the outpouring of public criticism of the decision on newspaper editorial pages, academic journal articles, and law review articles. Stone mentioned to Jackson that had the decision gone the other way, the complaints would have come from patriotic and veterans groups such as the American Legion. In other words, they would have received criticism no matter what they had done. (The fact that there was much less criticism of the *Barnette* decision contradicted Stone's point.) But Stone warned Jackson that public criticism should not affect the Court's judgment and that noting that criticism in the opinion would suggest to the public that the justices cared about what reporters and columnists thought.

Seeking to Shape Press Coverage

The fact that the justices followed the press and also, at least at times, were affected by news coverage does not prove they in turn sought to shape that coverage. One could argue that if the incidents previously described are evidence that the justices were seeking to shape press coverage, they also could be used as evidence that they were doing a poor job of it. It is unlikely that William O. Douglas sought the kind of negative coverage he obtained about his personal life or that Abe Fortas enjoyed the press coverage of his unsuccessful confirmation process or the ethics scandal that eventually drove him from the Court. It also is doubtful that the justices as a whole were pleased with the intense criticism of the *Gobitis* decision in 1940.

Yet these incidents actually suggest that the justices understood how the press could affect the image of the Court. They understood the connection between public opinion and their own work. They knew that their decisions existed within an environment influenced by public opinion. William O. Douglas once recounted that in a 1960 Court conference, Felix Frankfurter mentioned that had the segregation cases come in the 1940s rather than when they did, he would have voted that segregation was constitutional because "public opinion had not then crystallized against it." According to Douglas, Frankfurter said that the Eisenhower Court, as he called it, had demonstrated that public opinion had changed and he could vote against segregation.[179]

In a letter to a friend, Harlan Stone wrote: "I often wonder whether people at large will ever grasp what is going on in the work of our Court." Yet Stone concluded that "in the long run the tendencies of [the Court's] work would not go unnoticed." Stone believed it was important for the Court to affect the public's knowledge and attitudes about the Court.[180] For example, Stone recommended that Felix Frankfurter, before he joined the Court, write an article explaining the role of law vis à vis economic and social forces in society. Frankfurter did so, and the piece appeared in *The Forum*, a contemporary general opinion magazine, in June 1930. Stone went further by advising Frankfurter on what he should say in the piece and even mentioned an article in *Harper's* magazine that had appeared in April 1930 that Frankfurter could use as a reference.[181]

Even in seemingly trivial matters, the justices became concerned about publicity. In 1947, the law clerks wanted to hold a Christmas party and invite the messengers of the Court, who were African American. The secretaries objected because the messengers were their servants. Frankfurter suggested that the Court ban all social functions the justices did not organize themselves, but Fred Vinson objected to such a policy at that point because of the possible bad publicity of canceling a Christmas party because African Americans had been invited.[182]

As important as it was for the justices to understand that public opinion mattered, perhaps more important was their collective sense that they held the power to help mold public opinion. The desegregation and busing cases from the 1950s through the 1970s particularly vexed the justices as they sought to find a way to impose desegregation while not producing more resistance by the public. They felt they could achieve that balance. While considering a second set of desegregation cases in 1955, Felix Frankfurter argued for a "bare bones" decree with the desired result that "local passions aroused by last May's decisions would thereby be absorbed or tempered."[183] In 1971, William Brennan urged Warren Burger to be careful about the tone of the Court's opinion Burger was writing on school busing. Brennan worried that the opinion in *Swann v. Charlotte-Mecklenburg Board of Education*, which would uphold forced busing as a tool for school desegregation, might reverse the growing trend in the South to accept desegregation.[184]

Limitations on Affecting Press Coverage

Even if the justices possessed a desire to shape press and public attention, they had to come at the task in a way that preserved the dignity of their position. The justices in the twentieth century were expected not to appear before a press conference or make themselves available for repeated on-record interviews. The very image of the justices' seeking to shape coverage or responding publicly to coverage would undermine the content of their message; that is, that they did not pay attention to or care about what was said about them. Earl Warren explained the dilemma justices faced when seeking to influence press coverage, even when they were under external attack. He said that when the judiciary is maligned, "the Courts can't fight back. A man in politics can fight back. He can tell his story to the public . . . but the courts just can't fight back. It isn't in the nature of the position to do it."[185]

That explains why the justices agonized about how to respond to the Court-packing plan. They knew they could not issue press statements or give interviews because they would be seen not only as public opponents of the plan but also as diminishing the dignity of the Court by engaging in public debate about a policy issue, even one that affected them directly. They could not even testify against it in Congress, as that, too, according to Brandeis, would involve them directly in the public debate about the Court-packing plan. Rather, they sought ways to fight the plan without being public.[186]

This is true not only for the Court generally but also for individual justices. One example occurred in the late 1940s and early 1950s and involved Harold H. Burton. Fred Rodell, a Yale law professor, wrote articles in *The New Republic* and *Look* magazine criticizing the Truman appointees to the Court as inept. Rodell called Tom C. Clark "a smiling, superficial, opportunistic man on the move" and Harold Burton an "old-fashioned, narrow-gauged, precedent-worshipper who tries interminably to match cases as a woman shopper matches colors." The criticism stung, and a former Burton clerk urged Burton's friends and supporters to "do some answering to Rodell in public."[187] The criticism of Burton by Pearson and Rodell left its mark on Burton. When the chief justiceship became vacant in 1953, Burton was considered as a possible candidate. However, according to his biographer, the negative publicity about the quality of his work had left the image that he was "a middling justice who had not gained prestige while on the Court."[188] Even though Burton was the only Republican on the Court and the president was a Republican, he was passed over for the appointment.

Like others, justices who are attacked want to defend themselves in public. They even go so far as to draft press statements or letters to the editor. But then they usually hold back. For example, an editorial in the *Washington Post* criticized William O. Douglas' stay in a case in which another justice had already decided not to grant the stay. Douglas wrote a letter to the editor defending his decision. In the letter, he chastised the press, commenting that it was "amazing how little the press knows about Supreme Court procedures." Ultimately, Douglas thought better about it and never sent the letter.[189]

At other times, such as in the Robert Jackson-Hugo Black feud, they go ahead and launch their own defense in public. In 1968, Hugo Black gave a speech at Columbia University Law School rebutting those who said he had changed his constitutional philosophy over the years. He also specifically defended his dissenting opinion in *Griswold v. Connecticut*, explaining that "[e]ven though I like my privacy as well as the next person, I am nevertheless compelled to admit that the states have the right to invade it unless prohibited by some specific constitutional provision."[190]

Even when justices do seek to participate in the shaping of a story, they must convey the impression that they are not involved in such activities. If they are known to be engaged in seeking to shape coverage, then they cannot assert they are disinterested in it. One example was the case of Hugo Black while he was still a new justice. A journalist interviewed Black not long after he joined the Court. When the journalist sent Black a draft of the article based on the interview and sought the justice's approval, Black backed off any suggestion of involvement with the article. He wrote that he did "not wish to approve or disapprove any article" or have anything "appear which says it is my own story or is presented with my partial or full approval." Black emphasized again that he did not want to directly or even by implication appear to be giving approval to the story.[191]

Just because justices sometimes attempt to influence press coverage does not mean they are successful in the way they expect. In the summer of 1953, Felix Frankfurter told a reporter who phoned him that he would not want to stand in the way of Earl Warren becoming a Supreme Court justice. (In Eisenhower's first year in office, he had promised Warren a Supreme Court nomination, although no vacancy existed through most of 1953.) Frankfurter added that the reporter should get that message to Warren. Yet when news reports circulated that Frankfurter was planning to retire to provide a vacancy for Warren, the justice told the Associated Press that he had not hinted that he was leaving the Court.[192]

Like others who attempt to use the news media as a tool, justices also can be burned. One incident involved Harlan Stone's attempt to use a reporter to broadcast his views about the Court, other justices, and current events, particularly the president's Court-packing plan. For several months during 1937 and early 1938, Stone took daily walks with Marquis Childs, who covered Washington for the *St. Louis Post-Dispatch*. During those walks, Stone conveyed to Childs his views about the Court, the other justices, and the justices' opposition to Court packing. Childs published an article on January 22, 1938, discussing Stone's comments, although not quoting or mentioning Stone directly.[193] Rather than being disturbed by Childs' use of Stone's comments, the justice was pleased with the article. He called the piece "just what is needed to educate the public." In fact, he urged Childs to go further, asking why Childs didn't "publish something of the sort in a magazine having national circulation."[194]

Childs did just that when his article "The Supreme Court Today" appeared in *Harper's Magazine* in May of that year. Childs' article particularly mentioned Stone's comments that his colleagues were unhappy with the newest member of the Court, Hugo Black. The article stated that Black had made blunders that "shocked his colleagues" and that some of his opinions had to be rewritten by the other justices.[195]

The two stories led to intense speculation among the press as to who had provided Childs with information about the justices' private views, particularly about Black. Word of the daily walks spread, and attention turned to Stone. Stone's secretary was deluged by reporters seeking information about Stone's role in the articles. When she called Childs for advice, the secretary reminded him that she had "always told the Judge he talked too much."[196] Stone issued a statement denying that he was a source for the article. Childs also issued a similar public statement, although *Newsweek* reported that Childs privately was relating that Stone was his source inside the justice's conference room.[197] The stories led to criticism from the press about justices telling insider stories to the press. Stone was scarred by the incident, and he later related that he had learned that "many things can be said well enough in private conversation, but they take on a somewhat different complexion recorded in print."[198]

Objectives in Shaping Press Coverage

There are two types of objectives justices possess when they attempt to influence press coverage – one is institutional and the other individual. Individual objectives are more complex and varied, depending on the justice. Even the institutional objectives change depending on the political environment. Historically, when the Court has been under attack, the objective is to sustain the Court's power. Generally, that objective is universally shared by the justices, even though agreement on the means may be elusive.

Another objective is related to the institution, but it may not be widely accepted by the justices. That is opening the Court to greater public exposure to demystify the judicial process. It was a recurring theme in the twentieth century. From the 1940s on, some of the justices labored to make the Court and its work more accessible to the public. Several justices, such as William O. Douglas, Felix Frankfurter, and Hugo Black, were close to various news and editorial writers who covered the Court during the period. Frankfurter repeatedly urged his colleagues to do more to accommodate the press. Similarly, in the 1980s, Harry Blackmun began accepting on-the-record interviews because he felt the Court was not public enough. He justified his new approach to the press in a letter: "I have always felt that the Members of the Court are inclined to live too sheltered an existence. I find that the public is hungry for information about the Court."[199]

With the bicentennial of the Constitution in 1987, the justices generally viewed the occasion as an opportunity to discuss the document as well as to present their own institution to a largely uninformed public. William Rehnquist, as the new chief justice, published a book on the Court titled *The Supreme Court – How It Was, How It is*. At the behest of broadcast news organizations, three justices conducted an experiment of a mock oral argument in front of cameras, although the Court did not change its policy on cameras in the courtroom after the experiment. All of the justices also participated in a PBS documentary on the Court titled *This Honorable Court* during which they sat for television interviews to discuss the Court. Their efforts may have affected public opinion. Confidence in the Court rose during the mid-1980s at the same time the justices were taking to television cameras to explain their role.[200]

The institutional objectives were not the only ones important to justices in the twentieth century; they also had personal reasons for engaging the press. In fact, the institutional objective of opening the Court to the public, which was not widely accepted by the justices, also aided those justices who themselves wanted to be able to enjoy a more public presence and participate more fully in public debate. Some justices chafed over the practice of justices having to remain silent. Wiley Rutledge once complained in a speech about the limitations placed on justices. William O. Douglas simply broke the norm by giving some interviews and writing extensively off the bench. Douglas argued that he should have "full-fledged citizenship and therefore participate in all public affairs that didn't involve the work of the Court. . . . "[201]

One of these individual objectives had more to do with the internal dynamics of the Court than external constituencies. That was the use of the press by a justice to talk to other justices. That objective would seem odd when applied to the Supreme Court. Because the Court is an institution with only nine individuals, and those individuals work in close proximity to each other, it would seem safe to assume the justices talk to each other frequently. Hence, one would assume there would be no need to use the press to communicate when interpersonal communication is so readily available.

However, the press does have certain advantages over interpersonal communication for the justices. Given the fact that the justices follow press coverage, they are likely to receive the message from their colleague, particularly if it appears in a news outlet they follow, such as the *New York Times* or the *Washington Post*. Moreover, the importance of the message will be made clear if it is communicated in public. The receiving justice will understand that a response may be necessary, because the message has gone public and is being read or heard or viewed by many other political players. And, perhaps best of all, messages can be communicated anonymously. The justices' own fingerprints may not be visible, which allows them to say things to a colleague that would not otherwise be said personally. Of course, anonymity is difficult to maintain in a small institution, but not impossible if there is a situation where several justices could have been the instigators of the press message.

The justices in the twentieth century did, at times, talk to each other through reporters. One example was the previously mentioned incident of Harlan Stone commenting on his new colleague, Hugo Black. During those morning walks with Marquis Childs, who wrote for the *St. Louis Post-Dispatch*, Stone disparaged Black as someone who was not keeping up with the Court's work. He also related his view that Black didn't act much like a lawyer. Not surprisingly, Childs repeated the comments in his column, although he did not attribute them directly to Stone.[202] Similarly, forty years later, several justices used the interviews Bob Woodward and Scott Armstrong conducted with them for *The Brethren* to criticize Warren Burger's administration of the Court. Chief among them was Justice Potter Stewart.

Another objective in press coverage was to promulgate their views of current events. Harlan Stone privately expressed his delight at the controversy about the Court-packing plan. Stone wrote to a friend that, although he opposed the plan, he was "not displeased that the President has raised the issue. Perhaps I take a sort of sadistic delight in just retribution." It is likely that Stone passed his views on to the press. The popular Drew Pearson column reported that Stone was "pleased and openly defiant."[203]

Louis Brandeis, similarly, sought to shape current events to his liking via the press by suggesting that the press cover specific stories with certain angles that conformed to his views. For example, he sought to stop government spying on citizens. Once he urged an editor for the Scripps-Howard newspaper syndicate to launch a newspaper campaign against the practice. He also instructed Felix Frankfurter, before he joined the Court, to assist the reporter by helping him gain access to materials in the files of the American Civil Liberties Union.[204]

Still another objective of the justices appeared to be to write their own histories, which seemed to be an increasingly common practice in the late twentieth century. Some justices began to go public just before they left the Court to talk about their career contributions. William Brennan changed his mind about avoiding on-the-record sessions with the press a few years before retiring and was interviewed by NBC News, the *New York Times*, the *Hartford Courant*, and the *Village Voice*, among other media outlets.[205] He participated in a public debate through speeches (although never physically in the same place) with U.S. Attorney General Edwin Meese on how to interpret the Constitution. Brennan argued for a "living Constitution" approach, which had governed his career as a justice, whereas Meese promoted the "original text" model. Brennan knew, and expected, that his speeches debating Meese would receive press attention. He also arranged for his biography to be written by Stephen Wermiel, former Supreme Court correspondent for the *Wall Street Journal*. Thurgood Marshall became more open with the press in his last couple of years on the Court. He, too, cooperated with a journalist, Carl Rowan, on his biography. He also sat for press interviews. Harry Blackmun became increasingly public in a similar manner.

Justices had not engaged in such behavior throughout most of the twentieth century. And still, some justices near the end of the twentieth century continued to maintain that stance. Byron White and David Souter avoided the press during their respective service on the Court and did not deviate from that approach as they left. Warren Burger also maintained his public distance from the press when he left the Court.

For those who did engage in this late-career press involvement, one explanation may have been their sense that, because their tenure was ending anyway, the norms of the Court were less pressing on them. Moreover, they knew they would receive much less press attention for this task after they left the Court. Another reason justices may have felt freer to do so were changing norms caused by the institutional educational (and image-making) efforts surrounding the bicentennial, as well as Blackmun's own increasing public profile.

Strategies for Shaping Press Coverage

The twentieth-century justices had motives to seek to influence press coverage – both institutional and individual – and those motives were significant in the twentieth century as the Court was faced with recurring external criticism as well as internal incidents that became public and threatened to undermine the Court's legitimacy and, by association, the roles of individual justices. The question was how to affect press coverage to obtain those objectives, particularly those regarding individual justices and not just the institution as a whole. The justices employed a variety of methods to attain those ends.

Controlling Relations with Journalists

One strategy of justices was to cultivate, as well as control, relations with journalists. At times, associations with journalists had been acquired before a justice came to the Court. While on the Court, justices also forged relationships through social interaction or mutual friends. Those personal relationships sometimes became friendships with reporters, editors, and publishers that went beyond their jobs but also often proved useful to the justice. Some of these associations were with local journalists from their home states. Hugo Black had a friendship with an Alabama journalist, Grover Hall, a fact that was known among the other justices. When Felix Frankfurter retired, he asked Black to do him a favor and pass on to Grover Hall Frankfurter's gratitude for Hall's "use of his powerful pen to guide his fellow citizens toward decency and sanity. . . ."[206] However, most justice-journalist connections were with reporters and editors who had national significance. Louis Brandeis enjoyed a long friendship with Norman Hapgood, editor of *Harper's Weekly*. He termed Hapgood a "good friend" and called Irving Dilliard, of the *St. Louis Post-Dispatch*, "a good friend of Felix & mine...."[207] Felix Frankfurter commented in his diary that a popular Washington newspaper columnist in the 1940s "is in close relation with Douglas."[208]

Journalists were known around the Court for the tone of their coverage of the justices. Justices knew which reporters were sympathetic to them and, not surprisingly, gave high praise to those who were. Brandeis once called Irving Brant, editor of the *St. Louis Times-Star*, a "strong supporter of me generally."[209] He thought highly of those who agreed with him. Journalist Lincoln Steffens was "high-minded serious, fearless . . . a persistent progressive in politics . . . " and, according to Brandeis, Brant was "very intelligent, much more to the left...."[210]

Justices also got to know reporters because reporters themselves cultivated the link. It was common practice for a new reporter who belonged to the full-time press corps to solicit a meeting with each justice. In September 1965, Joseph Foote, a new reporter for *Congressional Quarterly* at the time, wrote to Earl Warren requesting an interview to "discuss with you what we have in mind for coverage."[211] This does not mean that all the justices granted such meetings, but it was one way for reporters to get to know justices. Similarly, new justices met with the existing reporters in the Supreme Court press corps. Earl Warren received the Supreme Court press corps in an off-the-record session shortly after he became chief justice.[212]

Reporters and justices became frequent correspondents with each other. Marquis Childs, who covered the Court for the *St. Louis Post-Dispatch*, wrote regularly to several justices, while sharing his columns, and praising them for their opinions. They reciprocated by congratulating him on his stories. On February 21, 1961, Hugo Black wrote to Childs and thanked him for sending a series of articles Childs had written. Black added that he would like to see the articles in a book because "they are well written in a way calculated to awaken many Bill of Rights-loving people who, I fear, have been unaware of the encroachments being made on constitutional safeguards...." In one letter, Childs thanked Hugo Black for a letter and added that Black was "most generous in what you say, both about me personally and about the articles that I wrote for the Post-Dispatch." Childs also thanked Black for a recent dissent: "Once again, may I express, as so many others have, my debt to you for speaking out so courageously in a time of fear and conformity."[213]

Childs' relationship with Black is one example of a reporter eventually ingratiating himself with a justice after a rocky initial relationship. After the controversy about the KKK and his early practice of dissenting, Black was criticized in the press in the late 1930s. The criticism seemed to emanate directly from the other justices. Childs' own stories transmitted other justices' negative views about Black. In one article in *Harpers Magazine*, Childs cited lawyers who stated that Black's opinions "read like his Senate speeches, more political essays than legal opinions" and that he was not carrying his share of the Court's work.[214] The latter claim likely originated with other members of the Court who talked with Childs "on background." As discussed, Childs eventually became a supporter of Black and acquired something close to the relationship he had had with the justices who were critical of Black.

Another journalist with close ties to justices was Irving Dilliard, a *St. Louis Post-Dispatch* editor. Dilliard wrote to Black frequently as well and sent him copies of his editorials. In one of Black's responses, he wrote that it was "encouraging to know that my work on the Court pleases men who think and believe what you do."[215] In another, he wrote that he wished the *St. Louis Post-Dispatch* had a wider circulation so that Dilliard's work could get a broader audience. Dilliard was well known among the justices. At Dilliard's request, William Brennan circulated several copies of a Dilliard column to his colleagues.[216]

Not surprisingly, *New York Times* reporters enjoyed a close proximity to justices. The twentieth-century justices were aware that the newspaper was a preeminent news source and that a news story in the *New York Times* about a sitting justice was a coveted opportunity. One popular *New York Times* reporter was Lewis G. Wood, who covered the Court during the 1930s, 1940s, and early 1950s. Wood became friends with several justices while covering the Court. When Wood returned from a vacation in South Carolina and appeared again in the press section of the courtroom, a Court messenger delivered a message to Wood from an associate justice that read, "Where did you get that tan, Lew?"[217] Wood's status with the justices aided him in covering the Court; he was granted a level of access that was not common for reporters. For instance, he wrote an article on Fred Vinson for the *New York Times Magazine*. The article followed the chief justice on a typical day, indicating the unusual level of access Wood enjoyed with Vinson.[218]

Another *New York Times* reporter who was well known to the justices and acquired friendships with several was Anthony Lewis. Lewis covered the Court during the late 1950s and early 1960s. Lewis was so well known that when he left the Court beat in 1964, Bert Whittington, the Court's public information officer, sent a memo to the justices notifying them of Lewis' departure. While covering the Court, Lewis wrote an apologetic for the Court that defended it against critics who felt it did not achieve the results some anticipated. Even after he left the beat, Lewis still wrote supportively of the justices. For example, when *The Brethren* appeared in 1979, Lewis panned the book in a review and defended the justices, particularly William Brennan, against Woodward and Armstrong's claims.[219]

Lewis was so well favored by the justices that when Bert Whittington, the Court's public information officer, found out that Lewis had made an interview request to Hugo Black, he wrote a memo to Black urging him to give on-the-record interviews to other journalists covering the Court as well, such as those from the Associated Press and the United Press International, and not just Lewis. Whittington suggested to Black that these other reporters "are regularly stationed here and would suffer from their Editors if Mr. Lewis were allowed a story exclusively." Black subsequently declined Lewis' interview request.[220]

There is evidence that reporters occasionally sought to use their stories to assist a justice internally. One case was Raymond Clapper, a columnist for the Scripps-Howard news service. Clapper discovered through mutual acquaintances that Hugo Black had expressed dismay about one of Clapper's columns. The column was written in response to Marquis Childs' article "The Supreme Court Today" in *Harper's Magazine*. It was unknown how Black's displeasure about Clapper's column was communicated to Clapper – whether it was through another justice, another reporter talking to Black, or some other source. The point was that Black was aware of the column. In fact, Black maintained a file of Childs' stories about him as well as of Clapper's column.[221] Clapper wrote to Black to explain that he had written the piece because he disliked Childs' article. Clapper called it "an outrageous piece of stabbing in the back and that if such an attack was coming out of the Court itself the situation deserved some airing." Clapper also told Black that he thought his article had created sympathy for Black and "that this incident will stop any further business like the Childs article."[222]

Some members of the Supreme Court press corps sent copies of their news stories to the justices. Similarly, editors often forwarded their columns to the individual justices. Both the news stories and the columns typically were highly positive about the justice personally or a particular opinion of the justice.[223] Richard Neuberger of *The Oregonian* sent Louis Brandeis copies of his work, stories related both to the Court and to other topics.[224] Miranda Spivack, Supreme Court reporter for the *Hartford Courant*, sent a copy of a story she wrote on the twentieth anniversary of the *Roe* decision to Harry Blackmun. Blackmun replied to Spivack to express his gratitude that she had sent the article and added that "you were very supportive."[225]

Some reporters sent notes to justices praising them for their opinions. Frank McNaughton, *Time* correspondent, wrote to Robert Jackson: "I want to compliment you on your Flag Salute opinion. I think it is one of the greatest that I have ever read. Some of the sentences have a power that is almost

Olympian. . . . " Jackson responded to McNaughton that "your letter is greatly appreciated."[226] Sometimes the praise seemed even more extreme than calling a justice's sentences "almost Olympian." Irving Dilliard of the *St. Louis Post-Dispatch* sent a telegram to Brandeis congratulating him on the thirtieth anniversary of a case Brandeis had won as a trial lawyer.[227]

The relationships between Hugo Black and Marquis Childs and Irving Dilliard, as well as between Harry Blackmun and Miranda Spivack, were not unique. Some justices reciprocated with praise for the kind of press coverage of the Court they enjoyed seeing. Earl Warren wrote thank-you notes to reporters. He told one ABC News reporter that he was "pleased beyond words" about the reporter's coverage of the Miranda decision.[228]

Reporters also sought to become informants for justices. The frequent social interactions already described, as well as background interviews, provided such opportunities. One recorded case involved Irving Brant of the *St. Louis Star-Times* and Hugo Black. Brant wrote to Black in the midst of the controversy regarding the *Harpers Magazine* article to assure Black that Harlan Stone was not the source of the criticisms of Black in the *Harpers* article. Brant told Black: "I can assure you that if it is based in any part on statements by Justice Stone, he [Childs] has completely twisted their implications."[229]

The professional relationship sometimes became more informal. Justices occasionally invited reporters to talk to them during the justices' vacations. Reporters sometimes followed William O. Douglas out West when he was on vacation to interview him. Similarly, Louis Brandeis gave interviews while on vacation. In 1935, he gave an off-the-record interview to two journalists and used the occasion to freely discuss the Court's decisions to overturn the Roosevelt administration's social programs and the inefficiencies of big business.[230]

Even in Washington, the interaction with reporters often was social as well as professional. Oliver Wendell Holmes, Jr. dined with well-known columnist Walter Lippmann. Felix Frankfurter lunched with Lewis Wood, James (Scotty) Reston, and Anthony Lewis of the *New York Times*; Joseph Alsop of *The New York Herald Tribune*; Brian Beedham of *The Economist*; and Neville Maxwell of *The Times* (London).[231] Frankfurter was close to Phil Graham, the publisher of the *Washington Post* during the 1950s. Graham had clerked for Frankfurter. Nor were justices only lunching with well-known reporters. Frankfurter also talked regularly with others in the press. In one diary entry, Frankfurter mentioned that Herbert Swope, an editor at *The New York World* had "called . . . on one of his long telephonic visits."[232]

Journalists reciprocated. Justices were invited to parties held by journalists.[233] They were guests at *Washington Post* publisher Katherine Graham's home. They attended correspondents' association dinners. Journalists sent personal greetings, such as on justices' birthdays. W. H. White, editor and publisher of *The Emporia Gazette*, wrote to Louis Brandeis on his eightieth birthday, telling him that "your work will live for a long time, in years, in decades, and I hope in generations. . . . "[234] In turn, justices acknowledged important events in journalists' lives. Arthur Goldberg wrote to congratulate Anthony Lewis when Lewis won the Pulitzer Prize for Supreme Court reporting. Goldberg also congratulated another reporter for winning an American Bar Association award.[235]

Reporters sometimes became protective of the justices. Lewis Wood of the *New York Times* wrote to Robert Jackson not long after the justice had joined the Court. Wood asked Jackson for a statement that he would not be involved in the New York gubernatorial race for two reasons. One was that Wood wanted an exclusive story for the *Times*, but the other was that Wood told Jackson, "I did not want you to get mixed up in it."[236] Another instance was when CBS News aired a special program about the Supreme Court in February 1963. Earl Warren assisted the network in the production of the show. However, in a subsequent letter to Earl Warren, CBS News producer Fred Friendly thanked the chief justice for his cooperation but also added that "[w]e have refrained from any public utterance in this regard because we felt that was the way you wished it."[237] In another case, the Alabama newspaper editor Grover Hall apologized to Hugo Black for reprinting a news syndicate article that was critical of Black. The editor wrote to Black that he hadn't noticed the story in time and would have omitted it if he had.[238]

Supreme Court beat reporters sometimes even expressed agreement with the Court's stated reluctance to be public. In 1955, Anthony Lewis asked for an interview with Black in conjunction with a story Lewis was writing on the solicitor general's office. However, Lewis added the caveat that even though he wanted Black's help with the piece, he was unsure whether it was "appropriate for members of the Court to speak with newspaper men on such a subject."[239] Seven years later, Lewis asked Black for an interview for an article he was writing for the *New York Times Magazine*. Lewis added that "[o]f course I am aware of your proper reluctance to discuss anything relating to the Court with newspaper men." However, Lewis stressed it was an historical piece and that Black's thoughts "would be most valuable."[240]

By controlling access and making Supreme Court beat reporters dependent on them for any information beyond the written opinions, justices placed reporters in the position of agreeing to an implicit professional bargain with the justices to preserve the reporters' positions on the beat. Failure to abide by the justices' rules of background or off-the-record interviews meant reporters could be shut out of any future interaction with the justices. Reporters in this highly controlled environment became desperate for news. Explaining why he agreed to the justices' rules of background interviews, *Baltimore Sun* reporter Lyle Denniston related that he was willing to make bargains to obtain news.[241]

The justices knew they had created this implicit bargain. Put succinctly, reporters who accepted the Court's practices and refrained from writing negatively about the justices were more likely to stay in the Court's good graces. Once, when a *Washington Post* reporter wrote stories suggesting that Felix Frankfurter's work volume was lower than that of other justices, Frankfurter lobbied the *Post* to remove the reporter from the Supreme Court beat.[242]

Another example occurred in 1987 when an ABC News crew was allowed to film the conference room when it was empty. While the crew was filming, Tim O'Brien, the network's Supreme Court reporter at the time, looked in the fireplace and pulled a piece of paper from the ashes. He appeared to be taking notes while perusing it. A Court public information officer confronted O'Brien and took the document. O'Brien denied taking notes on it. The incident led to a memo from the chief justice, William Rehnquist, to his colleagues informing them of the incident. Some justices responded with their own memos suggesting a response. Antonin Scalia urged that O'Brien be banned from the building. However, Lewis Powell and Harry Blackmun argued that the blame was partly on the justices for inviting reporters into the conference room without properly disposing of any confidential material first. John Paul Stevens weighed in that the incident was unlikely to have serious consequences for the Court: "My guess is that O'Brien will decide that the news value of what he may have seen is not worth the loss of our good will and that no serious harm will come from the incident."[243]

Leaking

To gain respect for their institution, justices need to direct the press' coverage away from the process by which they arrived at decisions and toward the end product. This did not originate in the twentieth century. As discussed earlier, John Marshall instituted the practice of delivering a single opinion for the Court rather than the individual opinions that had been common to that point. The practice masked the divisions among the justices.

Indeed, throughout its history, the Court has been surprisingly successful in using secrecy to focus attention where it wants and away from information that the justices believe could undermine their role. The Court is the most successful national government institution in filtering access to its deliberations. That success is aided by the fact that only the nine justices sit in the conference room where cases are discussed. Justices share their drafts with each other but usually not more broadly. The only additional participants are a relatively small number of clerks who are sworn to secrecy and face the prospect of dismissal from the Court and exile within the legal community as they are commencing their legal careers if they leak. Furthermore, they hold intense loyalties to their bosses that make it unlikely they would provide information to a reporter that, by the very act, might embarrass that justice.

That is not to say that clerks have not been sources for leaks about the Court. *The Brethren* is a view of the Burger Court that, to a large extent, emanates from the perspective of former clerks. However, it is unlikely that those clerks would have leaked had they not been allowed to do so by the justices they had worked for. The chief justice warns clerks each term about the hazards of leaking. Burger even promised to fire clerks who talked to the press.

Having said all that, there are individual reasons for justices to leak to the press. As discussed previously, justices do interact with reporters, and therefore the opportunities for leaking are frequent. The most egregious example in the twentieth century – one in which a majority of the justices participated – was *The Brethren*. This exposé of the Court was written by Bob Woodward and Scott Armstrong, two reporters for the *Washington Post*. It is significant that neither Woodward nor Armstrong had ever been part of the Supreme Court press corps. Therefore, neither had acquired the institutional relationships with justices that might have made them reticent to offend justices, sever future relationships, and inhibit their ability to report about that beat. According to Woodward, ultimately five of the nine justices sat for background or off-the-record interviews with the two journalists. Three of the justices – Harry Blackmun, Lewis Powell, and Potter Stewart – were identified by Woodward as sources after their deaths.[244]

The idea of the book began with a justice. Potter Stewart met Woodward at a cocktail party at *Washington Post* publisher Katherine Graham's house and began a personal relationship with Woodward. Stewart already thought highly of Woodward; during the Watergate investigation, he used a speech to praise Woodward and Carl Bernstein for uncovering the Watergate story.[245] Subsequent to their initial meeting, Stewart then arranged to spend hours with Woodward explaining the private behavior of the justices in Court conferences and detailing his criticisms of Warren Burger.[246] In an unusual move for a justice, Stewart promised Woodward that he would answer any question Woodward asked. Woodward later recounted that Stewart "knew what he was doing and I think he almost hoped that he could bring Warren Burger down by launching this inquiry into how he ran the Court."[247]

Word of the interviews for the book circulated throughout the Court. Burger was not one of the members of the Court with whom Woodward and Armstrong had spoken. He must have realized he would not be cast in a positive light. It was well known that Burger had no love for the media, nor did they have much for him. In a speech, Burger once said that lawyers were near the bottom in public esteem, but so were journalists. In return, the press had few kind words for him. When he retired, *Time* magazine called him "pompous and aloof." The *New York Times* characterized Burger's relationship with the press as "frosty."[248]

In the midst of the interviews Woodward and Armstrong were conducting, Burger decided to thwart their work. In conference, the chief justice proposed to the other justices that they institute an unwritten rule that no contact be made between justices and journalists. Apparently, the justices did not agree to the rule. Powell wrote a note to Burger, although he never sent it, that responded to the conversation in the Conference Room about Burger's proposal. Powell said he felt that the justices should not "foreclose all conversations with representatives of the media." He did say, however, that "if those who elect not to talk to media representatives are concerned that those of us who do may violate confidences, I would prefer a policy of no communication whatever – despite my own conviction that this is not in the best interest of the Court as an institution."[249]

The fact that so many justices, as well as many clerks, participated in the research on *The Brethren* indicated either a high level of dissatisfaction justices had with the current operation of the Court or their fear that they would be portrayed negatively if they did not cooperate with the reporters and provide their side of the story. Yet Burger's proposal may have dampened the enthusiasm for leaking. When Woodward sought a second round of interviews with Powell, the justice declined. Even Stewart began to have second thoughts about the book. Woodward told an interviewer that Stewart "realized he had started an avalanche of sorts that was going to cause the Court a lot of problems internally and externally."[250]

David Beckwith, then-editor of the *Legal Times* and a former *Time* magazine reporter, termed it "the biggest leak of all." Beckwith met regularly with Potter Stewart, and Stewart may have encouraged Beckwith to promote the book in the *Legal Times*. Stewart also may have been Beckwith's source when Beckwith mentioned in his promotion of the book that the justices had reacted negatively to it, even though it had not even been published yet.[251]

Lewis Powell sought to distance himself from the book. He wrote, but ultimately did not send, a note to Burger that he was "deeply distressed that my name is implicated" in the book, and that criticisms of Burger had been "manufactured from whole cloth." Powell also began to write a press statement that was intended to portray the book's content as fiction. Powell never issued the statement or even circulated it to others. He did send a note to Thurgood Marshall, who was heavily criticized in the book, to reassure him of his respect for him.[252]

The leaking that occurred through *The Brethren* affected the relations among the justices. Burger suspected that Stewart had initiated the project. Stewart's own retirement, at the age of sixty-five, only eighteen months after *The Brethren* appeared, may have been the result of those soured relations.[253] However, Stewart defended the book in an interview after he left the Court. Admitting there were inaccuracies, Stewart called them minor and said that "there's no reason on earth that the American people should not know these things."[254] Harry Blackmun also defended the book. He related in a television interview that his daughter had read *The Brethren* and learned what he did for the first time. "Now if that book did that for a lot of people, I think maybe it served a purpose."[255]

The Brethren was hardly the only time that secrecy was breached. For example in 1992, the deliberations on *Planned Parenthood v. Casey* were leaked prior to the decision. *Newsweek* magazine ran a short article describing the divided nature of the Court on the case, the possibility that no clear-cut decision would emerge, and the inside information that the decision would be handed down on the last day of the term.[256]

Nor was *The Brethren* the only time that justices began pointing incriminating fingers at each other as leaks appeared. In June 1972, William O. Douglas wrote a memorandum to the conference on the abortion cases. Shortly thereafter, the *Washington Post* published a story about the Court's deliberations on the abortion cases. The story included a discussion of Douglas' memorandum to the other justices. Douglas immediately was assumed to be the leaker. Douglas attempted to tamp down that speculation by writing to Burger and the other justices that he was "upset and appalled" because he had "never breathed a word concerning the cases, or my memo, to anyone outside the Court." He stated that the differences in the Court were "wholly internal" and that if they are disclosed, they come out in opinions, not press leaks.[257]

Douglas also felt the need to defend himself when the *National Observer* published an article on the Court by Nina Totenberg. Douglas explained to Burger that Totenberg had asked to interview him off the record. He replied that he would "never talk to anyone on-the-record or off-the-record about the Court." Douglas attempted to reassure Burger he was not the leak because previously he had been burned by a *National Observer* reporter. "I had seen one of the reporters several years back who wanted to do a piece about me. I saw him and it was a friendly visit. But as I suspected, it ended up with my decapitation."[258]

Those who were the most press friendly, as Douglas was, naturally were the most suspect. William O. Douglas related an incident when Owen Roberts asked the chief justice for a conference before the Court was set to announce a case. At the conference, Roberts passed around a Drew Pearson column from that morning predicting that the justices would announce that case and what the vote would be. Roberts accused a justice of leaking this information to the press. Felix Frankfurter suggested that Douglas or Frank Murphy had leaked. Whichever justice had leaked to Pearson likely did it again. In a later column, Pearson wrote that Roberts was "sputtering and fuming" about the leak.[259]

Another justice suspected of leaking regularly was Felix Frankfurter.[260] In the January 1947 issue of *Fortune* magazine, an article appeared about the Supreme Court written by Arthur Schlesinger, Jr. The article included information that clearly came from among the justices. Frankfurter was a prime suspect as the leak to Schlesinger. That prompted Frankfurter to write to at least one colleague denying that he was Schlesinger's source. Frankfurter wrote Frank Murphy that he had met with Schlesinger because he knew Schlesinger's father from Harvard and, as Frankfurter put it, "it would have been boorish not to see him. . . . " However, Frankfurter said he did not tell Schlesinger anything beyond a list of others to talk to and books to read. He denied having seen the manuscript before publication or even having read the article.[261]

At other times, secrecy was nearly breached. In 1953, William O. Douglas wanted to release a press statement asserting that Julius and Ethel Rosenberg, who had been sentenced to death as spies and whose appeal had been overturned by the Court, had not been given a fair trial. Douglas ultimately did not issue the statement. But the threat of the statement worried his colleagues. Felix Frankfurter wrote to Harold H. Burton that Douglas' letter would place the Court "in the position of being heedless to the pronouncement of a member of the Court that the pair were sentenced to death after a trial that violated the requisites of a fair trial. . . . Do you really think that that is a position in which the Court should be left under the condemnation that this would involve?"[262]

Yet Frankfurter himself was the potential target of a similar situation five years later when he wrote a concurring opinion in *Cooper v. Aaron* and incurred the wrath of Hugo Black and Justice William Brennan. In that case, the justices wanted a united front on the subject of racial desegregation, and Frankfurter's concurrence, which was more conciliatory toward desegregation opponents than the Court's unanimous opinion, threatened to dilute it. Black and Brennan were determined to issue a statement to the press asserting that

Frankfurter's opinion did not undermine the Court's decision. However, John Harlan talked the two out of the move.[263]

These examples suggest that each justice has significant power over his or her colleagues with regard to external relations. An individual justice's action can undermine the secrecy they are all expected to uphold and expose the other justices to public scrutiny. In these two cases, the justices who were ready to breach the tradition of secrecy acquiesced to the pressure of colleagues. The Robert Jackson incident discussed earlier in this chapter suggests even that pressure from colleagues is not always sufficient to maintain the norm of secrecy.

When a leak does occur, the justices seek to convey the impression that it did not happen in the first place. One way to do so regarding the timing of an announcement is to change it after the leak appears. William O. Douglas once related that when a case's outcome and timing were reported by Drew Pearson in advance, the justices delayed the announcement for several months "merely to avoid giving credence to Pearson's prediction."[264]

Another example of the ability of the power of a single justice to undermine secrecy is the issue of individual justices' policies on the opening of their personal papers after they retire or die. William Brennan's approach was to allow select researchers access to his papers, and Harry Blackmun's was to allow his papers to be opened five years after his death. Thurgood Marshall's decision to open his papers to full public access immediately following his death led to an outcry from the other justices, as many of the memos, case notes, and opinion drafts suddenly open to the public involved justices who were still sitting on the Court. Several justices sought to impose a policy that would prohibit justices from releasing their papers until ten years after their retirement. When the policy failed to be adopted because of a lack of unanimity, some justices unilaterally stripped their papers of information they did not want the public to see.[265]

Tools for Shaping Press Coverage

Symbolism

One indication of the justices' understanding of public opinion, and their role in shaping it, was the construction of the Court's own building. As discussed in Chapter 3, the Court did not have its own home during the eighteenth and nineteenth centuries. Not until 1935 did the Supreme Court meet in its own building on First Street and Maryland Avenue N.E. The building itself is a message in symbolism. Even though it was built during the midst of the Great Depression, the building looked like a marble temple.[266] The justices knew that the building would convey an important image for the Court. Harlan Stone joked that "whenever I look at that building I feel that the justices should ride to work on elephants."[267] It was significant that, even though the building had been initiated by William Howard Taft years before, it was completed when Franklin Roosevelt was declaring the Court out of touch with the public's will.

As discussed earlier, the use of the robe, the elevated bench, and legal terminology all reinforce the sense that the Court's pronouncements carry a weight that is supported by the U.S. Constitution and should be attended to by others in American government, including the public. The Court is the most formal of all governmental institutions in the United States. Formal wear is expected of counselors appearing before the Court. The sessions of the Court begin with a formal declaration. The justices are particular about how they are addressed. Decisions are "handed down." All of these symbols are efforts to invest the Court with an image of a legal rather than a political power whose will is not its own, but that of the Constitution.

Individual justices benefit from the institution's symbolism. The pronouncements of majority opinions are accorded a legitimacy that is not granted other institutions. When the president delivers the State of the Union address, a response is given immediately by the opposition party. Congressional acts are subject to lawsuit and efforts to enact repeal. But the Court is different. Although the Court's acts are criticized, those in the legal community still afford the Court a measure of deference that is not given to others. Opinions of individual justices are wrapped up in the authority of the institution, and even though those decisions can weaken the immediate image of the Court, those very decisions also can be legitimated by their association with the symbols of the institution.

The Timing of Decisions

In the twentieth century, both the Court collectively and justices individually used opinions for shaping press coverage. Justices knew their opinions could affect press coverage and hoped the press' attention to the story would influence public cognitions about the Court and law and, hence, public attitudes as well. Obviously, the vast majority of opinions never received much attention from the press. But those few with the potential for press notice could shape public knowledge and attitudes. Earl Warren once wrote in a letter that he hoped the Miranda decision would "have the effect of making the public realize the importance of good public work...."[268]

Even the timing of a decision was important. The justices battled between adhering to tradition and accommodating the demands of press coverage and public opinion. For many years, the justices issued opinions only on Mondays. By the end of the term, that practice resulted in several important decisions being delivered at the same time. Because reporters in the press corps would not be given extra space in their newspapers to cover them all (and broadcast journalism could cover even less), the journalists had to choose which decisions to cover. That meant that some never were noticed because reporters would not cover them the next day. By that time, the decisions were old news. Or, if several were reported, journalists would have to provide superficial coverage because of the time constraints of getting copy to an editor in time for the next deadline. That meant getting the facts wrong or simply not having enough time to provide an explanation of the Court's rationale in the decision.

Felix Frankfurter, the justice on the Warren Court most concerned about institutional press coverage, annually sent a memorandum to his colleagues urging them to change the Court's procedures to make it easier on the press. Frankfurter argued that the Court's practice of releasing several important decisions on one day resulted in "public indigestion, with consequent mis-information and mischievous reaction to decisions." He asserted that this problem had significant ramifications for the justices: "Greater sensationaliz-ing, because of the restricted space for reporting, normally follows a 'big day' at the court, and Congressional response – not merely talk but legislative pro-posals – is apt to be based on distorted and inadequate reporting of events."[269] Finally, in 1965, after Frankfurter had retired, the justices expanded decision announcement days beyond Mondays. Tom C. Clark was the instigator of the change.[270] Earl Warren, the chief justice, told Alfred Friendly, managing editor of the *Washington Post*, that the change was intended to help reporters. The effect was more significant than the justices might have expected. As a result, Friendly decided to post a full-time reporter at the Court.[271]

Also important was the timing of the release of specific decisions certain to receive expansive press attention. The *Roe* case could have come down in 1972; oral arguments initially were delivered in the 1971–72 term. Yet Warren Burger suggested that the case be held over to the next term. William O. Douglas suspected that Burger was seeking to avoid an election year announcement. Douglas wrote a memorandum to the conference arguing against putting off a decision on abortion. In the memo, Douglas noted to his colleagues that "this is an election year." He said it should not be their role to "make the path of any candidate easier or more difficult." Douglas suggested that delay actually would be as much a political signal as an announcement of the case. He argued, unsuccessfully, that the delay of the abortion cases into the next term, and beyond the 1972 election, would "in the eyes of many be a political gesture unworthy of the Court."[272]

Opinion Presentation

Not only the timing but also the manner of delivery are important for press coverage. Extended reading of an opinion is intended to emphasize its importance. Occasionally, justices wanted to go even further. Harry Blackmun sought to have his oral announcement of the *Roe* decision be recorded and distributed to the press. However, Brennan objected because it would have been a departure from current policy and might lead to the possibility that "the announcement will be relied upon as the opinion or as interpreting the filed opinion."[273]

As dissents are not the opinion of the Court, they are likely to receive less attention from reporters. Justices who issue one must find ways to emphasize the dissent to get coverage. John Paul Stevens once explained that the reading of dissents by justices in the courtroom was a way to make sure the dissent did not get lost among the other news of the day. Antonin Scalia commented that his objective with dissents was to "get it on record and get it attention."[274] Scalia took nine minutes to read his dissenting opinion in *Morrison v. Olson*, a case that addressed the constitutionality of the Ethics in Government Act of 1978. That was three times as long as Rehnquist took to read the majority opinion. Scalia did this again in the *Romer v. Evans* case on gay discrimination. As a result, his dissents were widely covered in news articles and editorials.[275] Frankfurter rarely read a dissent from the bench. When he did so in one case that deeply disturbed him, a fellow justice sent him a note indicating the reading had reached its intended target: "What you have just done, justifies continuance of the practice of announcing Decisions. If you suffered in its delivery, you can be assured its delivery caused suffering to those who differed with you."[276]

Revealing the Court through Writing

Because justices can write what they wish in their own individual concurrences or dissents, there is the prospect of a justice violating the norms of the Court by revealing too much about the internal deliberations. This is particularly true when a justice, as part of his or her critique of the Court's decision, wants to criticize not only the outcome but also the process by which it occurred and/or the motives of the other justices. Hugo Black wrote a concurrence designed to rebut a Frankfurter dissent. Specifically pointing to Frankfurter's dissent, Black lambasted justices who "rest their interpretation of statutes on nothing but their own conceptions of 'morals' and ethics.'"[277] Similarly, Owen Roberts used a dissent to accuse his colleagues of being capricious in their treatment of precedent. The justices' public criticisms of one another in the 1940s led the press to comment on the furor raging within the conference room. The *New York Times* noted that the justices' verbal battles were "no momentary judgment, but instead a carefully measured criticism, motivated by an unconcealed impatience or anger."[278]

In response to a bitter internal battle among the justices in 1991, Thurgood Marshall angrily dissented in the *Payne v. Tennessee* case regarding the constitutionality of victim impact statements. Marshall argued in his dissent that there was no justification for overruling two precedents that had been set within the previous four years on this issue. Marshall added that the law and the facts had not changed; "only the personnel of this court did." He concluded that the stability of the precedents of the past "depend on nothing more than the proclivities of the individuals who now comprise a majority of the Court."[279]

Other justices worried that opinions could be too frank. Hugo Black wrote a stinging dissent in his first case after taking his seat. The other justices worried that Black's harsh criticism of the Court's opinion would undermine the Court in the public's mind just as the Court was recovering from both the Court-packing plan and the controversy about Black's membership in the KKK.[280]

Justices also were concerned that opinion writing, particularly in dissents, could criticize the process of decision making as well as the outcome. Frank Murphy once objected to a Frankfurter written opinion that bemoaned the Court's decision as "unavoidably" late. Murphy wrote to the conference: "So far as the public is concerned, any decision rendered in the same term as that in which the case is argued is not 'unavoidably' late. . . . To say that such a decision is 'unavoidably' late is thus to stir up needless speculation and comment by the public."[281] In another case, Felix Frankfurter complained that he did not have enough time to write a dissent because the majority opinion in the case was not written until late in the term. Wiley Rutledge responded that, in an earlier case, he had complained similarly and wanted to mention brevity of time to write a dissent in his opinion and that Frankfurter had suggested he not do so. Rutledge wrote: "The basis for it was that you felt neither the Court nor any of its members should ever disclose or specifically acknowledge such a situation, even though the acknowledgment was in accordance with the actual fact."[282]

In their content, majority opinions still may reveal more about the justices' thinking than is intended. Joint documents can be vague because that is the only way to reach consensus. This is no less true of Supreme Court decisions.

One journalist suggested that "murky decision-reporting may be the reporting of murky decisions as well as the murky reporting of decisions."[283] After they take a case, justices are bound to make some kind of decision, even if they delay it. Ruling for one or the other of the two parties is less of a problem than determining the joint rationale for that decision. William O. Douglas admitted that the Court's opinions are sometimes opaque or not well developed logically "because of the patchwork that goes into their creation, satisfying this judge, getting a majority by putting in a footnote, striking out a sentence that would have made a paragraph lucid. . . . "[284]

Dissents as Vehicles

The very act of writing a dissenting opinion provides opportunities for justices to attract attention to their views. However, dissenting involves more than just announcing opposition to the Court's opinion and the reasons behind it. It is also part of the calculus of seeking to shape both the Court's opinion and public opinion. Louis Brandeis once confided to Felix Frankfurter that "there are all sorts of considerations that affect one in dissenting." Brandeis included "a limit to the frequency with which you can do it, without exasperating men" and that "you may have a very important case of your own as to which you do not want to antagonize on a less important case. . . . "[285] One example of antagonizing fellow justices was Hugo Black's early practice of dissenting. Black issued eight solo dissents in his first term as a justice. Harlan Stone was disturbed by the nature of the writing in Black's dissents. He accused Black of "using the judicial opinion as a political tract" and asked Frankfurter to tutor Black in the traditions of opinion writing.[286]

The amount of coverage given to a dissent varies depending on the newsworthiness of the case and the outlet. Broadcast news stories tend not to cover dissents. However, elite newspapers do. When a longer news story is written about a decision, dissents receive their own coverage from the press as a counterweight to the majority opinion. Yet this coverage rarely equals the attention given to the majority opinion, and in many cases the dissents are merely noted rather than explained.

Nevertheless, the fact that dissents receive attention can undermine the power of the majority opinion. Indeed, the prospect of public attention to the dissent can become a means of leverage for a justice seeking the ability to shape the Court's opinion. One example was the possibility of a Louis Brandeis dissent that ultimately reshaped the majority opinion. Brandeis' opinions were well respected and attracted the attention of the press because of their lucidity. In one case, Brandeis had written a stinging dissent that he was ready to issue in response to a majority opinion that was seriously flawed. The opinion, and Brandeis' dissent, worried the majority. As Brandeis recalled, "[T]hey [the majority] didn't want the Court shown up that way." The chief justice took over the opinion from the justice to whom it had originally been assigned and rewrote it to Brandeis' satisfaction.[287]

The tone expressed in the dissent also is a mechanism for attracting press attention. One of the most common users of pointed rhetoric in dissents has been Antonin Scalia. In one dissent, Scalia said the Court was "busy designing a Constitution for a country I do not recognize," and in another he accused his colleagues of acting on whim: "Today's opinion shows more forcefully than volumes of argumentation why our Nation's protection, that fortress which is our Constitution, cannot possibly rest upon the changeable philosophical predilections of the Justices of this Court. . . ."[288]

Scalia was criticized for the harshness of his verbal attacks on the majority. One law professor argued that Scalia's tone in dissents "sends exactly the wrong message to law students and attorneys about what type of discourse is appropriate in a formal legal setting."[289] However, Scalia seemed to know exactly what kind of rhetoric would attract attention from the press. He once commented that his objective with dissents was to "get it on record and get it attention." His biographer concluded that Scalia was "losing cases but winning a crowd beyond Washington, D.C."[290]

Justices used other means to attract the press' attention to their dissents. In the *Barnette* case, Frankfurter sent a note to two journalists he knew urging them to read his dissenting opinion in full, likely hoping they would give it attention in their coverage of the Court's decision.[291] Thurgood Marshall went even further. He had bitterly attacked the majority in the victim impact case mentioned earlier. Marshall then reinforced his words by announcing his retirement. The move gave his dissent even greater force and assured that his retirement announcement would include his strongly worded dissent. Indeed, the press responded as Marshall expected; his resignation was accompanied by coverage of his dissent in the *Payne* case.[292]

Concurrences as Vehicles

Perhaps even more important in asserting a justice's views for press and public consumption is the concurring opinion. On its face, a concurrence would seem to be unnecessary. The results of the case generally conform to the justice's preferences. So, why write separately?

One reason justices write concurrences is to distance themselves publicly from all or part of the rationale of the Court's opinion. This becomes necessary in some cases because of the presence of certain constituencies the justice seeks to communicate with to explain his or her reasoning for joining the Court's opinion. Clearly, the need is to make a public statement that provides the justice with an opportunity to explicate a personal rationale that is not embodied in the majority opinion. At the same time, the justice may have been influential in the direction and tone of the majority opinion. Yet such efforts would not be visible to the public if the justice did not author the majority opinion.

An example of the use of concurrence for public consumption in the twentieth century was the instance of William J. Brennan and the school prayer cases in the early 1960s. Brennan agonized over these cases. He was a devout Catholic. Indeed, he was the only Catholic on the Court at that time. He wrote a concurring opinion in the *Abington School District v. Schempp* case that went on for more than seventy pages, three times the length of the Court's opinion. Brennan used the concurrence to defuse potential criticism from Catholics, and perhaps others who were religious, who would not understand his position in the case. Brennan explained how a devoutly religious person would take the position of prohibiting compulsory Bible reading in public schools, which he could not have done through the majority opinion.[293]

In other cases, justices have decided against issuing concurrences to avoid drawing press attention toward the concurrence and away from the majority opinion. In 1954, Robert Jackson wrote his own concurring opinion for *Brown v. Board of Education*. Ultimately, Jackson decided not to issue the opinion precisely because it would attract press notice and diminish the image of unity the Court sought to convey in this momentous case and therefore potentially encourage public resistance.[294]

Using Surrogates

Another tactic was to work on the press through surrogates who lacked the constraints placed on justices. Whereas the justice was not supposed to take public stands on current issues or interact openly with the press, the surrogate could do so freely under the justice's direction. The most frequent user of surrogates likely was Louis Brandeis. While on the Court, Brandeis retained his deep interest in public policy and understood the role of the press in shaping public opinion relative to policy. However, he knew that as a justice, he was limited in how he could help shape such policy. Typically, Brandeis worked through others to influence press content. He did this through family and friends, particularly Felix Frankfurter prior to his own appointment to the Court. In 1937, Brandeis wrote to his daughter, Elizabeth Brandeis Rauschenbush, who lived in Wisconsin, that she should contact Charles Ross, a reporter for the *St. Louis Post-Dispatch*, to "make him see that the paper should make a great campaign for unemployment reserves. Induce him to come quickly to

Madison to investigate Wisconsin results & put him in touch with Wisconsin manufacturers and labor men."[295]

Because Felix Frankfurter was a contributing editor to *The New Republic*, Brandeis regularly gave Frankfurter suggestions about the editorial content. He passed on to Frankfurter whatever story ideas Brandeis wanted in the magazine, critiqued articles in the magazine in his correspondence with Frankfurter, and even urged Frankfurter to press the editors to launch campaigns on specific policy issues.[296] Frankfurter was not Brandeis' only contact with the magazine. Sometimes Brandeis met directly with Herbert Croly, the editor, to suggest content.

Granting Interviews

The justices were continually pressed by reporters to grant them interviews. On-the-record interviews were a rarity. When they did occur, justices were selective about who got them. When a journalist sought an interview for an article in the *New York Times Magazine*, Hugo Black agreed. But when a reporter for United Press wire service sought time with Black, the justice noted he had "told him I was seeing him as a friend only & that he could not write about anything I said or anything he saw. He said he would follow that."[297]

Reporters used a variety of means to get justices' participation in interviews. Some reporters used one justice as leverage to reach others. In an interview request to Black, Anthony Lewis mentioned that Potter Stewart had already met with him for an interview.[298] That leverage would communicate a sense of legitimacy in talking to the reporter if some other justice already had done so. It also might lead the justice to conclude that he or she needed to provide their view as well in self-defense.

Interview seekers also suggested that their stories would not embarrass the justices by their participation, either because they would be nonpolitical or because they would be positive about the justice. One reporter importuned Earl Warren for an interview by promising that the reporter's *Saturday Evening Post* piece would be "non-controversial, non-political, non-legal." Another journalist said his story would "not touch confidential information but would simply describe Court procedure, in a general way."[299] Duncan Aikman of the *New York Times* once wrote Hugo Black to ask for an interview and promised "there will be no conceivable embarrassment in it. . . ."[300] Similarly, Harry Blackmun agreed to an interview with Nina Totenberg for National Public Radio because Totenberg would not produce a "gotcha effort." To the contrary, Totenberg bent over backward to accommodate Blackmun. She contacted Blackmun's secretary prior to the interview and, according to the secretary, said "she would appreciate guidance from you [Blackmun] as to what questions you would like to have asked, where you want the conversation to go, etc."[301]

Broadcast media, particularly, were not venues justices used throughout most of the twentieth century. The first appearance by a justice on national radio probably was an address by Justice Oliver Wendell Holmes on March 9, 1931. It was the occasion of his ninetieth birthday, and Holmes said nothing about the Court or its work.[302] Television appearances also were extraordinarily rare. The one justice who granted a television interview during television's first decade was, not surprisingly, William O. Douglas. On May 11, 1958, Douglas was interviewed on national television by broadcast news reporter Mike Wallace. The justice did not talk much about the Court, but he did discuss his latest book about the loss of civil liberties by Americans in the wake of McCarthyism. This was one of Douglas' favorite topics, and he used the interview to bemoan the effects of McCarthyism on American's freedom of expression.[303]

The most unusual departure from the practice of avoiding television interviews was Hugo Black's CBS interview in 1968. After encouragement from CBS executive Fred Friendly, Hugo Black agreed to a television interview. Black later recounted that he "had grave doubts about delivering the interview." He said he was reassured when he received letters praising him for doing it.[304] The interview, with Eric Sevareid and Martin Agronsky, aired at 10:00 P.M. EST on December 3, 1968. It turned out to be the only television interview Black would give. Although Black's interview was a landmark event, as far as justices go, it went largely unnoticed by the general public. The interview was broadcast opposite a program with movie star Brigitte Bardot. According to Black, a *New York Times* reporter told him that his interview received 7 percent of the television audience, compared with Bardot's 75 percent.[305]

Black's television interview was a first because he agreed to talk about the Court and his own role as a justice, unlike Douglas' interview a decade earlier, which had focused on Douglas' new book. Black's interview occurred when he was eighty-two and not as liberal as he had been a decade or two earlier. Black criticized judges who go beyond the Constitution and the philosophy that judges should interpret the Constitution based on what fits the time period they are in. "Now that's a very prevalent philosophy. I'm not sure but what it's the controlling philosophy in this government."[306]

In the interview, Black discussed past events. He admitted that World War II was the only war he had supported. He also opined on current events. He initially deferred on the issue of whether demonstrators at the 1968 Democratic convention in Chicago had the right to assemble and demonstrate. However, he described the situation in such a way that indicated his own bias. He said:

"[Mayor Richard] Daley says they did so-and-so, and the other side says they're just a group of nice young idealists singing sweet songs of mercy and love, and I don't know. That's what the Press seemed to think and the television, that they were just young budding idealists. . . . " However, Black said the Constitution does not give a right to assemble on other's property, including government property.[307]

In the 1980s, a significant shift occurred in the justices' attitudes toward television. Justices like William Rehnquist and Harry Blackmun believed they should use the medium to educate the public about the Court. In 1984, Harvard Law professor Arthur Miller convinced the two justices to participate in an ABC News documentary on the Supreme Court. The involvement of Miller, who was not a journalist, led to Rehnquist's involvement. Rehnquist, who had not done a televised interview before, agreed only on the condition that he could edit his comments. Blackmun, who also participated, set no such conditions. The two justices only spoke generally about the Court.[308]

The justices began to perceive the broadcast media as a means for communicating their own messages to the public. This was particularly true of justices who were nearing the end of their careers. One example was Harry Blackmun's agreement to sit for a radio interview with National Public Radio. Blackmun used the 1993 NPR interview to announce that he had developed second thoughts about the constitutionality of the death penalty. In fact, Blackmun was the first justice to dramatically break from the no-television interview tradition by giving repeated television interviews during his last decade or so on the Court. Unlike Douglas and Black, Blackmun sat for interviews in his last decade or so on the Court with CNN, ABC News, and Bill Moyers.[309]

Harry Blackmun's agenda was clear. He wanted to humanize the Court and his colleagues. When veteran newscaster Daniel Schorr urged Blackmun to sit for the interview with him, he suggested the interview "would be refreshing and it would be a public service." Blackmun agreed.[310] In one interview, Blackmun said his colleagues were "all prima-donnas" and that their relationship was tense, particularly in the spring "when we're tired, when we're trying to get everything out. . . . "[311]

Such statements did not sit well with the other justices. It is possible that Blackmun felt some overt resentment from his colleagues. After a spate of interviews, Blackmun began to worry about the effect his public profile was having on his role on the Court. When turning down an interview request, he explained that if he accepted, it would "incur further enmity from the chief justice and perhaps from some of my colleagues."[312]

Yet Blackmun's example may have motivated Thurgood Marshall to appear on television, not to humanize the justices but to speak out on current events.

In 1990, Marshall sat for an interview on an ABC News program and used the opportunity to criticize President George H. W. Bush for his nomination of David Souter as William Brennan's replacement. Marshall said he had never heard of Souter and complained "I just don't understand what he's doing. I don't understand it."[313]

The much more common tool was the off-the-record interview or perhaps the background interview. The latter allowed the justice to hide behind eight colleagues or possibly the Court itself if the source was identified as someone close to the Court. The off-the-record interview was even better because it still facilitated the dissemination of the justice's views but without any possibility of connection to the justice. For instance, Louis Brandeis sat for an off-the-record interview with two journalists in the midst of the Court's rejection of Franklin Roosevelt's New Deal programs. Brandeis used the occasion to explain why he was joining the majority; he felt the NIRA was a mistake because real change had taken place in smaller units, particularly states, localities, and industry.[314] The interview provided a perspective to the press that might influence how they would write about Brandeis as well as about the New Deal.

Justices do not talk about such sessions, and true to the rules, reporters typically do not discuss them either. One exception was a *New York Times* reporter who reported on a background press conference Warren Burger held with reporters covering the Court. The story acknowledged that such press conferences were held regularly but that reporters who participated were not allowed to discuss them.[315] The story was rare and only occurred because the reporter writing the story did not attend the background session.

Holding Press Conferences

Justices almost never used the vehicle of a press conference for interacting with the press in the twentieth century. They typically occurred when a justice came to the Court or left it, although not all of the justices even did that. Byron White did not hold a press conference at his retirement in 1993. In the twenty-first century, Souter also abandoned the norm. He avoided the press when he retired in 2009. There were few other occasions in the twentieth century when justices sat for a press conference. Warren Burger held one in 1976 in St. Paul, Minnesota, to promote a national conference on judicial administration but avoided answering questions about interpretations of recent decisions of the Court. In 1989, William Rehnquist gave a news conference; however, he limited the press conference agenda to questions about judicial pay raises.[316]

William O. Douglas called a press conference less than a year before he retired to deny rumors that he was leaving the Court and to prove he was still capable of serving despite his advanced age. However, Douglas'

behavior – snapping at reporters, refusing to answer questions, or responding with one-word replies – only reinforced the sense that he was in poor
health, physically and mentally. The Court's press officer finally intervened to
end the press conference and spare Douglas further embarrassment.[317]

TWENTIETH-CENTURY PRESS RELATIONS

The moment when a justice actually became a major party nominee for
president occurred early in the twentieth century. But that event may have
produced an eventual backlash. Unlike during the previous century, only one
of the justices – Douglas – seemed to make any effort to get a major party
nomination. Indeed, Douglas was offered the vice presidency and could have
left the Court to run for vice president had he not concluded that Truman
was going to lose in 1948. Douglas' effort was the only example and the last to
date.

Additionally, by the end of the twentieth century, electoral involvement
was less likely given the dearth of political backgrounds of the vast majority of
justices. Sherman Minton was the last sitting member of Congress to become
a member of the Court. Fred Vinson was the last cabinet member, and Earl
Warren was the last sitting elected official for the rest of the twentieth century
and into the twenty-first century. The justices in the latter half of the twentieth
century came to the Court from backgrounds that might have minimized their
interaction with the press. Although cabinet members, senators, and governors
would have frequent interaction with the press and also be familiar with the
need to consider public opinion, appellate judges – either at the state or federal
level – would be expected to be more distant from and less concerned about
press coverage.

Yet these justices during the twentieth century – both in the earlier and latter
halves - utilized the tools available to them to implement their strategies for
individual external relations. They followed the press, were affected by press
coverage, and sought to shape that coverage of themselves. They interacted
with reporters. This interaction was not universal across justices. Some justices,
such as Byron White and David Souter, had less to do with the press during
their terms in office. Other justices possessed external relations strategies, cared
deeply about how the press covered them, and sought to mold the coverage of
themselves through their press relations.

Significant events occurred in the twentieth century that forced the justices to consider not only how their institution fared in the press coverage
and public opinion but also how they were perceived individually. Supreme
Court nominations were one example of such events. Still, there were others,

particularly scandals involving justices and external attacks on them, especially during the 1930s by other forces such as the president and Congress.

The justices' own views about going public seemed to change by the end of the twentieth century. The Bork nomination might be viewed as the pivotal point in that change. However, participation in U.S. Constitution bicentennial activities, as well as Blackmun's own efforts to go public to humanize the institution, occurred prior to the Bork nomination. Additionally, several justices neared retirement at the same time and began to "come out" to the press and to discuss the Court and their own views on issues related to the institution, including constitutional interpretation. Whatever the cause, the change occurred quickly. Brennan, Blackmun, and Marshall were all giving on-the-record interviews by the late 1980s and early 1990s.

As the justices moved out of the twentieth century, increasing pressure was placed on them to become relevant to the times by opening themselves up to greater scrutiny as human beings. Some justices were intent on lifting the shroud that the Court had placed around itself during the nineteenth and twentieth centuries. Others were not inclined to participate in such efforts. Yet, by the end of the twentieth century, the vast majority of the justices were engaged in public activities – televised interviews and speeches and on-the-record interviews – in which few of their colleagues in an earlier era would have participated.

6

Becoming Newsworthy

Chapter 5 suggests that the justices have been accorded increasing coverage in the news media, particularly in the last quarter century or so. This chapter provides empirical support for that assertion by reviewing the results of a study of news media coverage of Supreme Court justices during a forty-year period.

The unsuccessful confirmation process of Judge Robert Bork in 1987 is widely viewed as a seminal event in the history of the Supreme Court nomination process. The Bork nomination appeared to dramatically extend the time period for the confirmation process and attract expanded news coverage. But did it also raise the public profile of the individual justices? Did the justices, as well as the confirmation process itself, become more newsworthy in the period following the Bork nomination?

A content analysis of news stories about Supreme Court justices was conducted to answer these questions. A more detailed description of the methodology for this study is available in the appendix. Briefly, news stories about Supreme Court justices published in the New York Times and broadcast on NBC Nightly News from 1968 to 2007 were analyzed. The New York Times was chosen because it is considered the most prestigious daily newspaper. NBC Nightly News was selected as a representative of the three major broadcast networks. Moreover, through the Vanderbilt Television News Archives, NBC early-evening news programs are available dating back to 1968.

The criterion for inclusion in this study was that the story had to mention the name of at least one Supreme Court justice, which meant that stories about the institution of the Court without any mention of a particular justice or coverage of cases alone (again, without reference to an individual on the Court) were excluded. Many of these stories discussed cases as well. But this approach did allow for the inclusion of stories about the justices as individuals, as well as those related to oral arguments and decision announcements. These stories also incorporated coverage of the confirmation processes for those

TABLE 6.1. *Number of total stories about Supreme Court justices by decade*

	1968–77	1978–87	1988–97	1998–2007	% change 1968–87 to 1988–2007	% change 1988–97 to 1998–2007
NBC	204	253	244	137	(17)	(43)
New York Times	559	470	332	640	4	92

nominated and confirmed during this period. Unsuccessful nominees (Bork, Douglas Ginsburg, and Harriet Miers) were not included since the study focused on sitting justices during this time period. This forty-year period was chosen because it provided a twenty-year comparison on both sides of the 1987 Bork nomination. If the Bork nomination produced the expected change in news media coverage toward greater coverage of the justices, this historical analysis should reveal it.

THE TWENTIETH-CENTURY CHANGE

The first question is whether the number of stories about Supreme Court justices has increased, particularly post-1987. Table 6.1 shows the change in the number of news stories by decade for both NBC and the *New York Times*. The *New York Times* coverage of the Court increased only slightly (4 percent) during the two time periods. Not only did NBC coverage not increase between the pre-Bork and the post-Bork period, but it declined precipitously. NBC aired 457 stories about the justices from 1968 through 1987 and only 381 in the latter time period, constituting a 17 percent decrease in the number of stories.

The Bork nomination did not represent the landmark point that was hypothesized in terms of network news coverage; the *New York Times* coverage increase between the two periods was minimal, but the volume of NBC coverage declined. However, these results for NBC may say more about the state of network news generally than about coverage of the Court specifically. Broadcast news attention to the justices declined along with coverage of politics and government generally. Declining audience share and the resulting drop in revenue have led to shrinking news staffs and appeal to a general audience more interested in entertainment and less interested in complex public policy. The coverage of politics and government generally has suffered as a result of changes in whom network broadcast news programs appeal to and how stories are covered.[1] The Supreme Court coverage was a victim of those changes as well.

That does not mean change has not occurred, as Table 6.1 indicates. Rather, the difference came in the twenty-first century and not immediately following the Bork nomination. And it occurred in stunningly dissimilar ways. NBC News coverage of the justices fell substantially between the 1990s and the 2000s, and to a much greater extent than it had between the 1980s and the 1990s. The trends in broadcast television that were beginning in the 1980s and 1990s seemed to have hit in full force by the 2000s. News coverage of the justices also was affected. Simultaneously, however, the *New York Times* moved in the opposite direction, nearly doubling the number of stories discussing Supreme Court justices. For NBC News, the justices became less newsworthy; for the *New York Times*, they became much more so.

Table 6.1 reveals that the two media also moved in different directions earlier in this time period. NBC increased its coverage of the Court in the second time period (1978–87), which became the high point during this forty-year period. The difference for NBC may have been the presence of visuals, particularly the confirmation processes. John Paul Stevens was confirmed only twenty days after President Gerald Ford nominated him, but Sandra Day O'Connor and Robert Bork endured confirmation processes that stretched out over more than a hundred days.[2] William Rehnquist's and Antonin Scalia's were nearly as long. Part of those longer confirmation processes was the lengthy confirmation hearing during which the nominee spent several days in front of the Senate Judiciary Committee, and then other witnesses – both pro and con – spent additional days testifying about the nominee. Moreover, the O'Connor hearing was the first confirmation hearing offering gavel-to-gavel television coverage, a precedent that has been continued since.[3] Additionally, television news coverage added visuals by covering the background of a case as well as the Court's oral argument or decision. A television news reporter would find video for the story by interviewing the parties, going to the scene of the crime, and interviewing interest group representatives affected by the case's outcome. All of these provided new visuals that enhanced the story.

By contrast, the volume of *New York Times* coverage of the justices was very high in the first time period compared with the next two decades. There was a plethora of news stories that dominated *New York Times* coverage during the first decade of the study – the retirement of Earl Warren, the failed confirmation process of three nominees (Fortas, Haynsworth, and Carswell), the confirmation of five justices (Burger, Blackmun, Powell, Rehnquist, and Stevens), Fortas' resignation, and William O. Douglas' writings and the subsequent attempted impeachment effort. Of course, there were also several significant cases during that time period involving the death penalty, abortion, school

TABLE 6.2. *Type of news story by decade*

	1968–77	1978–87	1988–97	1998–2007	% change 1968–87 to 1988–2007	% change 1988–97 to 1998–2007
NBC						
Personal	72	58	91	43	3	(53)
Case Related	76	142	99	49	(49)	(51)
New York Times						
Personal	296	182	120	236	(26)	49
Case Related	167	189	138	130	(25)	(6)

busing, and presidential power that showed up in news coverage of the justices. The Court also played a central role in the Watergate crisis.

As mentioned earlier, these two news outlets approached the twenty-first-century coverage of the Court differently. While television news coverage declined, a high point for Supreme Court coverage for the *New York Times* was the beginning of the twenty-first century. What caused the *New York Times* to increase its coverage of Supreme Court justices? There were significant news stories about the justices in the twenty-first century that could explain this change – the *Bush v. Gore* case in 2000; the death of the chief justice, William Rehnquist; and the retirement of Sandra Day O'Connor. There were two Supreme Court confirmations – Roberts' and Alito's. Yet the difference may well rest with the higher public profile of individual justices. Table 6.2 demonstrates this point. The content analysis distinguished between types of stories. The two most prominent categories were stories primarily about the individual justices and those related to cases (such as case acceptance, oral argument, or decision announcement.) The individual justice stories also could discuss cases, but the frame of the story was primarily one or more of the justices. A story might have as its theme a speech by Harry Blackmun, but there also would be mention of *Roe v. Wade*. Many of these stories covered the confirmation process for a justice. Others discussed a justice's health, retirement, or death. Some were about a justice's statements, as indicated in Chapter 1 and Chapter 5. This table shows change over time in the number of these types of stories.

PEOPLE OR CASES?

According to Table 6.2, the attention to personal or case-related stories has fluctuated over time. The *New York Times* significantly increased the number of personal stories – stories about individual justices – between the 1988–97 and 1998–2007 time periods. The justices themselves, not just their work, became news. As Table 6.2 shows, the shift in attention appears even more dramatic when one examines the type of story on NBC and in the *New York Times*. Basically, what the two media – the *New York Times* and NBC *Nightly News* – discussed about the Court changed from an emphasis on cases to an emphasis on individuals. Yet the decline in NBC News coverage of cases meant that the overall portrait of the Court provided on NBC has changed. Whereas the picture of the Court in the 1968–77 period was focused on individuals, probably because of several nomination processes during that period, as well as coverage of William O. Douglas and Abe Fortas, the late 1970s and most of the 1980s saw a distinct shift toward case-oriented coverage. That may have been a result of the networks' assignment of legal affairs correspondents with legal backgrounds, a move the *New York Times* had made earlier with the appointment of reporters like Anthony Lewis and Fred Graham. Carl Stern, NBC's longtime Court correspondent, and Tim O'Brien, Stern's counterpart at ABC, both had law degrees prior to joining the Supreme Court press corps. Befitting their legal backgrounds, their focus may have been more case related. In addition, as mentioned earlier, reporters connected a visual component to an otherwise nonvisual story.

Then, by the 1990s (the period immediately after the Bork nomination), the case-related emphasis ceased and the more personal-oriented approach returned. Overall, NBC devoted less attention to both types of stories. There was a slight uptick in the news coverage of the individual justices in the 1990s. This may have been a result of the Thomas nomination, which captured saturation television coverage during 1991. During the last time period under study here – 1998 to 2007 – the extent of the news hole devoted to the individual justices did not decline. Rather, the news hole for the Court experienced a dramatic decline. Although coverage of cases was nearly three to one that of personal coverage from 1978 to 1987, that imbalance was gone by the 2000s.

THE NEED FOR VISUALS

Again, television news is a visual medium, which makes the job of covering a nonvisual story difficult. The Court does not readily provide visuals. Because it bans cameras in the courtroom, television news crews do not have much to work with in terms of visuals of the decision makers. The Court has been more accommodating with audio clips of key cases, although even that cooperation is rare. That still does not solve the visual problem. That problem became

TABLE 6.3. *Use of visuals in NBC stories by decade*

Percentage of stories with type of visual accompaniment			
	1968–77	1978–87	1988–97	1998–2007
Artists' Sketches	15	43	30	27
Photos	31	24	31	55
Video	16	25	40	61

more acute as television news reduced its production crews and cut back on the kinds of stories Supreme Court reporters had been doing. The Court would not provide the video of its handling of cases, and the networks increasingly found the process of obtaining those visuals too costly.

Despite the absence of change in the Court's formal approach to cameras, the portrayal of the justices on network television news has evolved over time. According to Table 6.3, the networks have moved away from sketch artists to the use of photographs or even video of the justices to tell their stories. This table includes the percentage for each decade of stories in which one or more justices were portrayed in a sketch, photograph, or video clip. Whereas photographs of the justices were used in one-third or fewer of NBC stories before 1998, more than half of the stories in the last decade included photographs of the justices. Similarly, usage of video clips including the justices has increased dramatically during the same time period. From at least the 1960s, the networks contracted with sketch artists to provide some visual accompaniment to television stories about the Court, particularly during oral arguments. The late 1970s and 1980s seemed to be the heyday for the use of these artists. Post-1987, however, fewer of the stories about Supreme Court justices included sketches, and far more used photographs and even video clips of the justices. The most dramatic shift came in the 2000s.

By prohibiting video cameras and even still photography from the courtroom, the justices forced broadcast television producers and reporters, who obviously thrive on visuals, to rely on artists' sketches of the justices in the courtroom. However, with the justices' increasing appearances in public forums, both recent photos and videos became more accessible for use by television news. As a result, the justices' faces are appearing more frequently in broadcast news stories about the Court, and the justices, as a group, eventually may lose a measure of anonymity they previously enjoyed.

COVERING INDIVIDUAL JUSTICES: THE BLACKMUN EFFECT

During the latter part of the twentieth century, some justices received broad public attention. When President Ronald Reagan nominated Sandra Day O'Connor in 1981, she became the first female justice in the history of the Court. That fact alone gave her a novelty that would attract press attention. Then O'Connor carved out a centrist position on the Court that made her the key justice to forge a majority. She became the voice for a majority anxious to have her fifth vote, or her concurrences defined law because they came from a justice who could tip the balance on the Court. Clarence Thomas also became well known because of his nomination process, which meant the press likely would cover him for some time after. Harry Blackmun made a conscious effort to raise his profile by accepting interviews. But did these actions actually attract press attention? Were those justices covered by the press more than their colleagues were?

Tables 6.4 and 6.5 show the extent to which individual justices who served during this period were covered by the *New York Times* and NBC. They detail the percentage of stories of each decade (as well as for the entire forty-year period) for each justice, as well as the percentage of change over time from decade to decade. That statistic allows us to see how coverage of each justice may have shifted over time. The tables are organized in descending order of the percentage of all stories mentioning that particular justice.

Table 6.4 clearly demonstrates that the *New York Times* offered an inordinate amount of coverage to Harry Blackmun. Blackmun was mentioned in nearly 27 percent of all stories about Supreme Court justices during this time period. That is particularly remarkable because Blackmun did not serve on the Court during sixteen of those forty years. The justice who served the longest during the forty years (William Rehnquist) and served as chief justice for nearly half of them was mentioned in nearly 26 percent of the stories, but still less than Blackmun.

Part of the reason for Blackmun's high coverage could be his "coming out" in the late 1980s and early 1990s, when he decided to accept some television interviews and used speeches to get attention. The decade when Blackmun received the most attention relative to his colleagues was the 1988–97 period. Blackmun was mentioned in 57 percent of *New York Times* stories about the justices during that time. No other justice came close to receiving that frequency of attention. Some of the attention was due to Blackmun's retirement in 1994.

However, his retirement does not explain why Blackmun got so much attention in the 1978–87 period. Four in ten *New York Times* articles about Supreme

TABLE 6.4. *Justices mentioned* – New York Times

Justice	1968–77 %*	1978–87 %	1978–87 % change**	1988–97 %	1988–97 % change	1998–2007 %	1998–2007 % change	Total No	Total %
Blackmun	21.6	41.7	162	57.5	(–3)	–		536	26.8
O'Connor	–	30.6	NA	44.3	102	37.3	163	530	26.5
Rehnquist	11.1	35.5	269	35.8	(29)	26.4	142	517	25.8
Burger	24.2	55.5	193	–		–		426	21.3
Marshall	22.2	34.7	132	35.8	(27)	–		421	21.0
Stevens	8.6	31.7	310	38.9	(13)	13.8	(32)	414	20.7
White	15.2	30.6	169	34.0	(22)	–		355	17.7
Scalia	–	6.8	NA	38.3	396	28.3	143	340	17.0
Brennan	16.6	31.7	160	24.4	(46)	–		339	16.9
Roberts	–	–		–		47.7	NA	305	15.2
Thomas	–	–		31.9	NA	23.1	140	254	12.7
Douglas	42.2	–		–		–		236	11.8
Kennedy	–	–		35.2	NA	18.1	(1)	234	11.7
Powell	11.4	32.1	236	–	–	–		223	11.1
Warren	25.4	–		–	–	–		190	9.5
Alito	–	–		–	–	29.8	NA	191	9.5
Ginsburg	–			21.1	NA	18.4	169	189	9.4
Souter	–	–		28.0	NA	14.7	101	187	9.3
Stewart	18.2	15.3	(29)	–	–	–		179	8.9
Fortas	27.0	–		–	–	–		165	8.2
Breyer	–	–		5.7	NA	16.3	547	123	6.1
Black	10.2	–		–		–		73	3.6
Harlan	6.3	–		–		–		44	2.2

* Percentage of all stories in the decade.
** Percentage change from previous decade in the number of stories the justice was mentioned in as compared to all of the stories for the decade.

Court justices during that period mentioned Blackmun. Only Burger received more attention. Also, Burger retired in 1986, which may have stimulated more coverage of him. No other justice merited such a high level of attention from the *New York Times* than Blackmun overall.

Emphasis on Blackmun may have stemmed from the *Roe* decision in 1973, but not directly. If that were so, we would expect Blackmun to have received an inordinate amount of mentions in the first decade under study. However, that did not happen. During the 1968–77 decade, Blackmun was overshadowed by several other justices in story mentions. Only later, perhaps as *Roe* was challenged in successive cases in the 1980s and early 1990s, did Blackmun get more frequent mentions from the *New York Times*.

TABLE 6.5. *Justices mentioned – NBC Nightly News*

Justice	1968–77 %*	1978–87 %	1978–87 % change**	1988–97 %	1988–97 % change	1998–2007 %	1998–2007 % change	Total No	Total %
Rehnquist	5.4	24.9	573	16.8	(35)	34.3	115	162	19.3
Burger	36.3	28.5	(3)	–		–		146	17.4
O'Connor	–	22.1	NA	16.0	(30)	30.7	108	137	16.3
Thomas	–	–		34.4	NA	17.5	(71)	108	12.9
Scalia	–	7.5	NA	16.4	211	22.6	(−23)	90	10.7
Stevens	8.3	11.1	165	8.2	(29)	10.9	(25)	80	9.5
Marshall	9.3	15.4	205	9.0	(44)	–		80	9.5
Blackmun	10.3	7.5	(10)	13.5	174	–		73	8.7
Brennan	5.9	17.4	367	6.6	(64)	–		72	8.6
White	3.4	14.6	529	9.4	(38)	–		67	8.0
Kennedy	–	–		11.1	NA	24.8	126	61	7.3
Souter	–	–		11.1	NA	18.2	(7)	52	6.2
Breyer	–	–		7.4	NA	19.7	150	45	5.4
Stewart	10.3	7.9	(1)	–		–		41	4.9
Fortas	18.6	–		–		–		38	4.5
Ginsburg	–	–		5.7	NA	12.4	121	31	3.7
Roberts	–	–		–		19.7	NA	26	3.1
Warren	11.8	–		–		–		24	2.9
Alito	–	–		–		13.9	NA	19	2.3
Douglas	6.9	–		–		–		14	1.7
Black	6.9	–		–		–		14	1.7
Harlan	3.4	–		–		–		7	.8

* Percentage of all stories in the decade.
** Percentage change from previous decade in the number of stories in which the justice was mentioned compared with all of the stories for the decade.

Another important point is that this level of coverage of Blackmun was only present in the *New York Times*. Table 6.5 shows that *NBC Nightly News* devoted its attention to the chief justices during the vast majority of this period – William Rehnquist and Warren Burger – and to the first woman, Sandra Day O'Connor, and to Clarence Thomas. As these figures show, the Thomas coverage was dominated by his confirmation hearings. Thomas' mentions on network news dropped significantly by the twenty-first century. Harry Blackmun was well below several other justices, in addition to the four just discussed, in the number of mentions on NBC. Even though Blackmun was considered newsworthy by the *New York Times*, he received about average attention from NBC given the length of time he served on the Court.

Table 6.6 represents the justices' identification in news stories with specific types of opinions and contrasts it with the overall number of opinions written by that justice. The table lists all the justices and the number of times they are mentioned in conjunction with a majority, concurring, or dissenting opinion. To construct the numbers, the number of mentions for that particular justice in relation to an opinion type was divided by the number of his or her years on the Court. This removes the issue of length of service on the bench and provides a relative statistic in comparing justices regardless of their time on the Court. Obviously, those who are on the Court longer during this period are likely to possess higher scores. For example, those at the low end are Earl Warren, Hugo Black, and John Harlan, who all served for only one to three years in this forty-year period. Yet this is not necessarily the case; the two lowest justices in *New York Times* coverage were Ruth Bader Ginsburg and Stephen Breyer, who served on the Court for fourteen and thirteen years, respectively, and who, on average, wrote more opinions than William Rehnquist.

Again, *New York Times* coverage heavily favored Harry Blackmun. Blackmun was most frequently mentioned as the author of a majority opinion, tied with Antonin Scalia as the justice most often mentioned as having issued a concurring opinion, and tied with Thurgood Marshall as the justice most frequently cited as having delivered a dissenting opinion. This was the case even though Blackmun's overall opinion output was lower than that of several other justices. On average, Blackmun wrote fewer majority opinions than Lewis Powell, Byron White, Warren Burger, Thurgood Marshall, and William Brennan. He wrote fewer concurring opinions than seven other justices and fewer dissenting opinions than six others. John Paul Stevens wrote, on average, twice as many dissents as Blackmun yet received only two-thirds of the coverage of his dissents in *New York Times* stories that Blackmun received. Blackmun ranked among the top ten in terms of total numbers of opinions and in each category, as measured by *New York Times* coverage, but his actual opinion writing in sheer volume did not match that of others such as Stevens, Powell, and Marshall.

Far fewer of NBC News' stories even mentioned a justice in reference to a type of opinion. NBC News stories more often just announced the results of decisions rather than naming the individuals writing the opinions. NBC News was more evenhanded in mentioning the names of authors of opinions. Burger, White, and Kennedy were mentioned slightly more often on NBC as authors of majority opinions. Burger's presence is not surprising, because he was the chief justice and had the power to assign opinions to himself when he was in the majority, particularly the most highly visible ones, which he often did. Burger, Marshall, and Brennan were the most frequently mentioned

TABLE 6.6. *News coverage of opinions compared with opinion writing by justice*
(Times mentioned by type of opinion divided by number of years on Court)

	New York Times			NBC News			Opinions*		
	Majority	Concurring	Dissenting	Maj. Conc.**	Dissent	Maj.	Concurring	Dissent	Total
Blackmun	**6.8***	**1.2**	**4.8**	0.3	0.6	12.1	4.4	10.2	27.9
White	5.3	0.7	2.5	1.1	0.3	14.8	3.5	9.6	23.4
Burger	4.9	0.6	2.5	**1.2**	**0.9**	13.7	4.2	6.5	25.8
Rehnquist	3.8	0.2	2.9	0.8	0.6	6.8	0.9	6.4	14.6
O'Connor	3.6	0.9	2.1	0.5	0.3	11.0	4.1	6.1	22.2
Stevens	3.5	0.4	3.2	0.7	0.5	11.0	4.9	20.4	**34.2**
Powell	3.3	0.5	2.4	0.7	0.3	**15.1**	6.8	9.5	33.5
Kennedy	3.1	1.0	0.7	1.1	0	9.3	3.8	3.9	15.5
Marshall	3.0	0.3	**4.8**	0.2	0.7	12.8	1.9	14.9	29.6
Brennan	2.8	0.4	4.5	0.6	0.7	12.6	4.3	18.6	24.0
Scalia	2.5	**1.2**	2.0	0.7	0.5	9.6	5.0	8.9	21.7
Souter	2.3	0.6	1.2	0.6	0.4	8.3	2.9	5.6	15.1
Stewart	2.2	0.3	1.1	0.3	0.1	7.8	2.2	6.6	12.1
Douglas	2.1	0.8	3.8	0	0	11.0	5.4	**31.2**	10.6
Thomas	1.1	0.6	1.5	0.6	0.4	8.2	3.2	8.0	17.3
Warren	1.5	0.0	0.0	0	0.5	6.0	0	2.0	1.0
Harlan	1.5	0.3	1.5	0	0.3	7.0	4.5	13.5	7.1
Black	1.5	0.8	1.0	0.2	0.3	7.7	**8.0**	19.2	3.7
Ginsburg	0.9	0.1	0.5	0.5	0.5	8.4	3.0	5.5	14.9
Breyer	0.8	0.1	0.0	0.5	0.5	7.9	3.4	8.7	17.5

* Data on opinions available from The Supreme Court Database at http://scdb.wustl.edu/index.php.
** NBC News mentioned only one justice having delivered a concurring opinion, and that occurred only once.
*** The boldface indicates the justice with the highest score in that particular category.

dissenters, although the difference between them and several other justices was minimal.

Not only was Blackmun mentioned more frequently by the *New York Times*, but he was also far likelier than his colleagues to be directly quoted, according to Table 6.7. During this forty-year time period, Blackmun was quoted in 13 percent of the stories about Supreme Court justices. This is more than double the percentage for the next closest justice – Sandra Day O'Connor. Blackmun was the most quoted justice in two of the three time periods when he was on the Court. In the middle time periods, Blackmun was quoted in one-fourth of *New York Times* stories about the justices. Only Warren Burger came close to Blackmun (20 percent) during one time period.

Blackmun quotes came not only from his decisions but also from his provocative statements and speeches. Furthermore, the associate justice received attention whenever abortion was discussed. As the Court dealt with several cases predicted to overturn or restrict *Roe*, Blackmun became the center of attention during the consideration of the case. He sometimes made himself the locus of press coverage because of his speeches discussing the Court's handling of *Roe* or the tone of his dissents or concurrences suggesting that *Roe* was in jeopardy.

The emphasis on Blackmun by the *New York Times* is also evident from a comparison with the number of times a justice was heard on NBC. (This meant that the justice's voice was actually heard. This could have been in a confirmation hearing or a speech or some other public event. In more recent cases after the Court released audio of highly controversial oral arguments, it would have included audio of the justices asking questions of counsel in oral argument, although these incidences are rare.) Those justices who were heard on NBC were the two chief justices during most of this time period – Warren Burger and William Rehnquist, who often would have spoken for the Court in various settings. The other two most prominent justices heard on camera were Clarence Thomas and Sandra Day O'Connor. Thomas received significant attention at his confirmation hearing, and O'Connor received NBC notice because of her unique position on the Court, as already discussed. Blackmun ranked among the lowest justices in terms of the number of times he was heard on NBC. This was despite Blackmun's television appearances. However, Blackmun did not give an interview to NBC during this period.

Why was Blackmun a star of *New York Times* Supreme Court coverage? The most likely explanation is the relationship Blackmun had with Linda Greenhouse, the *New York Times*' Supreme Court reporter for twenty-nine of the forty years of this study and for most of Blackmun's time on the Court. Greenhouse later became Blackmun's biographer. Greenhouse also was openly supportive

TABLE 6.7. *Justices quoted in New York Times stories or heard in NBC stories*
Percent of stories where the justice is quoted or heard in the story*

Justice	New York Times					NBC				
	1968–77	1978–87	1988–97	1998–2007	Overall	1968–77	1978–87	1988–97	1998–2007	Overall
Blackmun	7.9	25.5	26.9	–	13.1	0.5	0.4	0.8	0.7	0.6
O'Connor	–	8.1	14.2	6.7	6.4	–	4.0	0.4	9.5	2.9
Burger	5.2	20.2	–	–	6.4	3.9	5.2	–	–	2.7
Stevens	2.5	8.9	11.5	5.2	6.3	0.5	0	0	2.9	0.6
Scalia	–	1.3	10.9	9.2	5.0	–	2.0	0	7.3	1.8
Marshall	4.1	9.8	8.5	–	5.0	0.5	0	1.6	–	0.6
Rehnquist	2.0	6.4	8.5	3.3	4.5	0.5	4.4	0.8	10.2	3.3
Roberts	–	–	–	14.1	4.5	–	–	–	3.6	0.6
White	2.1	8.1	5.7	–	3.7	0	0	0.4	–	0.1
Kennedy	–	0.4	5.1	7.5	3.3	–	0.8	0.4	0.8	1.8
Brennan	2.7	8.1	3.3	–	3.2	0	0.8	0.4	–	0.4
Douglas	10.9	–	–	–	3.2	1.0	–	–	–	0.4
Powell	3.9	7.2	–	–	3.0	1.0	0.8	–	–	0.6
Ginsburg	–	–	7.3	4.9	2.7	–	–	0.4	1.5	0.4
Thomas	–	–	6.6	4.4	2.5	–	–	8.6	3.6	3.1
Stewart	4.5	4.7	–	–	2.4	0.5	1.6	–	–	0.6
Alito	–	–	–	6.9	2.2	–	–	–	6.6	1.1
Souter	–	–	5.1	4.1	2.1	–	–	2.1	2.2	1.0

* Those quoted or heard in 2 percent or more of stories overall.

of Blackmun's position in *Roe* and even marched in a pro-choice rally in 1989 while she was covering the Court's abortion decisions.[4] Not all stories about the Supreme Court during this time period were written by Greenhouse, but the vast majority would have been. Another piece of evidence that the Blackmun emphasis may have been related to Linda Greenhouse was the decreasing number of wire stories the *New York Times* used in covering Supreme Court justices. In the first decade under study, 23 percent of the stories came from the wire services. That percentage declined to 19 percent in the second decade, 11 percent in the third, and a mere 1 percent by the fourth. The *New York Times* increasingly was using its own staff and not the wire services to cover Supreme Court justices, suggesting that emphasis on Blackmun was a *New York Times* decision, likely Greenhouse's, rather than a function of wire service editorial decisions.

CONCLUSIONS

The justices have become newsworthy over time, but that newsworthiness is a recent phenomenon. The sheer volume of news coverage in the *New York Times* increased significantly as the twenty-first century began. NBC News did not increase its overall attention to the justices, but the proportion of stories primarily about justices rather than cases suggests that the justices as individuals became more newsworthy within the shrinking overall news coverage of the Court. The *New York Times* also devoted more attention to the justices as persons and not just to their connections to cases.

Public activity – writings, speeches, interviews – does spark greater attention to a justice. That is not the only reason, however. O'Connor received coverage because of her status as the first female justice, but also because of her swing position. Neither of those was necessarily the result of an external strategy. Abe Fortas did not seek press attention when ethics charges were lodged against him, and he eventually resigned under pressure.

In other cases, though, extrajudicial activity may well have resulted in increased press attention. Harry Blackmun may have been accorded coverage because he gave press interviews, but also because he cultivated a relationship with Linda Greenhouse that led to her status as his biographer, as well as extra attention for him as she covered the Court. William O. Douglas did warrant attention, not only because of his pending retirement (and then actual retirement) but also because of controversial actions and statements that led to an attempted impeachment effort.

The change in press attention to the Court did not occur following the Bork nomination but happened more recently. The anecdotes discussed at the beginning of the book appear to be not mere anecdotes, but actual examples of a larger shift that occurred in news coverage of justices of the U.S. Supreme Court. The timing suggests that the change was not caused by an event outside the Court – that is, a nomination process over which they had no control. Rather, it may have been the result of actions by the current justices themselves to become more public. But that is our next subject.

7

The Twenty-First Century and the Future

In 2000, Justice Clarence Thomas delivered a speech before a high school group and told the students that "the last political act we engage in is confirmation."[1] Thomas' statement was not that surprising. Despite a long history of political involvement by their predecessors, at least some justices today still like to perpetuate the myth that what they do has nothing to do with politics.

Nor is it the case that things have changed – that political involvement has become a thing of the past for twenty-first-century justices. It is highly unlikely that is the case. Of course, the extent of the current justices' political involvement is difficult to assess because of the shroud the justices place over their interactions. Obviously, scholars today lack the access to the papers of justices in the twenty-first century who have not retired or even those who have recently retired. It is likely to be many years before the papers of William Rehnquist, Sandra Day O'Connor, and John Paul Stevens become accessible. For example, only in 2010 did the papers of Potter Stewart become available to scholars. Stewart, who retired in 1981 and died in 1986, had stipulated that his papers remain closed until all justices who had sat with him had left the bench. John Paul Stevens, who retired in 2010, was the last of those justices who served with Stewart. Even when the papers of these justices become available, it is quite possible they will have removed evidence of political involvement because of their sensitivity over the release of previous justices' papers.

In one sense, justices in the twenty-first century might be inclined to be less politically involved than their predecessors. This is a result of the dearth of political backgrounds among the current justices. As discussed in Chapter 5, the number of justices with familiarity in elective or even appointed office declined dramatically throughout the twentieth century. That decline continued into the twenty-first century as well. Whereas in 1997, the Court had a majority (five – Rehnquist, O'Connor, Thomas, Scalia, and Souter) of its members possessing previous experience as executive political appointees or legislators, a little more than a decade later, there were only two – Thomas and newly appointed Justice Elena Kagan.[2] Except for a decade in the 1970s, it was the first time since its inception in 1790 that the Court lacked a member who previously had served as an elected official.

A previous political background often meant that the justices already brought with them some public familiarity when they were nominated. Some nominees had held high-profile elective office – for example, Hugo Black, U.S. senator from Alabama; Earl Warren, California governor and former vice presidential candidate; or Charles Evans Hughes, governor of New York. The lack of public name recognition prior to appointment means that justices today are less likely to be public figures before they come to the Court. Some quickly become public figures; Sandra Day O'Connor and Clarence Thomas each became well known overnight because she or he was a first or controversial nomination, respectively. Most do not, however.

Additionally, the involvement of justices as advisors to administrations may have diminished. Again, the extent of such activity may emerge in years to come when papers become available. But, unlike during the Fortas years, there is no public indication that Supreme Court justices are serving as ongoing advisors to presidents. One exception may be advising on Supreme Court nominations. Whether Republican justices advised President George W. Bush or Democratic justices did the same for President Barack Obama is unknown at the present. At least in the case of the chief justice vacancy in 2005, the former is unlikely because several of those associate justices who would have advised Bush – Scalia, Kennedy, and Thomas – were possible candidates for the post.

Nor is there any indication that justices are being touted for other office, particularly president, as occurred in the nineteenth and twentieth centuries. The most recent incident involved Sandra Day O'Connor. Some suggested that O'Connor run for vice president on the Republican ticket in 1988. That speculation increased to the point that O'Connor issued a statement asserting that she was not running for any office. No subsequent justice has been similarly mentioned since.[3] Listings of potential presidential candidates today do not include Supreme Court justices. And other offices – cabinet position, ambassadorship, or other elective office – also are not suggested for current justices, unlike their predecessors such as Charles Evans Hughes, Harlan Stone, and Arthur Goldberg.

OPPORTUNITIES FOR INCREASED EXPOSURE

As has been demonstrated, the justices in the twenty-first century are more public and more visible than their twentieth-century predecessors were. As discussed in earlier chapters, twenty-first-century justices give on-the-record interviews, deliver televised speeches, and occasionally make news for activities beyond their opinions. There also appear to be more justices "going public." Whereas William O. Douglas was the exception that proved the rule a half century ago, Douglas' raised profile today would be more the rule than the exception. Douglas' public exposure recently has been matched by those of several justices – Clarence Thomas, Sandra Day O'Connor, and Antonin Scalia. It should be made clear that the focus of news coverage today is not the same as it was with Douglas. With his frequent marriages and divorces, as well as his controversial writings, Douglas was more personally notorious than justices are today. It is true that some justices' personal activities are covered today, but there also is a significant emphasis on their role in judicial issues.

Moreover, justices today seem to be more open about their relationship with the press. They may appear to have given up attempting to disseminate the image that they are uninterested in and unaware of political events and issues generally. For example, whereas John Marshall said he "scarcely ever read a newspaper" and Lewis Powell suggested that he paid no attention to the press, Stephen Breyer told Larry King in a television interview that he reads newspapers. Speaking of the reaction to *Texas v. Johnson* (the 1989 flag burning decision), Anthony Kennedy admitted that he tracked newspaper editorials when he said in a speech that he noticed that during the course of the three months after that decision, the initial editorial reaction had changed to a more favorable stance toward the Court's position.[4] Of course, the justices' very presence at media outlets such as *Nightline*, *60 Minutes*, and Sean Hannity's show undermines the image that they are uninterested in the news media. They are aware of the various types of media, their ideological hue, and, apparently, which venues will serve their interests.

The most surprising shift has been in the approach of Antonin Scalia. For many years, he was well known among the press corps for his vehement opposition to audio or video recording of his public speeches. He had several run-ins with the press about his policy of banning cameras. When police officers acting under his orders attempted to enforce his ban by confiscating journalists' tape recorders, Scalia was roundly criticized by the press. Ironically, Scalia received a free speech award from a group in Cleveland but excluded broadcast coverage, including even C-SPAN, from the event.[5]

TABLE 7.1. *Appearances by U.S. Supreme Court justices on C-SPAN*

Justice*	1978–87	Decade 1988–97	1998–2007	Percent change from previous decade 88–97	98–07
Alito	NA	NA	47	–	–
Roberts	NA	NA	58	–	–
Breyer	NA	50	102	–	104
Ginsburg	NA	66	59	–	(11)
Thomas	NA	64	67	–	(5)
Souter	NA	33	28	–	(15)
Kennedy	10	38	55	280	46
Scalia	6	20	37	233	85
O'Connor	2	49	72	2350	46
Stevens	3	24	44	700	87
Rehnquist	13	75	75	477	0

* The list includes those justices who served in the twenty-first century. With the exception of Alito and Roberts, all of the justices served in more than one decade, which allows comparison across decades.

However, Scalia's attitude toward the press had changed by early 2005. According to Scalia's biographer, the outgoing justice was "reaching out to an audience beyond the Court."[6] Some accused him of going public in 2005 so he could succeed William Rehnquist as chief justice. But Scalia explained that his change was the result of encouragement from family and friends.[7] The fact that Scalia has remained public even after 2005 suggests that the change was not necessarily promotion related, but the result of a deliberate, long-term strategic shift in his approach to the press.

C-SPAN

One new and particularly friendly forum of exposure for justices is C-SPAN. Although Americans rarely heard the voices or saw video of their predecessors in the last half of the twentieth century, that is no longer the case in the twenty-first. The justices have become a regular presence on C-SPAN. Anthony Kennedy even joked about it in a speech. He said that a young man came up to him in a restaurant and said, "Are you Justice Kennedy?" Kennedy admitted that his first reaction was: "Oh, no. Here's a C-SPAN insomniac."[8]

As Table 7.1 illustrates, there has been a dramatic increase in the number of appearances by the justices on C-SPAN programs. The change has been in C-SPAN's interest in the Court and the individual justices, as indicated by the network's coverage of justices' various public appearances, but also in the justices' own responses to the presence of cameras. As discussed previously, justices were reluctant to be on camera, including for the delivery of public speeches. That reluctance has disappeared. Speeches to various groups are aired now, as is participation in various panel discussions, forums, and interviews. Additionally, when the justices testify before Congress on matters related to the federal judicial system or the Supreme Court's budget, that testimony is aired.

The table shows that the frequency of justices' appearances increased significantly between the third decade and the first and second of C-SPAN's existence, which began in 1978. Justices began appearing on C-SPAN regularly in the 1990s, but the number of times a justice came on C-SPAN increased again in the 2000s, at least for most justices. The number of appearances by Stephen Breyer more than doubled between the two time periods, and Scalia's and Stevens' nearly doubled. The number of times Kennedy was on C-SPAN rose by half, as did O'Connor's. The other justices' remained about the same, with none apparently shying away from C-SPAN.

C-SPAN's viewership does not mean that the justices receive saturation media coverage and will become celebrities matching entertainment or sports figures. Yet the presence of the justices on C-SPAN does mean they are more exposed than they were previously and that they are losing some of their anonymity, as Kennedy's anecdote indicates. That loss of anonymity, particularly in terms of face recognition, is a significant departure from the past, even if it only applies to the small segment of the general public who pay attention to C-SPAN programming.

Their seeming higher public profile in the twenty-first century may be not only a result of a strategic change on the part of individual justices to "go public" in a way previous justices did not but also a product of the increased opportunities for justices to become political players both on and off the bench. With high-profile nomination processes, television coverage of their speeches and forums, and a more positive approach to the utility of interviews (both televised and print), the justices can employ the media to attempt to shape public opinion about themselves and the Court.

The Special Case of Clarence Thomas

Even though the justice best known on C-SPAN may be Stephen Breyer, the best-known justice among the general public is Clarence Thomas. Following his confirmation hearings in 1991, Thomas became the most famous (or infamous) Supreme Court nominee. Even fifteen years after his nomination,

Thomas was better known than any other Supreme Court justice except Sandra Day O'Connor. Five years after his confirmation process, Thomas was known to 30 percent of Americans, a figure much higher than those for his colleagues, except O'Connor. Only by 2009 had Thomas begun to fade from public memory; only 14 percent could name him as a Supreme Court justice by that point. However, that level of name recognition still outstripped all of his colleagues.[9]

Thomas was unique among current or former justices for the continued attention to his confirmation process several years after it occurred, thus maintaining frequent press attention of Thomas. This included several popular books about the Thomas confirmation, as well as a television movie that aired in 1999. By the time of this writing, Thomas, who was only in his early sixties and potentially had many more years on the Court, already had been the subject of two biographies. Thomas' confirmation process guaranteed that he would continue to receive extra attention as a justice after he arrived at the Court. No other justice had become so well known to the American public and in such a negative way. Live television and radio broadcasting guaranteed that Anita Hill's sexual harassment accusations and Thomas' protests of a high-tech lynching would be etched in American minds for some time to come. Indeed, even though he at first sought to avoid the press after he was confirmed, Thomas was chased by television cameras covering his first day on the job.[10]

Yet the process of remaking Clarence Thomas' image began almost immediately. His wife, Virginia, sought to convey an image opposite the one left by Anita Hill's testimony. Within a month of her husband taking his seat on the Court, Virginia Thomas gave an interview to *People* magazine offering her views on Anita Hill's accusations. She accused Hill of being in love with Thomas but suffering from unrequited love: "In my heart, I always believed she was probably someone in love with my husband and never got what she wanted."[11] The other justices communicated that they were unhappy with the interview, but the process of Thomas' rehabilitation had just begun.[12]

However, the special case of Clarence Thomas also demonstrates the particularly difficult image-making job Supreme Court justices have, especially when others are attempting to set a justice's image as well. At the time of the Thomas confirmation hearings, more Americans believed Thomas was telling the truth about their relationship than believed Hill. One year later, after a pro-Hill campaign by her supporters and by Anita Hill herself, public opinion had reversed.[13]

Thomas himself undertook the job of altering his reputation. He worried about his public image. Former U.S. House Majority Leader Dick Armey once described Thomas as unhappy with the fact that so many people "think badly of him and think him to be a bad person."[14] Thomas began by delivering a series of speeches, particularly to friendly groups. Some of these were aired on C-SPAN. C-SPAN lacked the reach of venues Hill and her supporters were using, but the speeches likely helped to humanize Thomas to an audience of opinion leaders.

Three years after joining the Court, Thomas was called the "most media-shy of all the current justices." Thomas' usual avoidance of the press, however, was not actual shyness. Part of the explanation for his avoidance was a media strategy designed to enhance his star power by controlling his media appearances. That strategy was the product of advice by Armstrong Williams, a radio talk show host, newspaper columnist, and a close friend of Thomas.[15] The strategy seemed to work. Thomas appeared to have to do very little to get press notice. When he asked a question in oral argument, the first in eighteen months, *USA Today* noted the event, adding that the other justices "seemed startled when Thomas's deep voice resounded from the right side of the bench."[16]

Because Thomas had become a celebrity in whom the press was interested, he decided to use that inevitable news coverage for his own purposes. One such purpose was to excoriate those who opposed him. He gave a speech to the American Enterprise Institute in 2001, complaining about how he had been mistreated during the nomination process and in the ten years since. A biographer of Thomas, largely sympathetic to the justice, wrote that, following his confirmation process, "the magma of resentment inside Thomas had hardened into unforgiving wrath."[17]

STRATEGIC THEMES

Thomas' situation is unique, but his desire to establish his own reputation was not. The opportunities justices have today for press attention can be useful to them in sending certain messages about the Court as well as about themselves. As strategic players, the justices are conscious of what press coverage means and how it can be employed to their ends. The justices seem to be utilizing publicity about themselves for their own strategic purposes, primarily to convey certain themes. Indeed, one such theme is that the justices are not distant, but actually quite human.

Portraying Justices as Humans

In May 2010, Anthony Kennedy gave a talk to a Florida bar group and was asked by a high school student about the pros and cons of being a Supreme Court justice. Kennedy noted as one of the cons the fact that Supreme Court justices maintain a certain distance from others.[18] In an earlier age, that distance was viewed as a desirable thing. But Kennedy described it publicly as a negative. The justices appear to be seeking to bridge that distance by showing that they are human. For instance, Clarence Thomas makes public appearances in front of various groups – legal and otherwise – and talks freely about himself, including his background, habits, and personal likes and dislikes. Thomas once told a group of law students that he likes to go to "their joints, with dead animals on the wall, and . . . food I can't eat." He told another group that his favorite constitutional amendments were the post–Civil War amendments because, had it not been for them, "I'd be in a rice field right now."[19]

Kennedy and Thomas are not alone in seeking to close the gap between justices and ordinary people. Several justices have sought to convey that message today. As discussed in Chapter 5, in the last years of the twentieth century, some justices took upon themselves a specific mission to humanize the Supreme Court. Perhaps in response to public interest in their nomination processes as well as increased publicity about them personally, more recent justices also have opened up their lives to the public.

One method for doing so is the autobiography of a justice written for a general audience. Memoirs written by justices and published posthumously are not new. John Marshall, Roger Taney, and Charles Evans Hughes, among others, wrote memoirs for their families or posterity. However, they did not allow those writings to become public until after their deaths. Even an autobiography by a sitting justice is not new. Stephen Field wrote a book about his life in California prior to joining the Supreme Court. It was published in 1877 but likely was intended in preparation for Field's unsuccessful 1880 presidential campaign.[20] William O. Douglas authored three autobiographies, two of which appeared while he was on the Court. The first, titled *Of Men and Mountains*, was published in 1950 and discussed his childhood and his life before reaching the Supreme Court. The second covered his early years as well but also touched on his personal life after 1950. The third, published five years after he left the Court, featured his years as a justice. However, Douglas' autobiographies subsequently were viewed as filled with historical inventions intended to perpetuate public myths about the justice.[21] They seemed to work. One legal scholar concluded that, despite the negative news coverage about his personal life and writings, "Douglas retained much of the aura that he crafted for himself in *Of Men and Mountains*."[22]

However, in 2002 and 2007, two autobiographies from two different justices appeared: one from a justice who would not retire from the Court for another three years and a second from a justice not likely to retire for many years. Neither was running for president, as Field had done when his biography appeared and as Douglas wanted to do. But both were written by the best-known members of the Court.

Lazy B: Growing Up on a Cattle Ranch in the American Southwest, an autobiography of Sandra Day O'Connor, was published by Random House in 2002.[23] The book covers the period of her youth and tells the story of O'Connor's childhood and early years on an isolated Arizona ranch and then as a lonely high school student living in El Paso, Texas. According to her brother, O'Connor decided to write the book because she had been asked by many people how she could have come from a humble, rural background to serve on the Supreme Court.

Yet, the book was criticized for not achieving what O'Connor appeared to have set as its goal. One reviewer remarked that the book's "revelations about how the land, people, and values shaped Sandra Day O'Connor are as skimpy as the region's rainfall." Like the Supreme Court itself, O'Connor sought to tell a story, but similarly, she kept tight control of the message of that story.[24] Nor did O'Connor give any information about her time on the Court. The attention was focused on her as a person, not on her role as a justice.

Nevertheless, O'Connor went further in attempting to satisfy public interest in her as a person and transmit a message of humanness. She compiled a book of her speeches that Random House published in 2004. She also authored a children's book about her horse that appeared in print one year later.[25] All of these appeared while O'Connor was still on the Court.

In contrast with the O'Connor book, Clarence Thomas' autobiography was full of personal references and character insights. The book, like O'Connor's, was a *New York Times* best-seller. Unlike O'Connor's, Thomas' narrative included his tenure on the Court. The book, which appeared in print in 2007, detailed his life before being nominated to the Court but also continued on through his confirmation process and even addressed events in his life after his confirmation. He spoke candidly of his views about liberal interest groups who opposed his nomination in 1991 and his feelings about the accusations made by Anita Hill. A *New York Times* reviewer described the book as Thomas' attempt to "portray himself as a persecuted, almost Christlike figure singled out by the liberal establishment. . . . "[26]

These autobiographies were accompanied by book tours complete with bookstore signings and media interviews. Although Thomas' book tour was not as extensive as those for many other authors (nor did it need to be), he was interviewed on *60 Minutes*, ABC News, and talk radio programs including those hosted by Rush Limbaugh and Sean Hannity. Thomas's book was launched at a reception hosted by talk show host Armstrong Williams and attended by Washington political and media celebrities including then–Vice

President Dick Cheney. The event was even televised on C-SPAN and showed various justices mingling with reporters and politicians.[27]

In addition to the autobiographies, a remarkable number of biographies of justices have appeared recently. Not only have these biographies not been opposed by justices, but they usually have been the result of active or at least passive cooperation with biographers. ("Passive" meaning the justices did not discourage friends and associates from providing material for the books.) Interestingly, some of these biographies have been written by journalists, including those who cover the Court. Stephen Wermiel and Seth Stern co-authored a biography of William Brennan that was published in 2010. In 1986, several years before retiring, Brennan approached Wermiel about writing an authorized biography. Brennan subsequently sat for hundreds of hours of interviews with Wermiel for use in the book. Also, a journalist and an attorney co-authored a biography of John Paul Stevens that appeared the same month he announced his retirement from the Court.[28] Linda Greenhouse, the *New York Times* reporter who covered the Court for twenty-nine years, wrote an authorized biography of Harry Blackmun. The justices were shaping their historical record through cooperation with select journalists who not only wrote about them during their careers, but then would write what the justices expected would be the definitive accounts of them for posterity. Washington-area editor and publisher Herman J. Obermayer wrote a biography of William Rehnquist following the chief justice's death in 2005. Although Rehnquist did not commission nor help prepare a biography, as had Brennan, Stevens, and Blackmun, Obermayer and Rehnquist had been friends for many years, and the book, which does not address Rehnquist's jurisprudence, was written by a sympathetic news professional.[29]

A first in 2010 was the biography of a new justice. Sonia Sotomayor, with less than a year on the Court, became the subject of a biography of her rise to become a Supreme Court justice. Like Stevens, O'Connor, and Scalia, she participated in the making of the book.[30]

One of the most popular reporter-biographers among justices was Joan Biskupic, who covered the court for the *Washington Post* and then for *USA Today*. She authored two biographies of sitting justices. One was of Sandra Day O'Connor, which appeared in 2005, just before O'Connor retired from the Court; the other, published four years later, was a biography of Antonin Scalia. Again, both justices sat for interviews with Biskupic. The vast majority of the other justices cooperated with Biskupic as well.[31]

Thomas' autobiography was published after several unauthorized biographies appeared about Thomas and his confirmation process.[32] The first books about Thomas and his nomination process were largely critical of him.

Subsequently, Andrew Payton Thomas sought to portray Thomas positively. Similarly, Ken Foskett placed Thomas in a more positive light. More recently, Kevin Merida and Michael Fletcher offer an image of a conflicted Thomas, although still a more sympathetic figure than that characterized in the tomes appearing in the 1990s. Thomas did not cooperate with these biographers, but he did not appear to discourage others from assisting them.[33]

As most biographies do, these books show the justices as individuals much like others not in high public office, particularly the Supreme Court. From those biographies, readers learned that Clarence Thomas is a fan of Rush Limbaugh and listens to his radio show. Thomas also listens to country music and drives an RV. He enjoys watching football on television and eschews bridge and golf because he sees them as hobbies for rich people. Readers also discover that O'Connor tried to set up her new colleague David Souter on dates with eligible women in Washington.[34] Also, Antonin Scalia is a fan of the television series *24*.[35]

The interest in justices spilled over into those who had already retired and were generally less well known. A biography of Byron White, a justice for thirty years, appeared in 1998. Lewis Powell, who served for fourteen years, was the subject of a biography that appeared in 2001.[36] These were not written by journalists, however.

Public interest in the justices extended to justices as a group and the machinations on the Court. Such interest had occurred in the past, as mentioned previously. Interest in the inner workings of the Court led to the *Nine Old Men* in the 1930s and again to *The Brethren* in the late 1970s. But the 2000s saw several books about Supreme Court justices written for the general public. In *The Nine: Inside the Secret World of the Supreme Court*, Jeffrey Toobin attempted to reveal what the title implied – the story of the individual justices and their relationships with each other.[37] Toobin, who works as a legal analyst for CNN and *The New Yorker*, was far more respectful than Pearson and Allen had been. Nor was he as focused on insider gossip as Woodward and Armstrong were. Nevertheless, Toobin wanted to show the justices as humans who wrestle with personal relationships in the creation of judicial precedent, a point that justices previously rarely admitted. Toobin explained that he interviewed justices for the book, although he did not mention which ones or even how many. The interviews were conducted on a "not-for-attribution" basis.

The following year, ABC News reporter Jan Greenberg also wrote about the contemporary justices and their internal battles in *Supreme Conflict: The Inside Story of the Struggle for Control of the United States Supreme Court*.[38] Greenberg interviewed nine of the eleven current or former justices at that time. Toobin and Greenberg's access to the justices suggests a high level of cooperation between the justices and these journalist-commentators who were seeking an insider look at the Court. Greenberg's main revelation was that Clarence Thomas was not a clone of Antonin Scalia, but instead a major conservative force on the Court from the beginning of his service as a justice. That message was one that would have come primarily from the justices themselves.

Jeffrey Rosen's *The Supreme Court* does not concentrate exclusively on the current Court; he covers sets of justices from John Marshall on. But, importantly, his subject is, once again, the individual justices. And he does cover two Rehnquist Court justices – Rehnquist himself and Antonin Scalia.[39] Rosen explains that his emphasis on the individual justices is a product of his conclusion that "the Court is a deeply human institution, where quirks of personality and temperament can mean as much as ideology in shaping the law."[40]

The justices themselves also seem willing to talk publicly about their interactions with each other. Clarence Thomas told Biskupic that O'Connor organized a lunch for justices after their oral arguments. Thomas said he initially resisted but finally acquiesced to O'Connor's pleadings to attend. According to Thomas, the lunches enhanced the camaraderie on the Court. "Now you have a group of people who really enjoy each other's company." Also, Anthony Kennedy told an audience that the justices were part of a "happy court" right now.[41]

Defending the Institution

Another theme that justices in the twenty-first century are using publicity for is to defend the institution. As has been demonstrated throughout this book, this is hardly new. When the justices have felt that their institution was under attack, they have sought to protect it. John Marshall and his colleagues did so in the early years of the Court. Their successors acted similarly throughout the nineteenth and twentieth centuries. Ironically, the justices occasionally complain that they are defenseless in the face of attacks, yet they do defend themselves.

As mentioned in Chapter 5, in the 1980s, the justices decided to use the bicentennial of the Constitution to explain their institution to a public that was expecting greater democracy in their institutions and processes. And they used the medium of television to demonstrate they were still relevant in a rapidly changing television age. As chief justice, William Rehnquist took advocacy of the institution to a new level. Rehnquist wrote a series of popular books on the Court and its history, including the Court's role in key events in U.S. history.[42] Rehnquist also sat for interviews on C-SPAN explaining the role of the Court.

Justices in the twenty-first century have continued to use media sources to explain their rituals and practices, as well as the relevancy of the Court in a new age. They have given interviews on C-SPAN and elsewhere to have a forum to explain an institution that seems somewhat mysterious to many Americans. They have described the purpose of the symbols of the Court – the judicial robe and collar and architecture of the Court's building – as well as the Court's work: the process of granting cert, the role of oral argument, and how justices approach decision making.

Defense of the Court has not been conducted merely to address a general lack of public knowledge about how the Court works and why it exists in a democratic society. Rather, the justices' public statements about the institution also have been intended to rebut specific criticisms about the decisions they have made and the manner in which they judge. Several of the justices have taken exception to rhetoric about "activist judges" who need to be reined in by congressional action and public opinion. The most prominent has been Sandra Day O'Connor. Not long before her retirement in 2005, O'Connor began to deliver speeches on the importance of an independent judiciary. However, going further than giving mere civics lessons on the role of the Court, she also suggested that political forces were eroding that independence. She continued the campaign after she retired. In fact, O'Connor has been in a particularly advantageous position to wage a battle against critics of the Court because she is no longer a justice but has retained her celebrity status. Immediately after she left the bench, she began to rebut critiques of the judiciary being made by Republican leaders unhappy with recent Supreme Court decisions. Also, she chaired a conference on the judicial branch designed to discuss how to respond to complaints about the judiciary. She also has campaigned against the election of state judges.[43]

Yet, given her status as well as her willingness to speak out publicly, O'Connor can serve as a counterweight to the existing Court. A year after leaving the Court, O'Connor gave a speech reminding her colleagues, as well as others in the judiciary, that they needed to respect precedent and that if they did so, they would gain greater credibility in the eyes of the public. Also, following the *Citizens United v. FEC* decision in 2010, O'Connor expressed her opposition to the decision, predicting that it would make judgeship elections more expensive and diminish the impartiality of judges.[44] Retired justices usually have remained outside the public eye. Ironically, O'Connor's celebrity status has offered her a forum that provides the opportunity for her to criticize the decisions of an institution she set out to publicly defend.

O'Connor has been joined by other justices who use public forums to defend the institution against critics of the Court's decisions. Stephen Breyer assisted

O'Connor in heading a project to enhance civics education about the role of the judicial branch. He also accompanied O'Connor in a joint interview on the PBS *NewsHour* to argue for an independent judiciary and to blunt critics of the Court who wanted to limit its power. Ruth Bader Ginsburg has used public speeches to suggest that Republican critics were harming the judicial branch. She also argued that they were creating a culture that undermined the rule of law.[45]

Justices in the twenty-first century are continuing the tradition of defending the institution when they perceive it is under siege from others. There may be a critical difference, however, from the past. Unlike their predecessors, today's justices may be quicker to engage in public defense of the Court in the first place. By comparison, in the 1930s, the justices were reluctant to discuss Roosevelt's Court-packing plan. Charles Evans Hughes used the indirect approach of a letter to the chair of the Senate Judiciary Committee. By contrast, in the 1980s, William Brennan was willing to engage in a public debate with ideological conservatives about how to interpret the Constitution, and, in the twenty-first century, O'Connor, Breyer, and Ginsburg have decried Republican attacks on "activist judges." Also, they may be relying less on written opinions to express their views and more on other, non–opinion-related venues such as speeches, interviews, and forums.

Shaping the Policy Debate

Justices also have used their celebrity status to join a broader debate on issues and seek to direct that debate. For example, Stephen Breyer appeared on *Larry King Live* in the midst of a debate over whether a Protestant minister should be allowed to burn copies of the Qu'ran and asserted that such an act would be legal.[46] The justices use interviews, writings, and speeches to comment on policy issues, although typically they relate to the Court itself rather than areas such as foreign or domestic policy. Not surprisingly, these writings by justices today lack the controversial edginess of William O. Douglas' writings in the 1960s, but they do provide a forum for justices to discuss the Court as an institution or issues involving judicial decision making, including interpretation of the Constitution.

Not surprisingly, one popular topic of off-the-bench discussion is how judges should approach the Constitution. Antonin Scalia has entered the broader public constitutional debate with writings advocating originalism. Stephen Breyer responded with two books critiquing the originalist view held by Scalia and others. Breyer and Scalia also have used televised forums to engage in public debate about constitutional interpretation. Scalia, Breyer, and O'Connor participated in a televised "constitutional conversation" at the National Archives three months before O'Connor retired. The three justices sparred genially about constitutional interpretation. The appearance was unusual in that three justices appeared on camera simultaneously.[47]

Ruth Bader Ginsburg used a 2009 interview with Joan Biskupic of *USA Today* to enter the debate about the ideal composition of the Court. Specifically, Ginsburg commented on what type of nominee President Barack Obama should appoint to the Court when David Souter retired. Ginsburg suggested that the ideal Court would entail more of a gender balance. "Women belong in all places where decisions are being made," Ginsburg told Biskupic as Obama was contemplating whom to appoint before settling on Sonia Sotomayor.[48] Similarly, Anthony Kennedy contributed to the debate about the importance of empathy as a character trait for judges. Kennedy supported Obama's call for more empathetic justices on the Court who understand the real-world consequences of their decisions when he told a Florida audience that "[y]ou certainly can't formulate principles without being aware of where those principles will take you, what their consequences will be."[49]

The justices also have weighed in on broader subjects than those directly related to the judicial process. They sometimes have used the public forum to criticize the Court's own decisions. John Paul Stevens used a *New Yorker* interview to criticize the majority in *Citizens United* and expressed his unhappiness about the outcome of many recent cases on which he had dissented.[50]

The higher profile of justices means that they may be tempted to express a position on a policy issue that could come before the Court. In 2008, Antonin Scalia stated in an interview with a British radio channel that he believed torture was justified in some circumstances. In that situation, there was no current case before the Court, although this was a subject the Court was likely to handle at some future date. However, in other incidents where Scalia has spoken out, there were pending cases. In one 2004 speech, Scalia expressed his disapproval of an appellate court ruling that the phrase "under God" in the Pledge of Allegiance was unconstitutional. In another speech, he questioned the rights of detainees in Guantanamo. After the Pledge statement, he recused himself from the case, but he declined to do so in the Guantanamo case. William Rehnquist once opined in a book about whether civil liberties can be curtailed during wartime. John Paul Stevens used a speech to the American Bar Association to criticize the way the death penalty was used in the United States.[51]

One justice has become a participant in the debate about the role of the press. Antonin Scalia apparently thinks a lot about journalists. As mentioned in a previous chapter, he gave a speech criticizing press coverage of the Court. He also considers the press to be fundamentally antagonistic to those who share his views, suggesting it is a biased institution. He told Joan Biskupic that "much of the press is hostile to my message. I don't think it's a conspiracy. I do believe a large majority of the press consists of liberals, for whatever reason, that the profession attracts them."[52]

JUSTICES AS PARTICIPANTS IN DEBATES ABOUT THEMSELVES AND EACH OTHER

Some of the justices have used public venues to take part in public debate about themselves. Unlike justices of the past who typically ignored criticism, some current justices take the opportunity of a speech or an interview to defend themselves personally. For example, in an interview with Joan Biskupic, Scalia said he thought his proudest moment on the bench was not being chased off the case involving Vice President Dick Cheney by commentators in the press.[53] The fact that he would hold that interview is an indicator of the nature of the change that has occurred, but that he would use that interview to challenge the press is still another.

Another justice using the same approach was Clarence Thomas. Thomas' public settings typically were forums that were friendly to him. In 1993, he spoke to the convention of Concerned Women for America, a socially conservative group, and asked that the speech be closed to the media because he said "he just wants it to be among his friends."[54] Within a month of joining the Court, he sat for a televised interview with Paul Weyrich of the Free Congress Foundation. The interview was broadcast by satellite to conservative gatherings around the country. In his first eighteen months on the Court, he made three trips to Weyrich's conservative think tank. During the interview, Thomas thanked conservatives who "stood up for us and the love that you showed for us."[55] Obviously Thomas' autobiography, as well as the accompanying media tour for the book, was an opportunity for Thomas to express his side of the sexual harassment debate as well as his own legacy on the Court.

Still another example is the case of John Paul Stevens' public statements shortly before his retirement. Stevens was interviewed at length by Jeffrey Rosen for a *New York Times Magazine* article on the justice's service on the Court and later gave interviews about his pending retirement that appeared in *The New Yorker* and the *New York Times*. Stevens used the interviews to explain his career and defend his many votes throughout a thirty-four-year career. He even indicated that he expected to retire shortly, a public statement that is rare in the annals of justices' interactions with the press.[56]

Like their predecessors in the twentieth century, justices today also occasionally utilize the press to communicate with each other. John Roberts began his tenure by signaling his objectives as a new chief justice. He said publicly (which meant the message was heard by both the general public and his colleagues) that his goal was to create more consensus among the justices to avoid closely split decisions. Similarly, John Paul Stevens spoke to his colleagues after the *Citizens United v. FEC* case. Not only did Stevens issue a passionate dissent in the case but he also used the press to criticize the majority of his colleagues who voted against him in the decision, as well as the majority who had decided many other recent cases Stevens opposed.[57]

The justices also are going public about each other. When Joan Biskupic, Supreme Court reporter for the *Washington Post*, wrote books on both Sandra Day O'Connor and Antonin Scalia in 2005 and 2009, respectively, she found most of these justices' colleagues willing to sit for on-the-record interviews about O'Connor, Scalia, and the other justices.[58] Nor were they shy in providing detail that added to the public debate about the roles of particular justices. John Paul Stevens, for instance, revealed that "everyone on the Court from time to time has thought [Scalia] was unwise to take such an extreme position, both in tone and in position."[59]

SUMMARY

Relations between justices and the press are not new in the twenty-first century or even the twentieth. From the beginning of the Court, justices have possessed external strategies for shaping press coverage and public opinion regarding themselves as individuals and the Court as a whole. From the early Federalist justices appointed by George Washington and John Adams to those most recently appointed, the press has enjoyed some relationship with justices. That relationship has been fruitful for both reporters and justices.

This review of the history of those relations has not attempted to suggest that all justices have been so engaged. As mentioned throughout, some of the justices were distant from the press and, seemingly, from politics itself. In the nineteenth and twentieth centuries, some justices seemed disinterested in press coverage. Either they left little written record of that interaction (which may have been particularly true of eighteenth- or nineteenth-century justices without voluminous paper collections) or simply concentrated on their own opinions or the interaction among the justices and thought or wrote little about the external environment.

Some late-twentieth-century justices eschewed efforts to shape press coverage. Byron White avoided interviews with the press, even those "on background" or "off the record." He declined to hold a press conference when he retired, as other justices had done. He also destroyed most of his papers.

The irony is that few individuals have held as broad public name recognition before appointment to the Court and had as much interaction with the press as did Byron White, a former All-American halfback and professional football player.[60] White's distance from the press was due to his inherent shyness but also was a product of his disdain for journalists. When he retired, he told a friend that the rumor of his retirement was true, but he said, "I hate to confirm anything, *anything*, published in the Washington Post."[61] His contempt for the press was reciprocated. One journalist described White as someone who "scowls at people who call him 'Whizzer'" and glowers at people who don't."[62]

Others, however, were actively involved in thinking about the press and public opinion. They plotted to shape news coverage of themselves, their institution, and even public policy generally. Names such as Felix Frankfurter, Louis Brandeis, William O. Douglas, and Harry Blackmun recur in these pages because these were justices who thought a lot about public opinion and the press and were anxious to use the press to shape external opinion about the Court and themselves. But we also know about their interests and activities in this regard because their papers are open, and the correspondence between them and journalists, as well as their diary entries and appointment books, is available to peruse. It is likely that as the recent or current justices' papers become open, there may be more evidence that they, too, were (and are) engaged in more frequent interactions than we now are aware of. (Of course, they may redact their papers to eliminate just such information.)

The argument of this book has been that many of the justices have been externally strategic. Even if a majority of the justices have not fit into that category (which we likely will never know), there are those who do so at least some of the time. Linda Greenhouse once commented that "[w]hile the Justices naturally draw on their own values and perspectives in approaching cases, most of them, most of the time, act not as politicians but as judges. . . ."[63] Of course, most of the justices do not have to act as politicians most of the time to be strategic actors in external relations, and even successful actors. Like many others in national politics, they need only do so some of the time. And those who do not can rely on others who do to protect the external interests of the institution.

Moreover, many of those who were externally strategic also were the luminaries on the Court. It may be no coincidence that most of those justices whom we consider the greatest occupants of the bench are those whose names appear frequently in this account: John Marshall, Louis Brandeis, William O. Douglas, Hugo Black, and Felix Frankfurter, among others. These justices not only determined the direction of the Court when they sat on the bench but they also were active in seeking to shape the larger political environment in which that Court operated.

Justices do have motivations for interacting with the public – both institutional and individual – that propel them to engage in external relations. Public attitudes about the Court generally can affect the extent to which the institution is respected and deferred to by Congress, the president, and those at the state and local levels. Public opinion about individual decisions also can determine the extent to which a decision is understood and complied with. Obviously, that does not mean the Court does not take positions that are unpopular from time to time or may provoke intense controversy. Yet it is significant that the justices believe that how those decisions are crafted, explained, announced, and defended can make a difference in press coverage and public comprehension.

Finally, the perception of public opinion regarding an individual justice can affect each justice. By the early 1970s, William O. Douglas had become increasingly controversial, which inhibited his writing and led him to adopt a lower public profile. Even more serious, in 1969, Abe Fortas concluded that he was unable to continue in his position as an associate justice because of the constant attention to the ethical charges against him. Those situations are rare. What is more common is that public opinion affects the nature of a justice's reputation, as well as his place in history. When William Brennan wrote a concurrence in the school prayer case, he appeared to be seeking to preserve his reputation with Catholics who would not understand his vote unless he provided an explanation. And several justices in the late twentieth and early twenty-first centuries – such as William Brennan, Harry Blackmun, Thurgood Marshall, and John Paul Stevens – talked to reporters before leaving the Court and offered their own assessments of their careers on the Court. They also cooperated with journalist-biographers who would write their histories and help determine the records scholars would employ for years to come.

With these motivations, then, they engage in strategies designed to shape press coverage and the resulting public opinion. Those strategies are intended to support the institution, particularly when it is under external assault, or attempt to shape public policy on some issue. Such institutional strategies assist the individual justices in legitimating their roles because their own fortunes are intertwined with those of the institution.

Additionally, as we have seen, other strategies may serve the individual justice rather than the Court as an institution. These include pursuing higher office, seeking to shape the broader public policy debate, defining their own legacies as individual members of the Court, and seeking to communicate with each other to change their colleagues' attitudes or behavior. The pursuit of higher office was a feature of the Court for several justices through the nineteenth and twentieth centuries. The press became a mechanism for achieving that objective – from pseudonymous essays to campaign brochures to press coverage of speeches. Ambitious justices, such as John McLean, Stephen Field, Salmon Chase, and William O. Douglas, utilized these tools to run for the presidency. Interaction with the press became a necessary component of a presidential bid, although ultimately none of these bids met with success. Similarly, the press' role in chief justice appointments may not have been so successful in terms of securing the position for a chief justice. Press coverage may not have directly led to the appointment of a chief justice, but it may have prevented it in cases such as those involving Robert Jackson, Hugo Black, and Harold Burton. Jackson may have been successful in blocking Black, whereas Burton's failure to change his negative image may have scuttled his appointment.

Another objective was to influence the public policy debate. John Marshall's goal was to stabilize the Court's role as an arbiter of constitutional issues while expanding the power of the national government vis-à-vis the states. Marshall primarily used written opinions, as well as internal Court cohesion, to accomplish that task of shaping the larger debates about the role of the Court and the national government. However, he also turned to the press and the public, both through the tone of his opinions and by writing essays supporting the Court's decisions. Other justices at the time also used the forum of the Court to press their positions on current public policy issues. Similarly, justices throughout the nineteenth and twentieth centuries, such as John McLean, Louis Brandeis, and William O. Douglas, were involved in public debates about public policy in their respective time periods.

Some justices, particularly those serving in the latter half of the twentieth century, also sought to shape their own historical records as they left the Court. The justices know that journalists' accounts become a valuable resource for historians' accounts. That explains why, when *St. Louis Post-Dispatch* editorial page editor Irving Dilliard asked Hugo Black for cooperation in writing a retrospective on Black at the marking of his twentieth anniversary on the Court, the justice responded with suggestions of articles about him that would be useful to Dilliard.[64] It also explains why Black, at age eighty-two, sat for the CBS television interview. This tendency also appeared in the end-of-career press interviews Harry Blackmun, Thurgood Marshall, and John Paul Stevens gave where they separated themselves from the views of their colleagues. Even Stevens, who was one of the more active dissenters in the history of the Court, turned to the press to explain himself. Undoubtedly his interviews with venues like the *Washington Post*, the *New York Times*, and *USA Today* reached a broader audience than any of his written opinions had, a fact Stevens must have known.

As mentioned earlier, when Thurgood Marshall resigned, he left with an angry dissent. When asked at a press conference if he was leaving because of frustration, Marshall reacted angrily, calling the claim "a double-barreled lie," although his own biographer detailed Marshall's increasing anger at his inability to stop conservative justices from using their majority to overturn precedents he had helped create.[65] Marshall knew that his retirement would magnify the impact of his dissent, not only to the immediate case at hand but also to the string of cases with which he had disagreed.

Throughout history, justices used the press to communicate with one another. This was particularly true in the twentieth century. These efforts typically came in the form of background interviews. Fellow justices used the press to criticize Hugo Black when he was a relatively new justice. Raymond Clapper of the Scripps-Howard newspapers asked several of the other justices whether the Childs article about Black was accurate. Clapper reported that none of them "offered one word in Justice Black's defense, even privately."[66] Then the justices disavowed any role in lambasting Black. Harlan Stone issued a press statement that he was not responsible for Childs' articles. In another instance, Robert Jackson kept a clipping of a newspaper column by nationally syndicated columnist Frank R. Kent about Douglas' possible presidential bid in 1952. The column stated that some of the other justices were concerned about Douglas' presidential ambitions and felt that Douglas should not use the Court as a platform for a political campaign.[67] Whether Jackson was one of those who may have spoken directly or indirectly to the press about Douglas (and therefore had an interest in the article) is unknown. Even if Jackson was not involved, some other justice was.

Sometimes the communication was not private. Arthur J. Goldberg used a speech at New York University's James Madison lecture to chastise his fellow judges as well as others in government for not dealing sufficiently with the issue of equality in the administration of criminal justice. As he must have anticipated, Goldberg's speech was reported in the following day's *New York Times*.[68] Robert Jackson's criticism of Hugo Black discussed in Chapter 5 was another example of communication targeted at another justice, but not in a private manner.

The justices possess tools to implement those strategies. These include, first and foremost, the opinions they write. The issuance of an opinion, on its face, does not suggest any external strategy. Yet, as has been shown, opinions can become part of a justice's efforts to affect elite and public attitudes regarding the Court and/or the individual who is associated with the opinion. In addition to the direction of the opinion or the rationale for the result, press coverage can be affected by the language used as well as the presentation of the opinion at announcement.

In addition to opinions, justices can use background interviews to communicate messages to the public or even to each other. Off-the-record interviews may be useful for guiding the press in its coverage both of the Court generally and the individual justices. They also can reach the public through speeches (again primarily via press coverage), occasional on-the-record interviews, and even surrogates who communicate publicly what the justice may be encouraging privately.

This study shows that when a justice attempts to acquire a higher profile, he or she can do so, particularly with the help of the press. Harry Blackmun made a conscious effort to increase his visibility as a justice by giving broadcast interviews, opening his speeches to television, and making news with provocative statements, both in his speeches and his opinions. The *New York Times* accorded him that attention; they noted his opinions (above and beyond attention given to others) as well as his other public activities and statements. Other justices in the twenty-first century, such as Stephen Breyer and Antonin Scalia, also seem to have gone public in a way that suggests intent rather than coincidence. Scalia's own admission confirms that conclusion.

THE FUTURE

If norms have changed on the Court, then we can expect to see increasing use of a variety of tools available to justices. Nevertheless, it is likely that they will continue to be cautious about their venues. Although a sophisticated public television or C-SPAN interview program may be an acceptable forum, an afternoon talk show may not. Moreover, the justices still will be expected to avoid debating, or even discussing, pending cases unless they wish to be accused of bias and urged to recuse themselves. Yet the increased attention to the justices, and the justices' own participation in that expanded coverage, raises questions about what these norm changes may mean for the justices and the Court as an institution.

One question is how norm changes may affect the justices' relations with each other and their ability to function as a body. This question hinges on how justices use these forums to discuss one another. Will the higher public profile result in increased public criticism of each other? Such criticism is not a new phenomenon, as was discussed regarding the 1930s incident when some justices voiced in background interviews their dissatisfaction with their new colleague, Hugo Black, and the 1946 episode when Robert Jackson attacked

Hugo Black in public while others in turn took on Jackson. There must be internal pressure on the justices not to talk in their public appearances about their relations with other justices. Unlike Harry Blackmun, who seemed to take delight in publicly critiquing his colleagues but also was viewed as somewhat of a curmudgeon, justices today may be careful to express praise and respect for their fellow justices whom they must face again around the conference room table and from whom they may want to seek accommodation on opinion wording or joining. Yet it is likely that some future Court that may not be as happy as Anthony Kennedy describes the current justices to be will have its internal squabbles spill over into the press. The opportunity to do so, and the temptation, may be too strong for some future justices to resist.

Will this higher public profile lead justices increasingly to use this as an opportunity to criticize not only each other but also the decisions of the Court and perhaps even the Court itself? To some extent, this is already occurring. One feature of John Paul Stevens' 2010 interview with Jeffrey Toobin in *The New Yorker* was Stevens' criticism of many of the conservative majority's decisions. Similarly, as mentioned earlier, using her notoriety, Sandra Day O'Connor also expressed her opposition to the *Citizens United* decision in 2010. The issue is not the act of dissenting or the writing of a dissenting opinion. Dissent obviously has been a feature of the Court since its inception. The difference is in how that dissent is expressed. Justices have always done so through the medium of the written opinion. Yet going off the bench and giving an interview reiterating and expanding that dissent is something justices may be able to do more of as they acquire and utilize the opportunity to talk directly to the public.

Another issue is how the justices maintain the institution's tradition of secrecy. The justices' penchant for secrecy is not easy to uphold in a celebrity culture reinforced by television and the Internet. The Court's long-term traditions are scrutinized by the press, the public, and, as indicated earlier, even the justices themselves. They will need to decide which of their traditions are inviolable and which are expendable as they adjust to a new era of expected transparency for traditionally nontransparent institutions. How much can they share about the deliberations in conference while talking to the press? Can they explain the processes of the Court in an educational sense without providing specific examples with which they are familiar?

Still another challenge to the Court is handling television coverage. Although television is a fact of life for the president and Congress, as well as for governors and many large-city mayors, the medium is only now touching the lives of justices. An important question is whether the individual warming of the justices toward televised coverage of their speeches and other public events will lead them to adopt television coverage for their formal duties – opinion announcement and oral argument. Will they feel they are treated respectfully enough by television that they can trust that deference will be maintained if cameras are allowed in the courtroom?

Does television affect how the justices interact with the public? Will they use a televised forum to speak not just to the counsel in the room but also to the public watching at home? Obviously, high-profile oral arguments already receive news coverage. But television news coverage with the coveted visuals provided by the Court might well increase. Certainly, those oral arguments would be played in full not only on C-SPAN but also on cable news networks. One of the justices expected to use a televised forum would be Antonin Scalia. Joan Biskupic wrote about Scalia's testimony before the Senate Judiciary Committee confirmation hearing that Scalia "loved being onstage." That trait continued on the Court as Scalia has become the most active inquisitor during oral argument. But Scalia does more than just ask questions. Biskupic described Scalia as a justice who "played to the audience with jokes and put-downs. He could be a showman, a streetwise guy, and a pulverizer.... This was all very much a part of Scalia's persona ... "[69] Pamela S. Karlan, a frequent participant in oral arguments, also concluded that Scalia "plays to the crowd."[70] Scalia's showmanship did not endear him to his colleagues, particularly O'Connor. She was offended when he questioned the relevance of her line of questioning and directed pointed barbs at his colleagues' views in oral argument as well as in written opinions. But for Scalia, it was all part of the rough and tumble world of public discourse.[71]

Would future justices also become showmen playing to the crowd? Would the forum provide an opportunity to seek to influence public debate? Would a justice – now or in the future – view the presence of the cameras as a chance to speak to the public about the case as well as larger issues that may touch on public policy, much as their eighteenth-century predecessors did in a more limited way with grand jury charges.

The justices might not be the only performers in the room. Similarly, counsel participating in the oral arguments might utilize television coverage as an opportunity to speak beyond the Court. Such a strategy might well backfire, as it is the justices who ultimately decide each case. However, the televising of a counsel's arguments could place additional public pressure on the Court because it exposes the public to those arguments as well.

Furthermore, can the Court continue to withstand the pressure to televise its proceedings in the media age and the resulting celebrity culture? As the individual justices attain higher public profiles, will there be a greater clamor for these nine powerful individuals to allow observation by the public in numbers larger than the few hundred people able to sit in the courtroom of the Supreme Court building? Will this pressure become stronger because there is the existence of a medium – C-SPAN – that treats the justices respectfully and would constitute a more suitable televised venue for oral arguments than the previous limited options of network news story clips? How does the Court favor C-SPAN but exclude the other networks? This is the dilemma the Court has faced in terms of cameras in the courtroom.

Alternately, could televising of oral arguments actually benefit the Court institutionally? As shown in Chapter 6, news coverage of the Court has undergone a change toward more coverage of the individual justices. Would oral arguments focus more attention on the cases, and the legal issues they represent, than on the personalities on the bench?

Related to these questions is the issue of whether the change in norms that leads to a greater public presence of the justices will affect the Court's legitimacy in the public's mind. As the justices become more public, will the institution suffer? The currency for the Court is public legitimacy. In recent years, the justices may have been willing to become more public initially to explain their institution, but are there other ramifications that will deleteriously affect the work of the institution? The conventional wisdom has been that the Court's legitimacy is connected to the continuation of a mystique shrouding the Court. Jeffrey Rosen concluded: "The Court's resistance to publicity may or may not increase the public's understanding of how it goes about its business, but it hasn't hurt the Court's legitimacy."[72]

As the justices "go public," will the coverage of the Court become more political as it focuses on the individual justices and not just the product – that is, the written opinions the Court delivers to the press and, indirectly, the public? If the frame for press coverage of the justices is similar to that of other governmental figures, the result may be lower public regard for the Court as a legitimate arbiter.[73] The result could be harmful to the Court.

One example could be the case of Antonin Scalia's changing approach to television. The justice's argumentative and blunt personal style is well attuned to political battle. Previously, that personality had limited public exposure – nontelevised speeches, primarily to law schools and legal groups, as well as oral arguments. After Scalia decided in 2005 to become more public, he started presenting his personal style to a broad public audience. That got him in trouble. When, in March 2006, Scalia took a question on the rights of detainees in the war on terrorism, he responded with his own opinion about the need for such detainees to be tried in military rather than civilian courts. Because Scalia was about to hear a case directly on that topic, his remarks suggested that he was trying the case in public and drawing a conclusion even before he heard arguments. The image of a justice deciding a case before the counsel had the opportunity to argue it struck at the very image of impartial justice. News organizations criticized Scalia for making statements about pending cases beforehand.[74] Indeed, Scalia may well be the justice who does the most to undermine the image of the Supreme Court justice as an aloof figure distant from the public fray.

Will the public then become less deferential to the Court because of the public profile of the justices? The strategy of the justices through the history of the Court has been to maintain some measure of distance from the public to enhance a sense of mystery and awe toward the institution By not talking about the Court very much or even placing themselves out in front, the justices hoped to concentrate attention on their products and retain the shroud around themselves and how they arrived at their decisions. "The product should be transparent, but the process should not be" has been the mantra for maintaining the Court's power. John R. Hibbing and Elizabeth Theiss-Morse argue that the Court preserves its public support precisely because it keeps the press at bay. They present the example that if "someone made a videotape of the justices vigorously debating in conference and showed it to everyone in the nation, people would not feel warmed by the frank sharing of views. . . ."[75]

Emphasis on the image of distance on the part of the individuals, while simultaneously pushing forward the products of the Court (written opinions), has dominated the Court's approach to the press. When the new Supreme Court building was constructed in the 1930s, the justices added accommodations for the press and created the Public Information Office at the same time. Although the name suggests a broader reach, that office was designed for press relations. The new building design provided space within the building for the work of the press corps as well as within the courtroom itself. All of these accommodations were designed to aid the press in its role of covering the Court.[76] The justices also ensured that their written work was freely disseminated to the press corps at the time of the issuing of a specific decision or list of cases the Court had accepted, as well as other materials related to a case, such as the briefs by the parties and amici briefs. Reporters today still are provided with a calendar of oral arguments, including when each case will be heard. In addition, the reporters who cover the Court are provided with the weekly conference list so they can know what cases the justices will be deciding in each conference.

This feeding of the press corps is directed at the Court's institutional product. What the Court does not provide is a transcript of the discussion within the conference or even information about the results of a conference after it has occurred. The Court contends that journalists will get that information eventually. But if the Court provided it after a conference took place, journalists would have a better understanding of the decision-making process. They also could chart the changes that occurred in the opinions of the justices during the writing. They would know whether justices changed their minds during the course of the opinion writing, whether the majority switched hands, and whether the justices were fractured or united. (Or, if that information were public, perhaps the justices would not change their views during the opinion-writing stage.) All of that information speaks to the decision-making process, which justices typically seek to hide from the press and the public. That is why the Court is loath to produce it for public consumption.

Will the attention to the individual justices undermine the institution's product orientation? It would seem so. Already, the content of news coverage has shifted. The justices must consider the extent to which their adaptation to a changing media culture enhances or diminishes the legitimacy of their institution. On the one hand, the record of the past shows us that when justices "go public," they can assist the institution. John Marshall's presentation of a united front for the Court as well as the writing of essays in the face of external attacks on its role and legitimacy bolstered the Court's place as an independent third branch. Charles Evan Hughes' written communication to the Senate undermined support for the Court-packing plan. The Court may have enhanced its public approval in the 1980s by talking about the Court amidst the discussion of the bicentennial of the U.S. Constitution.

On the other hand, the Court's role is still a tenuous one. Public approval, although still higher than that for other institutions of government, waxes and wanes. Publicity for the Court can damage the image of the Court as well – be it possible impeachment of a justice; controversial writings, statements, or activities of justices that undermine the aura of impartiality; or personal feuding among justices. This historical review has included several examples making that point.

As today's justices encounter their new media environment, the question of how their unique institution, with its antiquated traditions and mores, survives in a highly contrasting media culture is one that will affect not only them personally but also the institution they represent. Whether the pressure from media forums to further their own individual objectives will prevail over institutional imperatives is the question that ultimately only they can answer.

APPENDIX

Methodology

This study included both an analysis of justices over time as well as an examination of recent press coverage. This project employed a two-method approach to the study of the relationships between justices and reporters. These methods were historical inquiry and content analysis of news stories about the Court.

HISTORICAL INQUIRY

Because this project examined possible change over time in the relationships between justices and reporters, secondary and primary sources related to the extrajudicial behavior of the justices throughout the history of the Court were employed. There are relatively few books and articles directly addressing the topic of justices and the press. In addition to biographies of the justices, articles, and monographs, I relied on the public papers of the coverage of the justices for insights into the attitudes of justices towards the press, as well as their public activities. These included speeches, writings, background interviews, rare on-the-record interviews, correspondence with the press, correspondence with colleagues, and letters to friends and acquaintances, among other sources. The Library of Congress Manuscript Division holds most of the extant papers of past U.S. Supreme Court justices, and I was able to examine most of the papers of the justices located there. Other justices' papers are available elsewhere. I also used the resources at the Special Collections Division, Harvard Law Library; Chicago Historical Society; the Tarleton Law Library, University of Texas; and the Yale University Sterling Memorial Library. I am grateful to the staff members at those libraries who assisted me in the location of materials relevant to this project.

CONTENT ANALYSIS

Another component of this project was the study of content of news coverage about justices. By analyzing the content of news stories, I was able to assess the amount of attention given to justices generally as well as press coverage of individual justices. I could determine the themes of stories about justices, such as discussion of cases versus discussion of individual justices. Additionally, I examined other features such as the presence of photos, sketches, or video of the justices, as well as whether the justices' voices were heard in the television news story or whether they were quoted in the print story. In addition, I linked the justice to the number and type of opinions they were associated with over this time period – majority, concurring, and dissenting – and compared that with news coverage of their opinions. In the *New York Times*, I coded for wire service stories versus *New York Times*–originated news stories. By conducting a longitudinal analysis, I tracked change over time in the nature of the news coverage.

Research assistants were used to code newspaper and television stories of individual justices from 1968 to 2007. Because the nomination of Robert Bork is viewed as a seminal event in the twentieth-century history of the judicial selection process, that point provided an approximate twenty-year period prior to the Bork nomination in 1987 and another twenty-year period subsequent to it. Whereas nineteenth-century nominees were routinely contested and rejected, the twentieth-century practice was the opposite. The president's nomination choices rarely were seriously opposed. The Bork nomination ended that practice. Since 1987, Supreme Court nominations have been highly publicized events. As a result, some recent Supreme Court justices, as nominees, became celebrities. Although that celebrity status fades somewhat after a justice dons judicial robes, there remains a standing with the public that their predecessors rarely acquired.

Two media – the *New York Times* and *NBC Nightly News* – were examined in the case study. The *New York Times* became representative of an elite daily newspaper's approach to Supreme Court justices. The paper is not typical of daily newspapers in its coverage of the Supreme Court. The paper has long assigned a full-time reporter to the Supreme Court beat. As a result, the *New York Times* is an example of the most thorough reporting by a general consumer news medium. *NBC Nightly News* was chosen as representative of the three broadcast network early-evening news broadcasts. NBC News also is the only one of the three major networks that has streaming online archived video available going back to 1968.

All news stories about justices in these two media between 1968 and 2007 were coded. *NBC Nightly News* video clips were obtained from the Vanderbilt

Television News Archive for that period. Using the index available at the archive, those news stories about one or more justices were retrieved and then coded. News stories about justices were determined by searching the archive's index by each justice's name. Those justices who served during this forty-year period of time were included. These were Hugo Black, William O. Douglas, Earl Warren, John Harlan, William Brennan, Potter Stewart, Byron White, Abe Fortas, Thurgood Marshall, Warren Burger, Harry Blackmun, Lewis Powell, William Rehnquist, John Paul Stevens, Sandra Day O'Connor, Antonin Scalia, Anthony Kennedy, David Souter, Clarence Thomas, Ruth Bader Ginsburg, Stephen Breyer, John Roberts, and Samuel Alito. Because many stories contained mention of more than one justice, duplicate stories were culled. The same process was used for the *New York Times* using the *New York Times* index. Each news story was coded independently by three different coders. Then a fourth individual took the majority view (or unanimous) of the three coders to produce the final code for each news story.

To assess reliability, a sample of news stories for both the *New York Times* and NBC News was examined to determine the extent of inter-coder agreement. For the *New York Times* stories, inter-coder agreement was high. For the dichotomous variables, inter-coder agreement for the three coders for each story was unanimous in 96 percent of the cases. As expected, agreement for non-dichotomous variables such as the themes and the type of story was slightly lower —93.1 percent unanimous agreement and 6.5 percent majority agreement. For NBC News, inter-coder unanimous agreement for dichotomous variables was 98.5 percent, and 95.8 percent unanimous agreement and 4.1 percent majority agreement for non-dichotomous variables.

Notes

PREFACE

1. See Charles Lane, "Once Again, Scalia's the talk of the Town; Justice Renders Frank Out-of-the Court Opinions on 2000 Presidential Election, 'Sicilian' Gesture," *Washington Post*, April 15, 2006, p. A2; Charles A. Radin, 'Scalia Gesture Not Obscene, Court Rep Says " *Boston Globe*, March 28, 2006; and Kenneth Jost, "Courts & the Law: Scalia v. Dignity," *CQ Weekly*, April 24, 2006, p. 1074.

2. Charles Lane, "Scalia' Refusal Sought in Key Detainee Case," *Washington Post*, March 28, 2006, p. A6; and "The Over-the-Top Justice, *New York Times*, April 2, 2006, section 4, p. 11.

3. Richard Willing, "In Memo, Scalia Stands Ground on Cheney Case," *USA Today*, March 19, 2005, p. A14; "Scalia Defends Involvement in Cheney Case," *Washington Post*, April 13, 2005, p. A6; Ashley Harrell and Pete Bowles, "Proud to be Italian!" *Newsday*, October 11, 2005, p. A14; and Adam Liptak, "Scalia Apologizes for Seizure of Recordings," *New York Times*, April 13, 2006, p. A13.

4. Jeffrey Rosen, "The Dissenter," *New York Times Magazine*, September 23, 2007, at http://select.nytimes.com/preview/2007/09/23/magazine/1154689944149.html; Joan Biskupic, "Sotomayor Keeps Community Bonds Tight," *USA Today*, December 28, 2009, at http://www.usatoday.com/news/washington/judicial/2009-12-28-sotomayor_N.htm?csp=34&utm_source=feedburner&utm_medium=feed&utm_campaign=Feed%3A±UsatodaycomWashington-TopStories±%28News±-±Washington±-±Top±Stories%29; and *Kelo v. City of New London*, 545 U.S. 469 (2005); "Group Seeks Souter Eviction as Protest," *USA Today*, January 21, 2006, at http://www.usatoday.com/news/nation/2006-01-21-souter-home_x.htm.

5. Adam Liptak, "Public Comments by Justices Veer Toward the Political," *New York Times*, March 19, 2006, section 1, p. 22.

6. Gina Holland, "Justice Ginsburg Concerned by Congressional Plan for Court Watchdog," *Associated Press*, May 4, 2006, at www.law.com.

7. Charles Lane, "The High Court Looks Abroad; As Congress Backs Bush Foreign Policy, Justices Voice Qualms," *Washington Post*, November 12, 2005, p. A5; Anne E. Kornblut, "Justice Ginsburg Backs Value of Foreign Law," *New York Times*, April 2, 2005, p. A10; and Joan Biskupic, "High Court Justices Hold Rare Public Debate," *USA Today*, January 14, 2005, p. A3.

8. Joan Biskupic, "Ginsburg: Court Needs Another Woman," *USA Today*, May 5, 2009, at http://www.usatoday.com/news/washington/judicial/2009–05–05-ruthginsburg_N.htm.

9. "Roberts Leading Court in More Media-Friendly Direction," *USA Today*, December 25, 2006, at http://www.usatoday.com/news/washington/2006–12–25-court-open_x.htm; and Tony Mauro, "Glimmers of Greater Openness at Secretive Court," First Amendment Center, October 9, 2006, at http://www.firstamendment center.org/analysis.aspx?id=17509.

10. Anne Gearan, "Rehnquist No Iron Man," *Boston Globe*, May 13, 2004, at http://www.boston.com/news/nation/washington/articles/2004/05/13/rehnquist_no_ iron_man/; "Clarence Thomas: The Justice Nobody Knows," CBS News, September 30, 2007, at http://www.cbsnews.com/stories/2007/09/27/60minutes/ main3305443.shtml; and "Justice Scalia on the Record," CBS News, April 27, 2008, at http://www.cbsnews.com/stories/2008/04/24/60minutes/main4040290.shtml.

11. Tony Mauro, "Souter: Republic is Lost Unless Civic Education Improves," *The National Law Journal*, May 21, 2009, at http://www.law.com/jsp/article.jsp?id= 1202430868164.

12. Matt Sedensky, "Justice Questions Way Court Nominees are Grilled," Associated Press, May 14, 2010, at http://news.yahoo.com/s/ap/20100514/ap_on_re_us/ us_supreme_court_kennedy.

13. Robert Barnes, "High Court: Justices Increasingly Speaking Outside the Classroom," *Washington Post*, April 5, 2010, at http://www.washingtonpost.com/wp-dyn/ content/article/2010/04/04/AR2010040402464.html?nav=rss_politics.

14. Stephanie Condon, "Clarence Thomas: State of the Union Too Partisan for a Justice," CBS News, February 4, 2010, at http://www.cbsnews.com/8301–503544_162– 6174857–503544.html.

15. Linda Greenhouse, "Telling the Court's Story: Justice and Journalism at the Supreme Court," *Yale Law Journal* 105 (April 1996): 1560.

16. Mauro, "Glimmers of Greater Openness at Secretive Court," op cit.

17. Mauro, "Glimmers of Greater Openness at Secretive Court," op cit.

18. Michael C. Dorf, "A TV Appearance by Two Supreme Court Justices Indicates How Much the Court Continues to Value Image Control," *FindLaw*, July 9, 2003, at Tony Mauro, "Glimmers of Greater Openness at Secretive Court," First Amendment Center, October 9, 2006, at http://www.firstamendmentcenter .org/analysis.aspx?id=17509; Joan Biskupic, *Sandra Day O'Connor: How the First Woman on the Supreme Court Became its Most Influential Justice*, New York: Harper Perennial, 2005; and Joan Biskupic, *American Original: The Life and Constitution of Supreme Court Justice Antonin Scalia*, New York: Farrar, Straus and Giroux, 2009, pp. 281–284.

19. See *The Federalist* no. 78, New York: J. & A. McLean, 1788.

20. Nor is this interaction unique to the U.S. Supreme Court. Most national courts issue press statements regarding their decisions. See Jeffrey K. Staton, "Constitutional Review and the Selective Promotion of Case Results," *American Journal of Political Science* 50 (January 2006): 98–112.

21. For a discussion of the Supreme Court's interaction with the press, see Eliot E. Slotnick and Jennifer A. Segal, *Television News and the Supreme Court: All the News That's Fit to Air?*, New York: Cambridge University Press, 1998; Linda

Greenhouse, "Telling the Court's Story," 1537–1561; and Richard Davis, *Decisions and Images: The Supreme Court and the Press*, Englewood Cliffs, N.J.: Prentice Hall, 1994.

22. See David L. Grey, *The Supreme Court and the News Media*, Evanston, Ill.: Northwestern University Press, 1968; Chester A. Newland, "Press Coverage of the United States Supreme Court," *Western Political Quarterly* 19 (March 1964): 15–36; Everette Dennis, "Another Look at Press Coverage of the Supreme Court," *Villanova Law Review* 20 (1974): 765–799.

1. EXTERNAL STRATEGIES

1. Joan Biskupic, *Sandra Day O'Connor: How the First Woman on the Supreme Court Became its Most Influential Justice*, New York: Harper Perennial, 2005, pp. 224–225.
2. For discussion of the attitudinal model, see Jeffrey A. Segal and Harold J. Spaeth, *The Supreme Court and the Attitudinal Model Revisited*, New York: Cambridge University Press, 2002.
3. C. Herman Pritchett, *The Roosevelt Court: A Study in Judicial Politics and Values 1937–1947*, New York: Macmillan, 1949.
4. *Minersville School District v. Gobitis* 310 U.S. 586 (1940) and *West Virginia Board of Education v. Barnette* 319 U.S. 624 (1943).
5. For campaign finance decisions, see *McConnell v. Federal Election Commission*, 540 U.S. 93 (2003) and *Citizens United v. FEC*, January 21, 2010, at http://www.supremecourtus.gov/opinions/09pdf/08-205.pdf. For partial birth abortion decisions, see *Stenberg v. Carhart* 530 U.S. 914 (2000) and *Gonzales v. Carhart*, 550 U.S. 124 (2007).
6. Linda Greenhouse, "Justice Stevens Renounces Capital Punishment," *New York Times*, April 18, 2008, at http://www.nytimes.com/2008/04/18/washington/18memo.html?ex=1366257600&en=4b5dce3ab9f0c476&ei=5124&partner=permalink&exprod=permalink.
7. Quoted in Walter F. Murphy, *Elements of Judicial Strategy*, Chicago: University of Chicago Press, 1964, p. 44.
8. Transcriptions of Conversations between Justice William O. Douglas and Professor Walter F. Murphy, cassette No. 13, December 17, 1962, at http://www.princeton.edu/~mudd/finding_aids/douglas/.
9. *Wirtz v. Hotel Employees*, 391 U.S. 492 (1968).
10. Memo from Hugo L. Black to William O. Douglas, June 3, 1968, Box 398, Hugo LaFayette Black Papers, Manuscript Division, Library of Congress, Washington, D.C.
11. Murphy, *Elements of Judicial Strategy*, pp. 57–58.
12. "Interview with Justice Antonin Scalia," June 19, 2009, C-SPAN, at http://supremecourt.c-span.org/assets/pdf/AScalia.pdf.
13. Transcript of Oral Interview with Jerry N. Hess, October 17, 1972, Tom C. Clark Papers, Tarlton Law Library, University of Texas, Austin, Texas.
14. Joan Biskupic, *American Original: The Life and Constitution of Antonin Scalia*, New York: Farrar, Straus and Groux, 2009, p. 176.
15. Murphy, *Elements of Judicial Strategy*, p. 59.

16. Philippa Strum, *Louis D. Brandeis: Justice for the People*, Cambridge Mass.: Harvard University Press, 1984, pp. 367–368.
17. Murphy, *Elements of Judicial Strategy*, pp. 84–85.
18. Jeffrey Rosen, "The Dissenter," *New York Times Magazine*, September 23, 2007, at http://select.nytimes.com/preview/2007/09/23/magazine/1154689944149.html.
19. Lee Epstein and Jack Knight, "Toward a Strategic Revolution in Judicial Politics: A Look Back, A Look Ahead," *Political Research Quarterly* 53 (September 2000): 625–661.
20. See Lawrence Baum, *Justices and Their Audiences: A Perspective on Judicial Behavior*, Princeton: Princeton University Press, 2006.
21. See Murphy, op cit; and Baum, *Justices and Their Audiences*, op cit. For criticism of the strategic model, see Saul Brenner and Joseph M. Whitmeyer, *Strategy on the United States Supreme Court*, New York: Cambridge University Press.
22. Lee Epstein and Jack Knight, *The Choices Justices Make*, Washington, D.C.: CQ Press, 1998, p. xiii.
23. Murphy, *Elements of Judicial Strategy*, pp. 7–8, 49–78.
24. Murphy, *Elements of Judicial Strategy*, pp. 123–175.
25. Brenner and Whitmeyer, *Strategy on the United States Supreme Court*, pp. 127–135.
26. See, for example, Robert McCloskey, *The American Supreme Court*, Chicago: University of Chicago Press, 1960; David G. Barnum, "The Supreme Court and Public Opinion: Judicial Decision Making in the Post-New Deal Period," *Journal of Politics* 47 (May 1985): 652-667; Thomas R. Marshall, "Public Opinion, Representation, and the Modern Supreme Court," *American Politics Research* 16 (1988): 296–316; and Neal Devins, "The Majoritarian Rehnquist Court?" *Law and Contemporary Problems* 67 (Summer 2004): 63–81.
27. McCloskey, *The American Supreme Court*, p. 224.
28. See, for example, William Leuchtenburg, *The Supreme Court Reborn: The Constitutional Revolution in the Age of Roosevelt*, New York: Oxford University Press, 1995; Stephen K. Shaw, William D. Pederson, and Frank J. Williams, eds., *Franklin D. Roosevelt and the Transformation of the Supreme Court*, Armonk, N.Y.: M.E. Sharpe, 2004; and James McGregor Burns, *Packing the Court: The Rise of Judicial Power and the Coming Crisis of the Supreme Court*, New York: The Penguin Press, 2009, 139–177.
29. Joseph Carroll, "Race and Education 50 Years After Brown v. Board of Education," Gallup News Service, May 14, 2004, at http://www.gallup.com/poll/11686/race-education-years-after-brown-board-education.aspx.
30. *Roe v. Wade* 410 U.S. 113 (1973); and Biskupic, *Sandra Day O'Connor*, pp. 272–274.
31. See William Mishler and Reginald S. Sheehan, "The Supreme Court as a Countermajoritarian Institution? The Impact of Public Opinion on Supreme Court Decisions," *American Political Science Review* 87 (March 1993): 87–101.
32. Letter from Wiley Rutledge to Malcolm E. Rosser, March 9, 1946, Box 137, Wiley Rutledge Papers, Manuscript Division, Library of Congress, Washington, D.C.
33. Barry Friedman, *The Will of the People: How Public Opinion Has Influenced the Supreme Court and Shaped the Meaning of the Constitution*, New York: Farrar, Straus and Giroux, 2009.

34. Friedman, *The Will of the People*, pp. 379–380; Gregory A. Caldiera and James L. Gibson, "The Etiology of Public Support for the Supreme Court," *American Journal of Political Science* 36 (1992): 635–664.

35. For a sample of this discussion, see James W. Stouterborough and Donald P. Haider-Markel, "Public Confidence in the U.S. Supreme Court: A New Look a the Impact of Court Decisions," *The Social Science Journal* 45 (March 2008): 28–47; James L. Gibson, Gregory A. Caldiera, and Lester Kenyatta Spencer, "The Supreme Court and the U.S. Presidential Election of 2000: Wounds, Self-Inflicted or Otherwise?" *British Journal of Political Science* 33 (October 2003): 535–556; and Caldiera and Gibson, op cit.

36. See Anke Grosskopf and Jeffery J. Mondak, "Do Attitudes Toward Specific Supreme Court Decisions Matter? The Impact of *Webster* and *Texas v. Johnson* on Public Confidence in the Supreme Court," *Political Research Quarterly* 51 (September 1998): 633–654; and Gibson, Caldiera, and Spencer. "The Supreme Court and the U.S. Presidential Election of 2000," 535–556.

37. Caldiera and Gibson, "Etiology of Public Support," p. 659.

38. Robert Barnes, "Reactions Split on Obama's Remark, Alito's Response at State of the Union," *The Washington Post*, January 29, 2010, at http://www.washington post.com/wp-dyn/content/article/2010/01/28/AR2010012802893.html?wprss=rss_politics.

39. See R. Kent Newmyer, *John Marshall and the Heroic Age of the Supreme Court*, Baton Rouge: Louisiana State University Press, 2001; and Francis N. Stites, *John Marshall: Defender of the Constitution*, New York: HarperCollins. 1981.

40. R. Kent Newmyer, *The Supreme Court Under Marshall and Taney*, 2d ed. Wheeling, Ill.: Harlan Davidson, Inc., 2006, p. 137; Bernard C. Steiner, *Life of Roger Brooke Taney: Chief Justice of the United States Supreme Court*, Westport, Conn.: Greenwood Press, 1970, p. 390; and Ben W. Palmer, *Marshall and Taney: Statesmen of the Law*, Minneapolis: University of Minnesota Press, 1939, p. 205.

41. Shaw, Pederson, and Williams, *Franklin D. Roosevelt and the Transformation of the Supreme Court*.

42. Baum, *Justices and Their Audiences*, pp. 64–65.

43. Memo from Felix Frankfurter to the Conference, April 14, 1955, Box A120, Tom C. Clark Papers, Tarlton Law Library, University of Texas, Austin.

44. Merlo J. Pusey, *Charles Evans Hughes*, vol. 2, New York: MacMillan, 1951, p. 756.

45. Brenner and Whitmeyer, *Strategy on the United States Supreme Court*, p. 153.

46. For text of the opinion, see U.S. Supreme Court at http://www.supremecourtus.gov/opinions/09pdf/08–205.pdf

47. Joan Biskupic, "Justice Stevens Bemoans Changed Court," *USA Today*, January 22, 2010, at http://www.usatoday.com/news/washington/judicial/supremecourt opinions/2010–01–21–court-analysis_N.htm?csp=34.

48. Biskupic, *Sandra Day O'Connor*, p. 251.

49. Jeffrey Rosen, "The Dissenter," at http://select.nytimes.com/preview/2007/09/23/magazine/1154689944149.html.

50. Philippa Strum, *Louis D. Brandeis: Justice for the People*, Cambridge, Mass.: Harvard University Press, 1984, p. 31.

51. "Justice Harry Blackmun's Papers," National Public Radio, at http://www.npr.org/news/specials/blackmun/#email.

52. Adam Liptak, "Stevens Contemplates Law, and How to Leave It," *New York Times*, April 3, 2010, at http://www.nytimes.com/2010/04/04/us/04stevens.html; Jeffrey Toobin, "After Stevens: What Will the Supreme Court be Like Without Its Liberal Leader?" *The New Yorker*, March 22, 2010, at http://www.newyorker.com/reporting/2010/03/22/100322fa_fact_toobin; and Joan Biskupic, "Justice Stevens Keeps Cards Close to Robe in Supreme Court," *USA Today*, March 12, 2010, at http://www.usatoday.com/news/washington/judicial/2009-10-18-stevens-supreme-court-justice_N.htm.

53. For a discussion of the Greenhouse Effect, see Baum, *Justices and Their Audiences*, pp. 139–145.

54. Baum, *Justices and Their Audiences*, pp. 145–150.

55. Howard Ball, *Hugo L. Black: Cold Steel Warrior*, New York: Oxford University Press, 1996, pp. 149–151; and Alpheus Thomas Mason, *Harlan Fiske Stone: Pillar of the Law*, New York: The Viking Press, 1956, pp. 473–474.

56. E. E. Schattschneider, *The Semisovereign People*, New York: Holt, Rinehart, and Winston, 1960.

57. Joan Biskupic, *American Original*, pp. 221–230.

58. Memorandum to the Court, May 7, 1954, Box 1241, Tom C. Clark Papers, Tarlton Law Library, University of Texas, Austin.

59. Speech to the University of Alabama Law School, March 9, 2010, at http://www.cspan.org/Recent/Supreme-Court-Judiciary.aspx.

60. "Interview with Justice Antonin Scalia," June 19, 2009, C-SPAN, at http://supremecourt.c-span.org/assets/pdf/AScalia.pdf.

61. Bernard Schwartz, *Super Chief: Earl Warren and His Supreme Court – A Judicial Biography*, New York: New York University Press, 1983, pp. 105–106.

62. Francis P. Weisenburger, *The Life of John McLean*, Columbus: Ohio State University Press, 1937, p. 197.

63. *U.S. v. Eichman*, 496 U.S. 310 (1990).

64. Joe Palazzolo, "Bush Tells Federalist Society Judicial Confirmation is Broken," *Legal Times*, November 19, 2007, at http://www.law.com/jsp/article.jsp?id=1195207444309.

65. Box 39, Folder 25, Arthur J. Goldberg Papers, Manuscript Division, Library of Congress, Washington, D.C.

66. Melvin I. Urofsky, ed., *The Douglas Letters: Selections from the Private Papers of Justice William O. Douglas*, Chevy Chase, Md.: Adler & Adler, 1987, p. 312.

67. Richard Davis, *Decisions and Images: The Supreme Court and the Press*, Englewood Cliffs, N.J.: Prentice-Hall, 1994, pp. 119–122.

2. THE PRESSURE TO GO PUBLIC

1. Richard Davis, *Decisions and Images: The Supreme Court and the Press*, Englewood Cliffs, N.J.: Prentice Hall, 1994, p. 113. Souter actually did not hold the traditional press conference when leaving the Court.

2. *The Federalist* no. 78, New York: J. & A. McLean, 1788.

3. Jeffrey Rosen, *The Supreme Court: The Personalities and Rivalries That Defined America*, New York: Times Books, 2006, pp. 5–6.

4. *Korematsu v. United States*, 323 U.S. 214 (1944); *Roe v. Wade*, 410 U.S. 113 (1973); and *Planned Parenthood of Southeastern Pa. v. Casey*, 505 U.S 833 (1992).

5. "C-SPAN Supreme Court Survey," C-SPAN, July 9, 2009, at http://www.c-span .org/pdf/C-SPAN%20Supreme%20Court%20Online%20Survey_070909_6pm .pdf; and "FindLaw's US Supreme Court Awareness Survey," FindLaw, at http:// public.findlaw.com/ussc/122005survey.html.

6. "New National Poll Finds: More Americans Know Snow White's Dwarfs Than Supreme Court Judges, Homer Simpson Than Homer's Odyssey, and Harry Potter Than Tony Blair, Zogby International, April 5, 2010, at http://www.zogby.com/ soundbites/ReadClips.cfm?ID=13498; "Fewer Than a Third of Americans Know Supreme Court Rulings are Final, a New Survey Finds," The Annenberg Public Policy Center of the University of Pennsylvania, September 13, 2007, at http://www.annenbergpublicpolicycenter.org/Downloads/Releases/ Release_ConstitutionDay07/CDaypressrelease_sept_307_version.pdf.

7. "C-SPAN Supreme Court Survey," C-SPAN, July 9, 2009, at http://www.c-span .org/pdf/C-SPAN%20Supreme%20Court%20Online%20Survey_070909_6pm. pdf.

8. Joan Biskupic, "Has the Court Lost Its Appeal?" *Washington Post*, October 12, 1995, p. A23.

9. *Newsweek* Poll, August 4, 1970.

10. Richard Davis, *Electing Justice: Fixing the Supreme Court Nomination Process*, New York: Oxford University Press, 2005, pp. 66–69.

11. For a discussion of the Nixon administration's role in the Fortas resignation, see John W. Dean, *The Rehnquist Choice: The Untold Story of the Nixon Appointment That Redefined the Supreme Court*, New York: Touchstone, 2001.

12. *Newsweek* Poll, May 17–18, 1987; and "High Court to Start Term with Near Decade-High Approval," Gallup, September 9, 2009, at http://www.gallup.com/ poll/122858/High-Court-Start-Term-Near-Decade-High-Approval.aspx.

13. Transcript, Knight-Ridder interview, October 29, 1973, Box 621, William O. Douglas Papers, Manuscript Division, Library of Congress, Washington, D.C.

14. Quoted in David Shaw, *Media Watch*, New York: MacMillan, 1984, p. 120.

15. Quoted in Davis, *Decisions and Images*, p. 103.

16. Davis, *Decisions and Images*, pp. 103–104.

17. Transcript of Lewis Powell press conference, June 26, 1987, Box 575, Thurgood Marshall Papers, Manuscript Division, Library of Congress, Washington, D.C.

18. "Justice Fears for Roe Ruling," *New York Times*, September 14, 1988, p. A24; Stuart A. Taylor, Jr., "Lifting of Secrecy Reveals Earthy Side of Justices," *New York Times*, February 12, 1988, p. A16; Stuart A. Taylor, Jr., "Justice Stevens Is Sharply Critical of Supreme Court Conservatives," *New York Times*, August 5, 1984, p. A1.

19. For a discussion of the political blogosphere, see Matthew Hindman, *The Myth of Digital Democracy*, Princeton: Princeton University Press, 2009; Antoinette Pole, *Blogging the Political: Politics and Participation in a Networked Society*, New York: Routledge, 2009; and Richard Davis, *Typing Politics: The Role of Politics in American Blogs*, New York: Oxford University Press, 2009.

20. "Holding Court: Dahlia Lithwick Dishes with Readers on the Supremes and the Start of a New Term," *Slate*, October 4, 2007, at http://www.slate.com/id/2175318/; and Dahlia Lithwick, "A Supreme Court Case That Puts Scalia and Gay Rights Advocates on the Same Side," *Slate*, April 28, 2010, at http://www.slate.com/id/2252251/.

21. For a discussion of the celebrity culture as it relates to politics, see Darrell M. West and John M. Orman, *Celebrity Politics*, Upper Saddle River, N.J.: Prentice Hall, 2002.

22. Virginia Lamp Thomas, "Breaking Silence," *People*, November 11, 1991, at http://www.people.com/people/archive/article/0,20111251,00.html; Debra Cassens Weiss, "Profs Protest Commencement Address by Justice Clarence Thomas," *ABA Journal*, April 25, 2008, at http://www.abajournal.com/news/article/profs_protest_commencement_address_by_justice_clarence_thomas/; Neil Lewis, "Justice Thomas Declines to Drop Speech to Bar," *New York Times*, June 17, 1998, p. 13.

23. Craig Allen, "News Conferences on TV: Ike-Age Politics Revisited," *Journalism Quarterly* 70 (Spring 1993): 13–25; and Stephen Frantzich, *The C-SPAN Revolution*, Norman: University of Oklahoma Press, 1996.

24. Henry J. Abraham, *Justices, Presidents, and Senators: A History of U.S. Supreme Court Appointments from Washington to Bush II*, 5th ed, Lanham, Md.: Rowman and Littlefield, 2008, p. 177.

25. For discussion of the changed nature of the Supreme Court nomination process post–Robert Bork, see Lee Epstein and Jeffrey A. Segal, *Advice and Consent: The Politics of Judicial Appointments*, New York: Oxford University Press, 2007; Davis, *Electing Justice*, op cit; and John Maltese, *The Selling of Supreme Court Nominees*, Baltimore: Johns Hopkins University Press, 1995.

26. *Estes v. Texas*, 381 U.S. 532 (1965).

27. Melivin I. Urofsky, ed., *The Douglas Letters: Selections from the Private Papers of Justice William O. Douglas*, Chevy Chase, Md.: Adler & Adler, 1987, pp. 64–65.

28. Quoted in Davis, *Decisions and Image*, p. 153.

29. Davis, *Decisions and Images*, p. 150.

30. Urofsky, ed., *The Douglas Letters*, pp. 325–326.

31. Joan Biskupic, *Sandra Day O'Connor: How the First Woman on the Supreme Court Became its Most Influential Justice*, New York: Harper Perennial, 2005, pp. 332–333; and Tony Mauro, "Breyer and Scalia Take Their Road Show Inside," *The National Law Journal*, March 24, 2010, at http://www.law.com/jsp/scm/PubArticleSCM.jsp?id=1202446761287&Breyer_and_Scalia_Take_Their_Road_Show_Inside.

32. "Interview with Justice Ruth Bader Ginsburg," July 1, 2009, C-SPAN, at http://supremecourt.c-span.org/assets/pdf/RBGinsburg.pdf. "Supreme Court Justice Stephen Breyer Interview," *CNN Larry King Live*, November 23, 2005, at http://transcripts.cnn.com/TRANSCRIPTS/0511/23/lkl.01.html.

33. "Interview with Justice Antonin Scalia," June 19, 2009, C-SPAN, at http://supremecourt.c-span.org/assets/pdf/AScalia.pdf.

34. See www.charlierose.com; and "Nightline Online: Chief Justice," *ABC News Nightline*, November 14, 2006, at http://abcnews.go.com/Nightline/video?id=2651301.

35. Joan Biskupic, *American Original: The Life and Constitution of Supreme Court Justice Antonin Scalia*, New York: Farrar, Straus and Giroux, 2009, p. 131.
36. "Justice Antonin Scalia," C-SPAN, May 4, 2008, at http://www.q-and-a.org/Transcript/?ProgramID=1178.

3 THE EARLY YEARS

1. Bernard Schwartz, *A History of the Supreme Court*, New York: Oxford University Press, 1993, pp. 15–18; *The Documentary History of the Supreme Court of the United States, 1789–1800*, New York: Columbia University Press, 1985, pp. 685–692.
2. Leon Friedman and Fred L Israel, *The Justices of the United States Supreme Court: Their Lives and Major Opinions*, New York: Chelsea House Publishers, 1969, p. 10.
3. Jean Edward Smith, *John Marshall: Definer of a Nation*, New York: Henry Holt, 1996, p. 325.
4. Smith, *John Marshall: Definer of a Nation*, p. 477.
5. David Loth, *John Marshall and the Growth of the Republic*, New York: W.W. Norton & Company, 1949, p. 158; Francis N. Stites, *John Marshall: Defender of the Constitution*, New York: HarperCollins, 1981, p. 80; and David Robarge, *A Chief Justice's Progress: John Marshall from Revolutionary Virginia to the Supreme Court*, Westport, Conn.: Greenwood Press, 2000, p. 249.
6. George Van Santvoord and William M. Scott, *Sketches of the Lives, Times and Judicial Services of the Chief Justices of the Supreme Court of the United States: Jay, Rutledge, Ellsworth, Marshall, Taney, Chase, and Waite*, 2d ed., New York: W.C. Little, 1882, pp. 8–105.
7. Henry J. Abraham, *Justices, Presidents, and Senators: A History of U.S. Supreme Court Appointments from Washington to Bush II*, 5th ed, Lanham, Md.: Rowman and Littlefield, 2008, pp. 59–61.
8. Smith, *John Marshall: Definer of a Nation*, p. 402.
9. Clare Cushman, ed., *The Supreme Court Justices: Illustrated Biographies 1789–1993*, Washington: CQ Press, 1993, pp. 22–23; Henry J. Abraham, *Justices, Presidents, and Senators: A History of U.S. Supreme Court Appointments from Washington to Bush II*, 5th ed, Lanham, Md.: Rowman and Littlefield, 2008, pp. 58–64; and Henry Flanders, *The Lives and Times of the Chief Justices of the Supreme Court of the United States*, vol. 2, rev. ed., New York: J. Cockcroft, 1875, pp. 124–132.
10. Schwartz, *A History of the Supreme Court*, pp. 7–11.
11. Peter Charles Hoffer et al, *The Supreme Court: An Essential History*, Lawrence: University Press of Kansas, 2007, p. 33.
12. Schwartz, *A History of the Supreme Court*, p. 18.
13. Schwartz, *A History of the Supreme Court*, pp. 18–19; Julius Goebel, Jr., *History of the Supreme Court of the United States: Volume I, Antecedents and Beginnings to 1801*, New York: Macmillan Co., 1971, pp. 552–556.
14. William R. Casto, *The Supreme Court in the Early Republic: The Chief Justiceships of John Jay and Oliver Ellsworth*, Columbia: University of South Carolina Press, 1995, p. 74; G. Edward White, "Recovering the World of the Marshall Court," *The John Marshall Law Review* 33 (2000): 785–787; Todd Estes, *The Jay Treaty*

Debate, Public Opinion, and the Evolution of Early American Political Culture, Amherst: University of Massachusetts Press, 2006, pp. 73–78; and William Garrot Brown, *The Life of Oliver Ellsworth*, New York: Da Capo Press, 1970, pp. 280–310.

15. Casto, *The Supreme Court in the Early Republic*, pp. 78–179.

16. Gerald T. Dunne, *Justice Joseph Story and the Rise of the Supreme Court*, New York: Simon and Schuster, 1970, p. 281; Stites, *John Marshall: Defender of the Constitution*, p. 152.

17. Walter Stahr, *John Jay: Founding Father*, London: Hambledon and London, 2005, p. 285.

18. Frank Monaghan, *John Jay: Defender of Liberty*, New York: Bobbs-Merrill, 1935, pp. 330–331.

19. Jane Shaffer Elsmere, *Justice Samuel Chase*, Muncie, Ind.: Janevar Publishing Company, 1980, pp. 128–129.

20. Casto, *The Supreme Court in the Early Republic*, p. 165; and James Haw and Francis F. Bierne, *Stormy Patriot: The Life of Samuel Chase*, Baltimore: Maryland Historical Society, 1980, pp. 207–208.

21. Dunne, *Justice Joseph Story and the Rise of the Supreme Court*, pp. 281–282.

22. Schwartz, *A History of the Supreme Court*, p. 16; and Loth, *John Marshall and the Growth of the Republic*, pp. 294–295.

23. Letter from Thomas Jefferson to Judge Spencer Roane, September 6, 1819, Electronic Text Center, University of Virginia Library, at http://etext.virginia .edu/etcbin/toccer-new2?id=JefLett.sgm&images=images/modeng&data=/texts/ english/modeng/parsed&tag=public&part=255&division=div1.

24. Ben W. Palmer, *Marshall and Taney: Statesmen of the Law*, Minneapolis: University of Minnesota Press, p. 125.

25. Stites, *John Marshall: Defender of the Constitution*, p. 132.

26. Scott Douglas Gerber, *Seriatim: The Supreme Court Before John Marshall*, New York: New York University Press, 1998, pp. 210–211.

27. R. Kent Newmyer, *John Marshall and the Heroic Age of the Supreme Court*, Baton Rouge: Louisiana State University Press, 2001, p. 295.

28. Stites, *John Marshall: Defender of the Constitution*, p. 90.

29. Robarge, *A Chief Justice's Progress*, pp. 268–269.

30. Stites, *John Marshall: Defender of the Constitution*, pp. 121, 132–133, and 135.

31. Newmyer, *John Marshall and the Heroic Age of the Supreme Court*, pp. 335–337; and Donald G. Morgan, *Justice William Johnson: The First Dissenter*, Columbia: University of South Carolina Press, 1954, p. 171.

32. Newmyer, *John Marshall and the Heroic Age of the Supreme Court*, pp. 338, 340.

33. Palmer, *Marshall and Taney: Statesmen of the Law*, pp. 126–127.

34. Robarge, *A Chief Justice's Progress*, pp. 288–289.

35. Casto, *The Supreme Court in the Early Republic*, p. 122.

36. F. Thornton Miller, "John Marshall in Spencer Roane's Virginia: The Southern Constitutional Opposition to the Marshall Court," *The John Marshall Law Review* 33 (2000): 1131.

37. Elsmere, *Justice Samuel Chase*, pp. 122–123; and Casto, *The Supreme Court in the Early Republic*, pp. 166–167.

38. Haw and Bierne, *Stormy Patriot*, 215.

39. Haw and Bierne, *Stormy Patriot*, p. 206.

40. Haw and Bierne, *Stormy Patriot*, p. 243.

41. Dunne, *Justice Joseph Story and the Rise of the Supreme Court*, pp. 298–299.

42. George Van Santvoord, *Lives, Times, and Judicial Services of the Chief-Justices of the Supreme Court of the United States*, Albany: Weare C. Little & Co., 1882, p. 205.

43. Van Santvoord, *Lives, Times, and Judicial Services*, p. 188.

44. Robarge, *A Chief Justice's Progress*, p. 279.

45. Stites, *John Marshall: Defender of the Constitution*, pp. 120, 135.

46. Smith, *John Marshall: Definer of a Nation*, p. 386.

47. Smith, *John Marshall: Definer of a Nation*, p. 419.

48. Smith, *John Marshall: Definer of a Nation*, p. 493.

49. Brown, *The Life of Oliver Ellsworth*, p. 239.

50. Brown, *The Life of Oliver Ellsworth*, p. 239.

51. Smith, *John Marshall: Definer of a Nation*, pp. 451–452.

52. Elsmere, *Justice Samuel Chase*, p. 113.

53. Stites, *John Marshall: Defender of the Constitution*, p. 152.

54. Edward S. Corwin, *John Marshall and the Constitution*, New Haven, Conn.: Yale University Press, 1919, p. 214.

55. Quoted in Smith, *John Marshall: Definer of a Nation*, p. 501.

56. Charles F. Hobson, "Editing Marshall," *The John Marshall Law Review* 33 (2000): 857.

57. John R. Cuneo, *John Marshall: Judicial Statesman*, New York: McGraw-Hill, 1975, p. 125.

58. Corwin, *John Marshall and the Constitution*, p. 183.

59. Palmer, *Marshall and Taney: Statesmen of the Law*, p. 127.

60. Stites, *John Marshall: Defender of the Constitution*, p. 135.

61. Smith, *John Marshall: Definer of a Nation*, p. 385.

62. Smith, *John Marshall: Definer of a Nation*, p. 448.

63. Haw and Bierne, *Stormy Patriot*, p. 252.

64. Robarge, *A Chief Justice's Progress*, pp. 259–260.

65. Dunne, *Justice Joseph Story and the Rise of the Supreme Court*, p. 282.

66. Miller, "John Marshall in Spencer Roane's Virginia," 1131.

67. Elsmere, *Justice Samuel Chase*, pp. 199–201.

68. Robarge, *A Chief Justice's Progress*, p. 269.

69. Loth, *John Marshall and the Growth of the Republic*, p. 174.

70. Charles F. Hobson, *The Great Chief Justice: John Marshall and the Rule of Law*, Lawrence: University Press of Kansas, 1996, p. 125.

71. Smith, *John Marshall: Definer of a Nation*, p. 493.

72. Robarge, *A Chief Justice's Progress*, p. 301; Hobson, *The Great Chief Justice*, pp. 176–177; and Stites, *John Marshall: Defender of the Constitution*, pp. 162–163.

73. Donald G. Morgan, *Justice William Johnson: The First Dissenter*, Columbia: University of South Carolina Press, 1954, p. 177, 185.

74. Robarge, A *Chief Justice's Progress*, p. 288.
75. Casto, *The Supreme Court in the Early Republic*, pp. 306–307, 310.
76. Frank Monaghan, *John Jay: Defender of Liberty*, New York: Bobbs-Merrill, 1935, p. 315.
77. Monaghan, *John Jay: Defender of Liberty*, p. 315.
78. Elsmere, *Justice Samuel Chase*, p. 164.
79. Richard B. Morris, *John Jay, The Nation and The Court*, Boston: Boston University Press, 1967, pp. 80–81; John E. O'Connor, *William Paterson: Lawyer and Statesman*, New Brunswick, N.J.: Rutgers University Press, 1979, p. 245; and Casto, *The Supreme Court in the Early Republic*, pp. 75, 128.
80. Quoted in Casto, *The Supreme Court in the Early Republic*, p. 128.
81. Monaghan, *John Jay: Defender of Liberty*, p. 315.
82. Stephen B. Presser, "The Verdict on Samuel Chase and His 'Apologist,'" in Gerber, ed., *Seriatim: The Supreme Court Before John Marshall*, p. 267; Casto, *The Supreme Court in the Early Republic*, pp. 165–166; and Elsmere, *Justice Samuel Chase*, p. 162.
83. Elsmere, *Justice Samuel Chase*, pp. 162–163; Robarge, A *Chief Justice's Progress*, p. 270; and Hobson, *The Great Chief Justice*, p. 50.
84. O'Connor, *William Paterson: Lawyer and Statesman*, pp. 239–241, 259; and Casto, *The Supreme Court in the Early Republic*, p. 179.
85. Stites, *John Marshall: Defender of the Constitution*, pp. 132–133; Newmyer, *John Marshall and the Heroic Age of the Supreme Court*, pp. 337–347; Robarge, A *Chief Justice's Progress*, pp. 286–287; and Corwin, *John Marshall and the Constitution*, p. 183.
86. Smith, *John Marshall: Definer of a Nation*, p. 452.
87. Willis P. Whichard, "James Iredell," in Gerber, ed., *Seriatim: The Supreme Court Before John Marshall*, p. 210; and G. Edward White, "Recovering the World of the Marshall Court," *The John Marshall Law Review* 33 (2000): 785–787.
88. Walter Stahr, *John Jay: Founding Father*, London: Hambledon and London, 2005, pp. 306–307.
89. Newmyer, *John Marshall and the Heroic Age of the Supreme Court*, p. 339.
90. Newmyer, *John Marshall and the Heroic Age of the Supreme Court*, p. 339.
91. Newmyer, *John Marshall and the Heroic Age of the Supreme Court*, p. 342.
92. Casto, *The Supreme Court in the Early Republic*, p. 150.
93. Casto, *The Supreme Court in the Early Republic*, pp. 152–153.
94. Haw and Bierne, *Stormy Patriot*, p. 192.
95. Haw and Bierne, *Stormy Patriot*, pp. 206–207.
96. Elsmere, *Justice Samuel Chase*, pp. 164–165.
97. See Milton Lomask, *Aaron Burr: The Conspiracy and Years of Exile 1805–1836*, New York: Farrar, Straus and Giroux, 1982; and Newmyer, *John Marshall and the Heroic Age of the Supreme Court*, p. 191.
98. Newmyer, *John Marshall and the Heroic Age of the Supreme Court*, p. 183.
99. Newmyer, *John Marshall and the Heroic Age of the Supreme Court*, p. 191.
100. Newmyer, *John Marshall and the Heroic Age of the Supreme Court*, p. 191.
101. Cuneo, *John Marshall: Judicial Statesman*, pp. 112–114; and Smith, *John Marshall: Definer of a Nation*, p. 373.

4. THE NINETEENTH CENTURY

1. Albert J. Beveridge, *The Life of John Marshall*, vol. IV, New York: Houghton Mifflin, 1919, pp. 589–591.
2. Quoted in George Van Santvoord, *Sketches of the Lives and Judicial Services of the Chief-Justices of the Supreme Court of the United States*, New York: Charles Scribner, 1854, p. 453.
3. Quoted in Beveridge, *The Life of John Marshall*, p. 589
4. See Richard L. Rubin, *Press, Party, and Presidency*. New York: W.W. Norton, 1981; and Culver Smith, *The Press, Politics, and Patronage: The American Government's Use of Newspapers 1789–1875*, Athens: University of Georgia Press, 1977.
5. See Michael Schudson, *Discovering the News*, New York: Basic Books, 1978.
6. W. Stephen Belko, *The Invincible Duff Green: Whig of the West*, Columbia: University of Missouri Press, 2006, p. 178.
7. Belko, *Invincible Duff Green* p. 178.
8. Robert C. Williams, *Horace Greeley: Champion of American Freedom*, New York: New York University Press, 2006.
9. David Healy, *James G. Blaine & Latin America*, Columbia: University of Missouri Press, 2001, pp. 1–16.
10. Francis P. Weisenburger, *The Life of John McLean*, Columbus: Ohio State University Press, 1937, pp. 6–7, 12–13.
11. Donald Malcolm Roper, *Mr. Justice Thompson and the Constitution*, New York: Garland Publishing Inc., 1987, p. 235; and Donald Grier Stephenson, Jr., *The Waite Court: Justices, Rulings, and Legacy*, Santa Barbara, Calif.: ABC-CLIO, 2003, p. 123.
12. James W. Ely, Jr., *The Chief Justiceship of Melville W. Fuller, 1888–1910*, Columbia: University of South Carolina Press, 1995, p. 5.
13. Clare Cushman, ed., "Melville W. Fuller 1888–1910," in *The Supreme Court Justices*, Washington: CQ Press, 1995, pp. 246–247.
14. Wirt Armistead Cate, *Lucius Q. C. Lamar: Secession and Reunion*, New York: Russell and Russell, 1935, pp. 101–102.
15. John Niven, *Salmon P. Chase: A Biography*, New York: Oxford University Press, 1995, p. 9.
16. Niven, *Salmon P. Chase: A Biography*, p. 34
17. Niven, *Salmon P. Chase: A Biography*, pp. 93, 117; and Albert Bushnell Hart, *Salmon Portland Chase*, Boston: Houghton Mifflin and Company, 1899, pp. 61–62.
18. Niven, *Salmon P. Chase: A Biography*, p. 117.
19. Niven, *Salmon P. Chase: A Biography*, p. 204.
20. Niven, *Salmon P. Chase: A Biography*, p. 113.
21. John Niven et al., eds, *The Salmon P. Chase Papers*, vol. 1, Kent, Ohio: Kent State University Press, 1993, p. 707.
22. Bushnell Hart, *Salmon Portland Chase*, pp. 138–139.
23. Bushnell Hart, *Salmon Portland Chase*, p. 179.
24. Clare Cushman, ed., "Melville W. Fuller 1888–1910,' pp. 246–247.

25. G. Edward White, *The American Judicial Tradition*, 3rd ed., New York: Oxford University Press, 2007, p. 107.

26. Grier Stephenson, Jr., *The Waite Court: Justices, Rulings, and Legacy*, p. 74.

27. Stephenson, *The Waite Court: Justices, Rulings, and Legacy*, p. 14.

28. Alexander A. Lawrence, *James Moore Wayne, Southern Unionist*, Chapel Hill: University of North Carolina Press, 1943, pp. 210–211.

29. Bruce R. Trimble, *Chief Justice Waite: Defender of the Public Interest*, Princeton: Princeton University Press, 1938, p. 141.

30. Frederick J. Blue, *Salmon P. Chase: A Life in Politics*, Kent, Ohio: Kent State University Press, 1987, pp. 247–282.

31. Trimble, *Chief Justice Waite: Defender of the Public Interest*, pp. 140–142.

32. Blue, *Salmon P. Chase: A Life in Politics*, pp. 281–287.

33. Letter to Mr. Grannis, November 11, 1888, Melville Fuller Papers, Chicago Historical Society, Box 4, Folder 31.

34. Trimble, *Chief Justice Waite: Defender of the Public Interest*, p. 147.

35. Trimble, *Chief Justice Waite: Defender of the Public Interest*, p. 293.

36. Letter to Grover Cleveland, March 12, 1891, Melville Fuller Papers, Chicago Historical Society, Box 5, Folder 37; and Letter to Grover Cleveland, May 4, 1892, Melville Fuller Papers, Chicago Historical Society, Box 5, Folder 39.

37. J. W. Schuckers, *The Life and Public Services of Salmon Portland Chase*, New York: D. Appleton and Company, 1874, pp. 563–564.

38. Willard L. King, *Lincoln's Manager David Davis*, Cambridge, Mass.: Harvard University Press, 1960, p. 277; and Blue, *Salmon P. Chase: A Life in Politics*, p. 320.

39. Blue, *Salmon P. Chase: A Life in Politics*, p. 247.

40. Blue, *Salmon P. Chase: A Life in Politics*, pp. 284, 286.

41. Schuckers, *The Life and Public Services of Salmon Portland Chase*, pp. 579–580.

42. Schuckers, *The Life and Public Services of Salmon Portland Chase*, pp. 582–583.

43. Blue, *Salmon P. Chase: A Life in Politics*, pp. 288–291.

44. Schuckers, *The Life and Public Services of Salmon Portland Chase*, pp. 588–589.

45. R. Kent Newmyer, *The Supreme Court Under Marshall and Taney*, 2d ed., Wheeling, Ill.: Harlan Davidson, Inc., 2006, p. 140; and Carl B. Swisher, *Roger B. Taney*, New York: Macmillan, 1935, pp. 491–492.

46. Francis P. Weisenburger, *The Life of John McLean*, Columbus: Ohio State University Press, 1937, pp. 69–70, 75–76, 84, 103–104, 135–137.

47. Weisenburger, *The Life of John McLean*, pp. 124–125.

48. Weisenburger, *The Life of John McLean*, p. 197.

49. Newmyer, *The Supreme Court Under Marshall and Taney*, pp. 491–492.

50. Henry G. Connor, *John Archibald Campbell*, New York: Da Capo Press, 1971, p. 109.

51. King, *Lincoln's Manager David Davis*, p. 272.

52. King, *Lincoln's Manager David Davis*, pp. 278–279.

53. King, *Lincoln's Manager David Davis*, p. 281.

54. King, *Lincoln's Manager David Davis*, pp. 282–283.

55. Swisher, *Roger B. Taney*, pp. 283–299; and Charles Fairman, *Mr. Justice Miller and the Supreme Court 1862–1890*, Cambridge, Mass.: Harvard University Press, 1939, pp. 297–298.

56. Quoted in Swisher, *Roger B. Taney,* pp. 284–285.

57. Carl Brent Swisher, *Stephen J. Field, Craftsman of the Law,* Washington, D.C.: The Brookings Institution, 1930, p. 269.

58. Swisher, *Stephen J. Field, Craftsman of the Law,* p. 295.

59. Swisher, *Stephen J. Field, Craftsman of the Law,* pp. 288–289.

60. Swisher, *Stephen J. Field, Craftsman of the Law,* pp. 296–297.

61. Swisher, *Stephen J. Field, Craftsman of the Law,* p. 298.

62. Swisher, *Stephen J. Field, Craftsman of the Law,* p. 300.

63. Quoted in Swisher, *Stephen J. Field, Craftsman of the Law,* pp. 301–302.

64. Swisher, *Stephen J. Field, Craftsman of the Law,* pp. 304–305.

65. Lawrence, *James Moore Wayne, Southern Unionist,* pp. 158–159.

66. Weisenburger, *The Life of John McLean,* pp. 102–203.

67. Letter to Grover Cleveland, January 2, 1893, Melville Fuller Papers, Chicago Historical Society, Box 6, Folder 41.

68. Weisenburger, *The Life of John McLean,* p. 71.

69. Weisenburger, *The Life of John McLean,* p. 71.

70. Weisenburger, *The Life of John McLean,* p. 77.

71. Lawrence, *James Moore Wayne, Southern Unionist,* p. 174.

72. Lawrence, *James Moore Wayne, Southern Unionist,* p. 173; and Connor, *John Archibald Campbell,* pp. 122–132.

73. Lawrence, *James Moore Wayne, Southern Unionist,* p. 173.

74. King, *Lincoln's Manager David Davis,* pp. 201–203.

75. Quoted in Cate, *Lucius Q. C. Lamar: Secession and Reunion,* p. 487.

76. James B. Murphy, *L. Q. C. Lamar: Pragmatic Patriot,* Baton Rouge: Lousiana State University Press, 1973, pp. 261–262.

77. William D. Bader and Roy M. Mersky, *The First One Hundred Eight Justices,* Buffalo, N.Y.: William S. Hein & Co., Inc, 2004, pp. 55–56.

78. Quoted in Swisher, *Roger B. Taney,* p. 377.

79. Ben W. Palmer, *Marshall and Taney: Statesmen of the Law,* Minneapolis: University of Minnesota Press, 1939, pp. 146–147.

80. Palmer, *Marshall and Taney: Statesmen of the Law,* pp. 222–223.

81. Palmer, *Marshall and Taney: Statesmen of the Law,* pp. 186–187.

82. Palmer, *Marshall and Taney: Statesmen of the Law,* pp. 222–223.

83. Palmer, *Marshall and Taney: Statesmen of the Law,* pp. 253–254.

84. Quoted in Lawrence, *James Moore Wayne, Southern Unionist,* p. 98.

85. Lawrence, *James Moore Wayne, Southern Unionist,* p. 173.

86. Lawrence, *James Moore Wayne, Southern Unionist,* p. 182.

87. King, *Lincoln's Manager David Davis,* pp. 254–256.

88. Quoted in Lawrence, *James Moore Wayne, Southern Unionist,* p. 210.

89. Lawrence, *James Moore Wayne, Southern Unionist,* p. 209.

90. Swisher, *Roger B. Taney,* p. 488.

91. Bernard C. Steiner, *Life of Roger Brooke Taney: Chief Justice of the United States Supreme Court,* Westport, Conn.: Greenwood Press, 1970, pp. 389–390.

92. Newmyer, *The Supreme Court Under Marshall and Taney,* p. 137; and Palmer, *Marshall and Taney: Statesmen of the Law,* p. 205.

93. Bernard C. Steiner, *Life of Roger Brooke Taney,* p. 390.

94. *The Richmond Enquirer*, March 10, 1857. Quoted in Charles W. Smith, Jr., *Roger B. Taney: Jacksonian Jurist*, Chapel Hill: University of North Carolina Press, 1936, p. 174.

95. Palmer, *Marshall and Taney: Statesmen of the Law*, pp. 206–207.

96. Weisenburger, *The Life of John McLean*, p. 209.

97. See Michael F. Holt, *By One Vote: The Disputed Presidential Election of 1876*, Lawrence: University Press of Kansas, 2008; and William H. Rehnquist, *Centennial Crisis: The Disputed Election of 1876*, New York: Knopf, 2004.

98. Swisher, p. 275.

99. Holt, pp. 229–232; and Swisher, *Stephen J. Field, Craftsman of the Law*, pp. 271–277.

100. Rehnquist, *Centennial Crisis: The Disputed Election of 1876*, p. 164.

101. Swisher, *Stephen J. Field, Craftsman of the Law*, p. 278.

102. Swisher, *Stephen J. Field, Craftsman of the Law*, pp. 278–279.

103. Quoted in Swisher, *Stephen J. Field, Craftsman of the Law*, p. 279.

104. *Chicago Tribune*, March 6, 1877. Quoted in Swisher, *Stephen J. Field, Craftsman of the Law*, pp. 281–282.

105. Schuckers, *The Life and Public Services of Salmon Portland Chase*, pp. 582–583.

106. Niven, *Salmon P. Chase: A Biography*, p. 423.

107. Steiner, *Life of Roger Brooke Taney*, p. 210.

108. King, *Lincoln's Manager David Davis*, p. 263.

109. Niven, *Salmon P. Chase: A Biography*, p. 448

110. Box 50, Morrison Waite Papers, Manuscript Division, Library of Congress, Washington, D.C.

111. Edward Mayes, *Lucius Q. C. Lamar: His Life, Times, and Speeches*, Nashville, Tenn.: AMS Press, 1974, p. 566.

112. King, *Lincoln's Manager David Davis*, p. 262.

113. Trimble, *Chief Justice Waite: Defender of the Public Interest*, pp. 269–270.

114. Fairman, *Mr. Justice Miller and the Supreme Court 1862–1890*, p. 278.

115. Fairman, *Mr. Justice Miller and the Supreme Court 1862–1890*, p. 300.

116. Fairman, *Mr. Justice Miller and the Supreme Court 1862–1890*, p. 288.

117. Steiner, *Life of Roger Brooke Taney*, p. 206

118. Letter from John Marshall Harlan, May 11, 1888, Melville Fuller Papers, Chicago Historical Society, Box 4, Folder 30.

119. Connor, *John Archibald Campbell*, pp. 102–103.

120. Weisenburger, *The Life of John McLean*, pp. 156–157.

121. Weisenburger, *The Life of John McLean*, pp. 193.

122. Weisenburger, *The Life of John McLean*, pp. 124–125, 140–141.

123. John P. Frank, *Justice Daniel Dissenting: A Biography of Peter V. Daniel, 1784–1860*, Cambridge, Mass.: Harvard University Press, 1964, p. 257

124. Newmyer, *The Supreme Court Under Marshall and Taney*, p. 136.

125. *Chicago Tribune*, December 2, 1888, Melville Fuller Papers, Chicago Historical Society, Box 4, Folder 31.

126. Lawrence, *James Moore Wayne, Southern Unionist*, pp. 152–153.

127. Swisher, *Roger B. Taney*, pp. 488–489.

128. Swisher, *Roger B. Taney*, pp. 489–490.

129. *Justice George Shiras, Jr. of Pittsburgh*, Pittsburgh Pa.: University of Pittsburgh Press, 1953, pp. 169–171, 180.

130. *Nashville American*, April 8, 1895, Melville Fuller Papers, Chicago Historical Society, Box 6, Folder 46.

131. Mayes, *Lucius Q.C. Lamar: His Life, Times, and Speeches*, p. 550.

132. Niven, *Salmon P. Chase: A Biography*, p. 385.

133. Trimble, *Chief Justice Waite: Defender of the Public Interest*, pp. 276–277.

134. Mayes, *Lucius Q. C. Lamar: His Life, Times, and Speeches*, p. 490.

135. Fairman, *Mr. Justice Miller and the Supreme Court 1862–1890*, pp. 286–287.

136. Fairman, *Mr. Justice Miller and the Supreme Court 1862–1890*. p. 287.

5. THE TWENTIETH CENTURY

1. Merlo J. Pusey, *Charles Evans Hughes*, vol. 1, New York: MacMillan, 1951, p. 239.

2. Alpheus Thomas Mason, *Harlan Fiske Stone: Pillar of the Law*, New York: The Viking Press, 1956, pp. 262–289.

3. March 11, 1952, Diary entry, Box 2, Reel 3, Harold H. Burton Papers, Manuscript Division, Library of Congress, Washington, D.C.

4. Letter from Hugo L. Black to Sherman Minton, December 13, 1948, Box 61, Hugo LaFayette Black Papers, Manuscript Division, Library of Congress, Washington, D.C.

5. Box 2, Reel 3, Harold H. Burton Papers, Manuscript Division, Library of Congress, Washington, D.C.

6. William Howard Taft to George Sutherland, July 7, 1925, and William Howard Taft to George Sutherland, July 25, 1928, Box 4, George Sutherland Papers, Manuscript Division, Library of Congress, Washington, D.C.

7. Letter from Horace H. Lurton to Horace Van Deventer, December 3, 1910, Box 1, Horace H. Lurton Papers, Manuscript Division, Library of Congress, Washington, D.C.

8. Pusey, *Charles Evans Hughes*, vol. 1, pp. 273–274.

9. Samuel Hendel, *Charles Evans Hughes and the Supreme Court*, New York: King's Crown Press, 1951, p. 68.

10. Pusey, *Charles Evans Hughes*, vol. 1, p. 316.

11. Pusey, *Charles Evans Hughes*, vol. 1, pp. 316–325.

12. Pusey, *Charles Evans Hughes*, vol. 1, p. 329.

13. Quoted in Hendel, *Charles Evans Hughes and the Supreme Court*, p. 69.

14. Quoted in Pusey, *Charles Evans Hughes*, vol. 1, p. 332.

15. Pusey, *Charles Evans Hughes*, vol. 1, p. 267.

16. Mason, *Harlan Fiske Stone*, pp. 402–404.

17. Bruce Allen Murphy, *Wild Bill: The Life and Legend of William O. Douglas*, New York: Random House, 2003, pp. 188–190, 212–230, and 251–265; and Tom Twitty, "Douglas Vice-Presidential Bandwagon Rolling," *New York Herald Tribune*, May 2, 1948.

18. Melvin I. Urofsky, ed., *The Douglas Letters: Selections from the Private Papers of Justice William O. Douglas*, Chevy Chase, Md.: Adler & Adler, 1987, pp. 216, 218.

19. Murphy, *Wild Bill: The Life and Legend of William O. Douglas*, pp. 284–286.
20. Urofsky, ed., *The Douglas Letters*, p. 214.
21. Newspaper clipping of Alsop column "From Cloister to Convention," n.d., Reel 1, Felix Frankfurter Papers, Manuscript Division, Library of Congress, Washington, D.C.
22. Felix Frankfurter, Diary entry, December 30, 1947, and Felix Frankfurter, Diary entry, April 7, 1947, Reel 1, Felix Frankfurter Papers, Manuscript Division, Library of Congress, Washington, D.C.
23. *Hirabayashi v. U.S.*, 320 U.S. 81 (1943); and Murphy, *Wild Bill: The Life and Legend of William O. Douglas*, p. 207.
24. Felix Belair, Jr., "Mr. Truman's Friend – And His Nominee?" *New York Times*, December 16, 1951, p. 185.
25. James E. St. Clair and Linda C. Gugin, *Chief Justice Fred M. Vinson of Kentucky*, Lexington: University Press of Kentucky, 2002, pp. 195–196.
26. Gallup Survey, June 13, 1956.
27. Transcriptions of Conversations between Justice William O. Douglas and Professor Walter F. Murphy, cassette No. 14, April 5, 1963, at http://www.princeton.edu/~mudd/finding_aids/douglas/.
28. Mason, *Harlan Fiske Stone*, pp. 267–268.
29. Transcriptions of Conversations between Justice William O. Douglas and Professor Walter F. Murphy, cassette No. 9, May 23, 1962, at http://www.princeton.edu/~mudd/finding_aids/douglas/; and St. Clair and Gugin, *Chief Justice Fred M. Vinson*, pp. 194–195.
30. Transcript, Arthur J. Goldberg Oral History Interview I, 3/23/83, by Ted Gittinger, Internet Copy, LBJ Library.
31. Transcriptions of Conversations between Justice William O. Douglas and Professor Walter F. Murphy, cassette No. 5, December 27, 1961, at http://www.princeton.edu/~mudd/finding_aids/douglas/.
32. Alpheus Thomas Mason, *Brandeis: A Free Man's Life*, New York: The Viking Press, 1946, p. 536.
33. Mason, *Brandeis: A Free Man's Life*, p. 529.
34. H. N. Hirsch, *The Enigma of Felix Frankfurter*, New York: Basic Books, 1981, pp. 40, 99–126.
35. Bruce Allen Murphy, *Fortas: The Rise and Ruin of a Supreme Court Justice*, New York: William Morrow and Company, Inc., 1988, p. 219.
36. Kim Isaac Eisler, *A Justice for All: William J. Brennan, Jr. and the Decisions That Changed America*, New York: Simon and Schuster, 1993, p. 189.
37. Mason, *Brandeis: A Free Man's Life*, p. 606.
38. Mason, *Harlan Fiske Stone*, pp. 335–336.
39. Hirsch, *Enigma of Felix Frankfurter*, pp. 155, 162, 166.
40. Mary Frances Berry, *Stability, Security, and Continuity: Mr. Justice Burton and Decision-Making in the Supreme Court 1945–1958*, Westport, Conn.: Greenwood Press, 1978, p. 46; and John W. Dean, *The Rehnquist Choice: The Untold Story of the Nixon Appointment that Redefined the Supreme Court*, New York: Touchstone, 2001, pp. 13, 137–138, 181–184.
41. Mason, *Brandeis: A Free Man's Life*, p. 522.
42. Mason, *Harlan Fiske Stone*, p. 265.

43. Mason, *Harlan Fiske Stone*, pp. 267, 270; and Urofsky, ed., *The Douglas Letters*, pp. 224–225.
44. Mason, *Harlan Fiske Stone*, p. 707.
45. Hirsch, *Enigma of Felix Frankfurter*, pp. 99–126
46. Felix Frankfurter, Diary entry, April 8, 1947, Reel 1, Felix Frankfurter Papers, Manuscript Division, Library of Congress, Washington, D.C.
47. St. Clair and Gugin, *Chief Justice Fred M. Vinson*, pp. 197–198.
48. Transcript, Abe Fortas Oral History Interview, 8/14/69, by Joe B. Frantz, Internet Copy, LBJ Library.
49. See Murphy, *Fortas: The Rise and Ruin of a Supreme Court Justice*, op cit.
50. Murphy, *Fortas: The Rise and Ruin of a Supreme Court Justice*, p. 188.
51. Murphy, *Fortas: The Rise and Ruin of a Supreme Court Justice*, pp. 202–203, 235.
52. Transcript, Abe Fortas Oral History Interview, 8/14/69, by Joe B. Frantz, Internet Copy, LBJ Library.
53. Clarinda Pendleton Lamar, *The Life of Joseph Rucker Lamar 1857–1916*, New York: G.P. Putnam's Sons, 1926, pp. 247–265; and Mason, *Harlan Fiske Stone*, 1956, p. 707.
54. William Domnarski, *The Great Justices, 1941–1954: Black, Douglas, Frankfurter, and Jackson in Chambers*, Ann Arbor: University of Michigan Press, 2006, p. 51.
55. Transcript, Earl Warren Oral History Interview I, 9/21/71, by Joe B. Frantz, Internet Copy, LBJ Library.
56. For treatment of the Bork nomination, see Ethan Bronner, *Battle for Justice: How the Bork Nomination Shook America*, New York: W.W. Norton, 1989; Patrick McGuigan and Dawn M. Weyrich, *The Ninth Justice: The Fight for Bork*, Washington, D.C.: Free Congress Research and Education Foundation, 1990; and Michael Pertschuk and Wendy Schaetzel, *The People Rising. The Campaign Against the Bork Nomination*, New York: Thunder Mouth Press, 1989.
57. Philippa Strum, *Louis D. Brandeis: Justice for the People*, Cambridge, Mass.: Harvard University Press, 1984, p. 291.
58. Pusey, *Charles Evans Hughes*, vol. 2, p. 651.
59. Pusey, *Charles Evans Hughes*, vol. 1, p. 279.
60. Fred P. Graham, "Stewarts Tells of Barring His Elevation," *New York Times*, May 28, 1969, p. 36.
61. Laura Kallman, *Abe Fortas: A Biography*, New Haven, Conn.: Yale University Press, 1990, p. 328.
62. Kallman, *Abe Fortas: A Biography*, pp. 337- 338.
63. Kallman, *Abe Fortas: A Biography*, pp. 328–333.
64. Kallman, *Abe Fortas: A Biography*, pp. 342–345.
65. Quoted in Henry J. Abraham, *Justices, Presidents, and Senators: A History of U.S. Supreme Court Appointments from Washington to Bush II*, 5th ed, Lanham, Md.: Rowman and Littlefield, 2008, p. 276.
66. Quoted in Mason, *Brandeis: A Free Man's Life*, p. 470.
67. Mason, *Brandeis: A Free Man's Life*, p. 465.
68. Mason, *Brandeis: A Free Man's Life*, p. 467; and Strum, *Louis D. Brandeis: Justice for the People*, pp. 296–297.
69. See Kenneth W. Goings, *The NAACP Comes of Age: The Defeat of Judge John J. Parker*, Bloomington: Indiana University Press, 1990.

70. Abraham, *Justices, Presidents, and Senators*, pp. 236–237.
71. For a discussion of the Haynsworth and Carswell nominations, see Abraham, *Justices, Presidents, and Senators*, pp. 10–14; and Bruce H. Kalk, "The Carswell Affair: The Politics of a Supreme Court Nomination in the Nixon Administration," *American Journal of Legal History* 42 (July 1988): 261–287.
72. John Anthony Maltese, *The Selling of Supreme Court Nominees*, Baltimore: Johns Hopkins University Press, 1998, p. 14.
73. Quoted in Abraham, *Justices, Presidents, and Senators*, p. 12.
74. "From Obscure to Unknown," *New York Times*, January 21, 1970, p. 46.
75. Gallup Poll, June 22–27, 1967; and Gallup Poll, May 22–27, 1969.
76. See note 56 for Bork nomination. For discussion of the Thomas nomination, see Christopher E. Smith, *Critical Judicial Nominations and Political Change: The Impact of Clarence Thomas*, Westport, Conn.: Praeger, 1994; Jane Meyer and Jill Abramson, *Strange Justice: The Selling of Clarence Thomas*, Boston: Houghton Mifflin, 1994; and Timothy M. Phelps and Helen Winternitz, *Capitol Games: The Inside Story of Clarence Thomas, Anita Hill, and a Supreme Court Nomination*, New York: HarperPerennial, 1993.
77. For a discussion of the evolution of the Court-packing plan, see William E. Leuchtenburg, "The Origins of Franklin D. Roosevelt's 'Court-Packing' Plan," *The Supreme Court Review* (1966): 347–400.
78. Franklin D. Roosevelt, "Fireside Chat on Reorganization of the Judiciary," March 9, 1937, at http://www.mhrcc.org/fdr/chat9.html.
79. Quoted in Barry Friedman, *The Will of the People: How Public Opinion Has Influenced the Supreme Court and Shaped the Meaning of the Constitution*, New York: Farrar, Straus and Giroux, 2009, pp. 3–4.
80. Quoted in Barbara A. Perry and Henry J. Abraham, "Franklin Roosevelt and the Supreme Court: A New Deal and a New Image," in Stephen K. Shaw et al., eds., *Franklin D. Roosevelt and the Transformation of the Supreme Court*, vol. 3, Armonk, N.Y.: M.E. Sharpe, 2004, pp. 25–26.
81. Drew Pearson and Robert Allen, *Nine Old Men*, New York: Doubleday, 1936.
82. Pearson and Allen, *Nine Old Men*, pp. 116, 186.
83. Perry and Abraham, "Franklin Roosevelt and the Supreme Court: A New Deal and a New Image," pp. 30–33; and Gallup Poll, November 13, 1936; and Gallup Poll, February 22, 1937.
84. Mason, *Harlan Fiske Stone*, p. 446.
85. Pusey, *Charles Evans Hughes*, vol. 2, pp. 756.
86. Quoted in Melvin I. Urofsky, *Louis D. Brandeis: A Life*, New York: Pantheon, 2009, p. 717.
87. Pusey, *Charles Evans Hughes*, vol. 2, p. 766.
88. Pusey, *Charles Evans Hughes*, vol. 2, pp. 756–757; and Urofsky, *Louis D. Brandeis: A Life*, pp. 716–718.
89. For an insider's account of Nixon's selection of Supreme Court nominees, see Dean, *The Rehnquist Choice*, op cit.
90. Howard Ball, *Hugo L. Black: Cold Steel Warrior*, New York: Oxford University Press, 1996, p. 94
91. Ball, *Hugo L. Black: Cold Steel Warrior*, p. 96.

92. Box 63, Hugo LaFayette Black Papers, Manuscript Division, Library of Congress, Washington, D.C.

93. Message from R. Rose, Ship Master, to Justice H. L. Black, September 29, 1937, Box 250, Hugo LaFayette Black Papers, Manuscript Division, Library of Congress, Washington, D.C.

94. Box 63, Hugo LaFayette Black Papers, Manuscript Division, Library of Congress, Washington, D.C.

95. Ball, *Hugo L. Black: Cold Steel Warrior*, pp. 149–151; "Quarrel on the High Bench," *The New York Times*, June 12, 1946, p. 26; and Lewis Wood, "Jackson's Attack on Black Stirs Talk of Court Inquiry," *New York Times*, June 12, 1946, p. 1.

96. Letter from Felix Frankfurter to Wiley Rutledge, March 7, 1944, Box 109, Wiley Rutledge Papers, Manuscript Division, Library of Congress, Washington, D.C.

97. Letter from Felix Frankfurter to Wiley Rutledge, May 10, 1945, Box 121, Wiley Rutledge Papers, Manuscript Division, Library of Congress, Washington, D.C.

98. Transcriptions of Conversations between Justice William O. Douglas and Professor Walter F. Murphy, cassette No. 3, December 20, 27, 1961, at http://www.princeton.edu/~mudd/finding_aids/douglas/.

99. Ball, *Hugo L. Black: Cold Steel Warrior*, pp. 12–13.

100. Alexander H. Pekelis, "The Supreme Court Today," *The New Republic*, April 17, 1944, Hugo LaFayette Black Papers, Manuscript Division, Library of Congress, Washington, D.C.

101. Drew Pearson, "Washington Merry-Go-Round," unknown and undated newspaper, Box 26, Robert Houghwout Jackson Papers, Manuscript Division, Library of Congress, Washington, D.C.

102. Edwin A. Lahey, "Black's Threat to Take His Feud with Jackson to Public Revealed," *Washington Star*, June 11, 1946.

103. James E. St. Clair and Linda C. Gugin, *Chief Justice Fred M. Vinson of Kentucky*, Lexington: University Press of Kentucky, 2002, p. 158.

104. St. Clair and Gugin, *Chief Justice Fred M. Vinson*, p. 156.

105. St. Clair and Gugin, *Chief Justice Fred M. Vinson*, pp. 158–160.

106. Mason, *Brandeis: A Free Man's Life*, p. 613.

107. R. L. Duffus, "Brandeis: Crusader at Eighty," *New York Times*, November 8, 1936, p. SM4.

108. G. Edward White, *Oliver Wendell Holmes, Jr.*, New York: Oxford University Press, 2006, p. 114.

109. Murphy, *Wild Bill: The Life and Legend of William O. Douglas*, pp. 336–337.

110. Sandra Day O'Connor speech to the University of Florida Law School, September 9, 2005, at http://www.law.uf.edu/dedication/speechtext.shtml; and Box 1455, Harry A. Blackmun Papers, Manuscript Division, Library of Congress, Washington, D.C.

111. Murphy, *Wild Bill: The Life and Legend of William O. Douglas*, p. 293.

112. Murphy, *Wild Bill: The Life and Legend of William O. Douglas*, pp. 376, 641.

113. Murphy, *Wild Bill: The Life and Legend of William O. Douglas*, pp. 399–400.

114. "Ethics and the Supreme Court," *Los Angeles Times*, October 19, 1966, Box 59, Hugo LaFayette Black Papers, Manuscript Division, Library of Congress, Washington, D.C.

115. Murphy, *Fortas: The Rise and Ruin of a Supreme Court Justice*, pp. 546–556; and Kallman, *Abe Fortas: A Biography*, pp. 322–325.
116. Kallman, *Abe Fortas: A Biography*, p. 365.
117. Murphy, *Fortas: The Rise and Ruin of a Supreme Court Justice*, pp. 556–575; and Kallman, *Abe Fortas: A Biography*, pp. 360–366.
118. Kallman, *Abe Fortas: A Biography*, pp. 370–372.
119. Kallman, *Abe Fortas: A Biography*, pp. 370–372; Dean, *The Rehnquist Choice*, pp. 4–10.
120. Quoted in Kallman, *Abe Fortas: A Biography*, p. 368.
121. Letter from Marvin L. Arrowsmith (Associated Press) to Hugo L. Black, May 20, 1969, Box 59, Hugo LaFayette Black Papers, Manuscript Division, Library of Congress, Washington, D.C.
122. Memorandum to the Conference, November 22, 1966, Box 59, Hugo LaFayette Black Papers, Manuscript Division, Library of Congress, Washington, D.C.
123. Quoted in Murphy, *Wild Bill: The Life and Legend of William O. Douglas*, p. 429.
124. Dean, *The Rehnquist Choice*, pp. 24–26.
125. Murphy, *Wild Bill: The Life and Legend of William O. Douglas*, pp. 433–434.
126. Daniel Seligman, "Revolution, Rant, and Justice Douglas," *Life*, May 1, 1970, Box 59, Hugo LaFayette Black Papers, Manuscript Division, Library of Congress, Washington, D.C.
127. Edwin P. Hoyt, *William O. Douglas*, Middlebury, Vt.: P.S. Eriksson, 1979, pp. 147–148; and Murphy, *Wild Bill: The Life and Legend of William O. Douglas*, pp. 433–434.
128. Hoyt, *William O. Douglas*, pp. 75–76.
129. Urofsky, ed., *The Douglas Letters*, pp. 236–237.
130. Dean, *The Rehnquist Choice*, p. 25.
131. Murphy, *Wild Bill: The Life and Legend of William O. Douglas*, pp. 435–442; and Hoyt, *William O. Douglas*, pp. 147–149.
132. Quoted in Friedman, *The Will of the People*, p. 5.
133. Quoted in Friedman, *The Will of the People*, p. 269.
134. Murphy, *Fortas: The Rise and Ruin of a Supreme Court Justice*, p. 190.
135. Letter from George Sutherland to Glenn Frank, January 16, 1933, Box 7, George Sutherland Papers, Manuscript Division, Library of Congress, Washington, D.C.
136. Letter from Wiley Rutledge to Helen Lamont, February 15, 1946, Box 137, Wiley Rutledge Papers, Manuscript Division, Library of Congress, Washington, D.C.
137. Richard Davis, *Decisions and Images: The Supreme Court and the Press*, Englewood Cliffs, N.J.: Prentice-Hall, 1994, p. 112.
138. Davis, *Decisions and Images: The Supreme Court and the Press*, pp. 111–112.
139. Alpheus Thomas Mason, *Harlan Fiske Stone*, p. 305; Robert M. Mennel and Christine L. Compston, eds., *Holmes and Frankfurter: Their Correspondence, 1912–1934*, Hanover, N.H.: University Press of New England, 1996, p. 216; and Richard A. Posner, ed., *The Essential Holmes: Selections from the Letters, Speeches, Judicial Opinions, and Other Writings of Oliver Wendell Holmes, Jr.*, Chicago: University of Chicago Press, 1992, p. 30.
140. For examples, see Mason, *Harlan Fiske Stone*, p. 593; and Box 151, Harry A. Blackmun Papers, Manuscript Division, Library of Congress, Washington, D.C.

141. Letter from Wiley Rutledge to Hugo L. Black, March 20, 1944, Box 109, Wiley Rutledge Papers, Manuscript Division, Library of Congress, Washington, D.C.

142. Letter from Louis D. Brandeis to Oliver Wendell Holmes, May 18, 1925, and Letter from Louis D. Brandeis to Oliver Wendell Holmes, May 19, 1925, Melvin I. Urofsky and David W. Levy, eds., *Letters of Louis D. Brandeis*, vol. 5, Albany: SUNY Press, 1980; Robert M. Mennel and Christine L. Compston, eds., *Holmes and Frankfurter: Their Correspondence, 1912–1934* Hanover, N.H.: University Press of New England, 1996, pp. 86, 240.

143. Letter from Felix Frankfurter to Tom C. Clark, November 6, 1951, Reel 1, Felix Frankfurter Papers, Manuscript Division, Library of Congress, Washington, D.C.

144. Felix Frankfurter, Diary entry, January 16, 1948, Reel 1, Felix Frankfurter Papers, Manuscript Division, Library of Congress, Washington, D.C.; Box 376, Harold H. Burton Papers, Manuscript Division, Library of Congress, Washington, D.C.; and Letters to David Sarnoff, March 10, 1960, and October 29, 1965, B1041, Tom C. Clark Papers, Tarlton Law School, University of Texas, Austin, Texas.

145. Box 1442, Folder 1, Harry A. Blackmun Papers, Manuscript Division, Library of Congress, Washington, D.C.

146. Burnett F. Anderson, "An Interview with Chief Justice Burger on the Judiciary and the Press," *American Bar Association Journal* 61 (November 1975): 1352–1353.

147. Antonin Scalia, "A Justice Critiques the Press," in Richard Davis, ed., *Politics and the Media*, Englewood Cliffs, N.J.: Prentice Hall, 1994, pp 262–267.

148. Letter to the justices from Felix Frankfurter, November 10, 1944, Box 121, Wiley Rutledge Papers, Manuscript Division, Library of Congress, Washington, D.C.

149. Felix Frankfurter, Diary entry, November 20, 1947, Reel 1, Felix Frankfurter Papers, Manuscript Division, Library of Congress, Washington, D.C.

150. Joan Biskupic, *An American Original: The Life and Constitution of Antonin Scalia*, New York: Sarah Chrichton Books, 2009, pp. 131–132.

151. Letter to William O. Douglas from Hugo L. Black, n.d., Box 59, Hugo LaFayette Black Papers, Manuscript Division, Library of Congress, Washington, D.C.

152. Letter from Wiley Rutledge to John Frank, February 13, 1946, Wiley Rutledge Papers, Manuscript Division, Library of Congress, Washington, D.C.

153. Box 151, Harry A. Blackmun Papers, Manuscript Division, Library of Congress, Washington, D.C.

154. Boxes D177–183, Tom C. Clark Papers, Tarleton Law Library, University of Texas, Austin, Texas.

155. Carl T. Rowan, *Dream Makers, Dream Breakers: The World of Justice Thurgood Marshall*, Boston: Little Brown, 1993, p. 340.

156. Memorandum to the Conference, December 10, 1962, Box 59, Hugo LaFayette Black Papers, Manuscript Division, Library of Congress, Washington, D.C.

157. Laura Kallman, *Abe Fortas: A Biography*, New Haven, Conn.: Yale University Press, 1990, p. 362.

158. Letter from Wiley Rutledge to George K. Gardner, March 13, 1946, Box 137, Wiley Rutledge Papers, Manuscript Division, Library of Congress.

159. Mason, *Harlan Fiske Stone*, p. 391.

160. Letter from Felix Frankfurther to Sherman Minton, October 8, 1953, Felix Frankfurter Papers, Harvard Law School Library; and Mason, *Harlan Fiske Stone*, New York: The Viking Press, 1956, p. 532.

161. Melvin I. Urofsky, *Division and Discord: The Supreme Court Under Stone and Vinson, 1941–1953*, Columbia: University of South Carolina Press, pp. 152–153; Berry, *Stability, Security, and Continuity*, pp. 88–89; and Box 59, Hugo LaFayette Black Papers, Manuscript Division, Library of Congress, Washington, D.C.

162. Urofsky, ed., *The Douglas Letters*, p. 124.

163. Kevin Merida and Michael A. Fletcher, *Supreme Discomfort: The Divided Soul of Clarence Thomas*, New York: Doubleday, 2007, pp. 213, 291–292.

164. Box 151, Folder 10, Harry A. Blackmun Papers, Manuscript Division, Library of Congress, Washington, D.C.; and Box 176, Folder 4, Box 176, Folder 4, Robert Houghwout Jackson Papers, Manuscript Division, Library of Congress, Washington, D.C.

165. Box 176, Folder 4, Box 176, Folder 4, Robert Houghwout Jackson Papers, Manuscript Division, Library of Congress, Washington, D.C.; and Box 151, Folder 10, Harry A. Blackmun Papers, Manuscript Division, Library of Congress, Washington, D.C.

166. Box 1355, Harry A. Blackmun Papers, Manuscript Division, Library of Congress, Washington, D.C.

167. Letter from Harlan Stone to Louis Brandeis, June 23, 1936, Reel 52, Papers of Louis D. Brandeis at the University of Louisville located at Harvard University Law School.

168. Box 127, Folder 11, Robert Houghwout Jackson Papers, Manuscript Division, Library of Congress, Washington, D.C.

169. 343 U.S. 579 (1952); Box 176, Folder 4, Robert Houghwout Jackson Papers, Manuscript Division, Library of Congress, Washington, D.C.

170. Box 363, Hugo LaFayette Black Papers, Manuscript Division, Library of Congress, Washington, D.C.

171. Box 127, Folder 11, Robert Houghwout Jackson Papers, Manuscript Division, Library of Congress, Washington, D.C.

172. "Senate Committee on the Judiciary: S. Hrg. 103–482, Nomination of Ruth Bader Ginsburg to be Associate Justice of the Supreme Court of the United States," 303, GPO Access, at http://www.gpoaccess.gov/congress/senate/judiciary/sh103–482/296–305.pdf.

173. R. W. Apple, Jr., "Justices Are People," *New York Times*, April 10, 1989, p. A1.

174. G. Edward White, *Justice Oliver Wendell Holmes: Law and the Inner Self*, New York: Oxford University Press, 1993, pp. 426–427.

175. Hirsch, *The Enigma of Felix Frankfurter*, p. 152.

176. Eisler, *A Justice for All*, pp. 198–201.

177. Felix Frankfurter, Diary entry, December 30, 1947, Reel 1, Felix Frankfurter Papers, Manuscript Division, Library of Congress, Washington, D.C.

178. Memo from Harlan Stone to Robert Jackson, March 31, 1943, Box 127, Folder 10, Robert Houghwout Jackson Papers, Manuscript Division, Library of Congress, Washington, D.C.

179. Urofsky, ed., *The Douglas Letters*, p. 169.

180. Mason, *Harlan Fiske Stone*, pp. 302–303.

181. Mason, *Harlan Fiske Stone*, pp. 302–303.

182. Felix Frankfurter, Diary entry, December 20, 1947, Reel 1, Felix Frankfurter Papers, Manuscript Division, Library of Congress, Washington, D.C.

183. Memorandum to Conference, April 14, 1955, Box 574, Earl Warren Papers, Manuscript Division, Library of Congress, Washington, D.C.

184. 402 U.S. 1 (1971); and Joan Biskupic, *Sandra Day O'Connor: How the First Woman on the Supreme Court Became Its Most Influential Justice*, New York: Harper Perennial, 2005, p. 246.

185. Transcript, Earl Warren Oral History Interview I, 9/21/71, by Joe B. Frantz, Internet Copy, LBJ Library.

186. Mason, *Harlan Fiske Stone*, pp. 447–455.

187. Berry, *Stability, Security, and Continuity*, pp. 148–150.

188. Berry, *Stability, Security, and Continuity*, p. 153.

189. Urofsky, ed., *The Douglas Letters*, pp. 65–66.

190. Sidney F. Zion, "Justice Black Denies Change in Basic Constitutional Philosophy," *New York Times*, March 21, 1968, p. 43.

191. Letter from Hugo L. Black to William H. Hendrix, October 30, 1937, Box 250, Hugo LaFayette Black Papers, Manuscript Division, Library of Congress, Washington, D.C.

192. Earl C. Behrens, "Frankfurter Won't Say He's Retiring," *San Francisco Chronicle*, July 31, 1953, p. 2.

193. Mason, *Harlan Fiske Stone*, pp. 472–474.

194. Mason, *Harlan Fiske Stone*, pp. 472–473.

195. Mason, *Harlan Fiske Stone*, p. 473.

196. Mason, *Harlan Fiske Stone*, p. 474.

197. Mason, *Harlan Fiske Stone*, p. 474.

198. Mason, *Harlan Fiske Stone*, pp. 476, 701.

199. Box 1441, Folder 5, Harry A. Blackmun Papers, Manuscript Division, Library of Congress, Washington, D.C.

200. Stuart Taylor, Jr., "The Supreme Court; Lifting of Secrecy Reveals Earthy Side of Justices," *New York Times*, February 22, 1988, at http://www.nytimes.com/1988/02/22/us/washington-talk-supreme-court-lifting-secrecy-reveals-earthy-side-justices.html?pagewanted=all?pagewanted=all; and "Three Justices Show Interest in Camera Demonstration," *The News Media & The Law* 13 (Winter 1989): 23–24; and Gallup surveys, August 5–8, 1983; May 17–20, 1985, October 24–27, 1986.

201. Quoted in Davis, *Decisions and Images*, pp. 40–41.

202. Urofsky, *Division and Discord*, p. 17.

203. Mason, *Harlan Fiske Stone*, p. 447.

204. Strum, *Louis D. Brandeis: Justice for the People*, p. 326.

205. Davis, *Decisions and Images*, pp. 118–119.

206. Letter from Felix Franfurter to Hugo L. Black, September 12, 1963, Box 59, Hugo LaFayette Black Papers, Manuscript Division, Library of Congress, Washington, D.C.

207. Mason, *Brandeis: A Free Man's Life*, pp. 141, 465, 605; Letter from Louis D. Brandeis to Rufus Daniel Isaacs, January 8, 1922, and Letter from Louis Brandeis to Elizabeth Brandeis Raushenbush, January 25, 1937, Urofsky and Levy, eds. *Letters of Louis D. Brandeis*, vol. 5, pp. 42–43, 585–586.

208. Felix Frankfurter, Diary entry, December 30, 1947, Reel 1, Felix Frankfurter Papers, Manuscript Division, Library of Congress, Washington, D.C.

209. Letter from Louis Brandeis to Elizabeth Brandeis Raushenbush, January 25, 1937, Urofsky and Levy, eds. *Letters of Louis D. Brandeis*, vol. 5, pp. 585–586.

210. Letter from Louis Brandeis to Elizabeth Brandeis Raushenbush, January 25, 1937, and Letter from Louis D. Brandeis to Rufus Daniel Isaacs, January 8, 1922, Urofsky and Levy, eds. *Letters of Louis D. Brandeis*, vol. 5, pp. 42–43, 585–586.

211. Letter from Joseph Foote to Earl Warren, September 17, 1965, Box 666, Earl Warren Papers, Manuscript Division, Library of Congress, Washington, D.C.

212. Letter from Charlotte G. Moulton to Earl Warren, October 23, 1953, Box 666, Earl Warren Papers, Manuscript Division, Library of Congress, Washington, D.C.

213. Letter from Marquis Childs to Hugo Black, March 9, 1961, Box 23, Hugo LaFayette Black Papers, Manuscript Division, Library of Congress, Washington, D.C.

214. Box 23, Hugo LaFayette Black Papers, Manuscript Division, Library of Congress, Washington, D.C.

215. Letter from Irving Dilliard to Hugo Black, November 15, 1957, Box 25, Hugo LaFayette Black Papers, Manuscript Division, Library of Congress, Washington, D.C.

216. Letter from Hugo L. Black to Irving Dilliard, November 25, 1958, Box 25; and Memo from William Brennan to The Chief Justice, Mr. Justice Black, and Mr. Justice Douglas, December 11, 1959, Box 25, Hugo LaFayette Black Papers, Manuscript Division, Library of Congress, Washington, D.C.

217. "Lewis G. Wood Dies: Veteran Newsman," *New York Times*, June 8, 1953, p. 29.

218. Lewis G. Wood, "Mr. Chief Justice and Mr. Vinson: It is Just a Year Since He Was Named to His High Post and He Is Still the Amiable 'Judge,'" *The New York Times*, June 8, 1947, p. SM11.

219. Memorandum from Bert Whittington, November 6, 1964, Box 39, Hugo LaFayette Black Papers, Manuscript Division, Library of Congress, Washington, D.C.; Anthony Lewis, "The Supreme Court and Its Critics," *Minnesota Law Review* 45 (1961): 305; and Anthony Lewis, "Supreme Court Confidential," *The New York Review of Books*, at http://www.nybooks.com.erl.lib.byu.edu/articles/archives/1980/feb/07/supreme-court-confidential/?page=1.

220. Letter from Anthony Lewis to Hugo L. Black, November 30, 1959, and Memo from Bert Whittingham to Hugo L. Black, December 1, 1959, Box 39, Hugo LaFayette Black Papers, Manuscript Division, Library of Congress, Washington, D.C.

221. Box 23, Hugo LaFayette Black Papers, Manuscript Division, Library of Congress, Washington, D.C.

222. Letter from Raymond Clapper, Scripps-Howard Newspaper reporter, to Hugo L. Black, May 12, 1938, Box 250, Hugo LaFayette Black Papers, Manuscript Division, Library of Congress, Washington, D.C.

223. Letter from Irving Dilliard, *St. Louis Post-Dispatch*, to Louis D. Brandeis, March 16, 1938, Papers of Louis D. Brandeis at the University of Louisville located at Harvard University Law School.

224. Letter from Richard Neuberger to Louis D. Brandeis, March 20, 1937, Reel 53, Papers of Louis D. Brandeis at the University of Louisville located at Harvard University Law School.

225. Box 1355, Folder 12, Harry A. Blackmun Papers, Manuscript Division, Library of Congress, Washington, D.C.

226. Letter from Frank McNaughton, *Time* magazine correspondent, to Robert H. Jackson, June 19, 1943, Box 127, Folder 11, Robert Houghwout Jackson Papers, Manuscript Division, Library of Congress, Washington, D.C.

227. Telegraph from Irving Dilliard to Louis D. Brandeis, February 23, 1938, Papers of Louis D. Brandeis at the University of Louisville located at Harvard University Law School.

228. Davis, *Decisions and Images: The Supreme Court and the Press*, p. 41.

229. Letter from Irving Brant to Hugo L. Black, May 10, 1938, Box 250, Hugo LaFayette Black Papers, Manuscript Division, Library of Congress, Washington, D.C.

230. Hoyt, *William O. Douglas*, p. 59; and Mason, *Brandeis: A Free Man's Life*, p. 620.

231. Mason, *Brandeis: A Free Man's Life*, p. 513; and Letter from Lewis Wood to Robert H. Jackson, June 9, 1944, Box 21, Robert Houghwout Jackson Papers, Manuscript Division, Library of Congress, Washington, D.C.; and various Felix Frankfurter Diary entries, Reel 2, Felix Frankfurter Papers, Manuscript Division, Library of Congress, Washington, D.C.

232. Felix Frankfurter, Diary entry, November 2, 1947, Reel 1, Felix Frankfurter Papers, Manuscript Division, Library of Congress, Washington, D.C.

233. Letter from Frank Kent to Robert H. Jackson, November 25, 1946, Box 15, Robert Houghwout Jackson Papers, Manuscript Division, Library of Congress, Washington, D.C.

234. Letter from W. H. White to Louis Brandeis, October 12, 1936, Reel 52, Papers of Louis D. Brandeis at the University of Louisville located at Harvard University Law School.

235. Letter to Anthony Lewis from Arthur J. Goldberg, May 6, 1963, and Box 34, Letter from Dana Bullen, The *Evening Star*, to Arthur J. Goldberg, July 21, 1964, Box 29, Arthur J. Goldberg Papers, Manuscript Division, Library of Congress, Washington, D.C.

236. Letter from Lewis Wood to Robert H. Jackson, July 27, 1942, Box 21, Robert Houghwout Jackson Papers, Manuscript Division, Library of Congress, Washington, D.C.

237. Letter from Fred W. Friendly, CBS News Executive Producer, to Earl Warren, February 25, 1963, Box 666, Earl Warren Papers, Manuscript Division, Library of Congress, Washington, D.C.

238. Letter from Grover Hall to Hugo L. Black, May 16, 1938, Box 250, Hugo LaFayette Black Papers, Manuscript Division, Library of Congress, Washington, D.C.

239. Letter from Anthony Lewis to Hugo L. Black, March 19, 1955, Box 39, Hugo LaFayette Black Papers, Manuscript Division, Library of Congress, Washington, D.C.

240. Letter from Anthony Lewis to Hugo L. Black, January 3, 1962, Box 39, Hugo LaFayette Black Papers, Manuscript Division, Library of Congress, Washington, D.C.

241. David Margolick, "Phantom News Conference Where Burger Sets the Tone," *New York Times*, February 15, 1984, p. A23.

242. Transcriptions of Conversations between Justice William O. Douglas and Professor Walter F. Murphy, cassette No. 14, April 5, 1963, at http://www.princeton .edu/~mudd/finding_aids/douglas/.

243. Box 1441, Folder 14, Harry A. Blackmun Papers, Manuscript Division, Library of Congress, Washington, D.C.

244. David J. Garrow, "The Brethren: Inside the Supreme Court," *Constitutional Commentary* 18 (Summer 2001): 303.

245. "Watergate Case Newsmen Hailed by Justice Stewart," *New York Times*, May 10, 1973, p. 36.

246. Garrow, "The Brethren: Inside the Supreme Court," 305–306.

247. Garrow, "The Brethren: Inside the Supreme Court," p. 306.

248. David Margolick, "Phantom News Conference Where Burger Sets the Tone," p. A23; and "Reagan's Mr. Right," *Time*, June 30, 1986, at http://www.time.com/ time/magazine/article/0,9171,961645-1,00.html.

249. Quoted in Garrow, "The Brethren: Inside the Supreme Court," p. 306.

250. Quoted in Garrow, "The Brethren: Inside the Supreme Court," p. 307.

251. Potter Stewart Appointment Books, 1977, 1978, 1979, Potter Stewart Papers, Manuscript Division, Sterling Memorial Library, Yale University, New Haven, Conn.; and Garrow, "The Brethren: Inside the Supreme Court," p. 307.

252. Garrow, "The Brethren: Inside the Supreme Court," pp. 309–310.

253. Garrow, "The Brethren: Inside the Supreme Court," p. 317.

254. Quoted in Garrow, "The Brethren: Inside the Supreme Court," pp. 317–318.

255. Box 1441, Folder 3, Harry A. Blackmun Papers, Manuscript Division, Library of Congress, Washington, D.C.

256. Biskupic, *Sandra Day O'Connor*, p. 271.

257. Urofsky, ed., *The Douglas Letters*, pp. 185–186.

258. Urofsky, ed., *The Douglas Letters*, pp. 69–70.

259. Transcriptions of Conversations between Justice William O. Douglas and Professor Walter F. Murphy, cassette No. 4, December 27, 1961, at http://www .princeton.edu/~mudd/finding_aids/douglas/.

260. Transcriptions of Conversations between Justice William O. Douglas and Professor Walter F. Murphy, cassette No. 6, January 18, 1962, at http://www.princeton .edu/~mudd/finding_aids/douglas/.

261. Letter from Felix Frankfurter, to Frank Murphy, January 6, 1947, Felix Frankfurter Papers, Harvard Law School Library.

262. Letter from Felix Frankfurter to Harold H. Burton, May 23, 1953, Box 314, Folder 3, Harold H. Burton Papers, Manuscript Division, Library of Congress, Washington, D.C.

263. Eisler, *A Justice for All*, pp. 154–156.

264. Transcriptions of Conversations between Justice William O. Douglas and Professor Walter F. Murphy, cassette No. 6, January 18, 1962, at http://www.princeton .edu/~mudd/finding_aids/douglas/.

265. Biskupic, *Sandra Day O'Connor*, pp. 297–302.

266. Perry and Abraham, "Franklin Roosevelt and the Supreme Court: A New Deal and a New Image," pp. 18–19.

267. Pearson and Allen, *Nine Old Men*, p. 9.

268. Letter to Louis H. Pollack, June 23, 1966, Box 617, Earl Warren Papers, Manuscript Division, Library of Congress, Washington, D.C.
269. Berry, *Stability, Security, and Continuity*, p. 214.
270. Memorandum for the Brethren from the Chief, April 5, 1965, B 1241, Tom C. Clark Papers, Tarlton Law Library, University of Texas, Austin, Texas.
271. Davis, *Decisions and Images: The Supreme Court and the Press*, pp. 36–37.
272. Urofsky, ed., *The Douglas Letters*, p. 185.
273. Box 151, Folder 3, Harry A. Blackmun Papers, Manuscript Division, Library of Congress, Washington, D.C.
274. Biskupic, *Sandra Day O'Connor*, p. 251.
275. Biskupic, *An American Original*, pp. 137, 218.
276. Hirsch, *The Enigma of Felix Frankfurter*, p. 159.
277. Mason, *Harlan Fiske Stone*, p. 606.
278. Mason, *Harlan Fiske Stone*, p. 611.
279. Rowan, *Dream Makers, Dream Breakers: The World of Justice Thurgood Marshall*, pp. 402–404.
280. Mason, *Harlan Fiske Stone*, p. 468.
281. Letter from Wiley Rutledge to the conference, June 18, 1947, Box 137, Wiley Rutledge Papers, Manuscript Division, Library of Congress, Washington, D.C.
282. Letter from Wiley Rutledge to Felix Frankfurter, June 18, 1947, Box 137, Wiley Rutledge Papers, Manuscript Division, Library of Congress, Washington, D.C.
283. John P. MacKenzie, "The Warren Court and the Press," *Michigan Law Review* 67 (December 1968): 305.
284. Transcriptions of Conversations between Justice William O. Douglas and Professor Walter F. Murphy, cassette No. 12, December 18, 1962, at http://www.princeton.edu/~mudd/finding_aids/douglas/.
285. Strum, *Louis D. Brandeis: Justice for the People*, p. 365.
286. Mason, *Harlan Fiske Stone*, p. 469.
287. Strum, *Louis D. Brandeis: Justice for the People*, p. 368.
288. Biskupic, *American Original*, pp. 140, 219.
289. Biskupic, *American Original*, p. 138.
290. Biskupic, *American Original*, pp. 217, 220.
291. Hirsch, *The Enigma of Felix Frankfurter*, p. 175.
292. See Linda Greenhouse, "High Court Widens Evidence Allowed in Capital Cases," *New York Times*, June 28, 1991, p. A1; and Ruth Marcus, "High Court Ends Term with Conservative Push," *Washington Post*, June 28, 1991, p. A1.
293. Eisler, *A Justice for All*, pp. 182–183.
294. Domnarski, *The Great Justices*, p. 59.
295. Letter from Louis Brandeis to Elizabeth Brandeis Raushenbush, January 25, 1937, Urofsky and Levy, eds. *Letters of Louis D. Brandeis*, vol. 5, pp. 585–586.
296. Strum, *Louis D. Brandeis: Justice for the People*, pp. 375–377.
297. Box 250, Hugo LaFayette Black Papers, Manuscript Division, Library of Congress, Washington, D.C.
298. Letter from Anthony Lewis to Hugo L. Black, November 30, 1959, Box 39, Hugo LaFayette Black Papers, Manuscript Division, Library of Congress, Washington, D.C.

299. Letter from Paul F. Healy to Earl Warren, October 30, 1958, and Letter from Robert Donovan to Earl Warren, September 17, 1957, Box 666, Earl Warren Papers, Manuscript Division, Library of Congress, Washington, D.C.

300. Letter from Duncan Aikman, *New York Times*, to Hugo L. Black, October 26, 1937, Box 250, Hugo LaFayette Black Papers, Manuscript Division, Library of Congress, Washington, D.C.

301. Box 1441, Folder 11, Harry A. Blackmun Papers, Manuscript Division, Library of Congress, Washington, D.C.

302. Harry C. Shriver, ed., *Justice Oliver Wendell Holmes: His Book Notices and Uncollected Letters and Papers*, New York: Da Capo Press, 1973, p. 142.

303. "William O. Douglas, "The Mike Wallace Interview," ABC Television, May 11, 1958, at http://www.hrc.utexas.edu/multimedia/video/2008/wallace/douglas_william_t.html.

304. Letter from Hugo L. Black to Richard S. Salant, CBS News President, December 6, 1968, Box 490, Hugo Lafayette Black Papers, Manuscript Division, Library of Congress, Washington, D.C.; and "CBS News Special: Justice Black and the Bill of Rights" as broadcast over the CBS Television Network, Tuesday, December 3, 1968, 10:00–11:00 P.M. EST, Box 490, Hugo Lafayette Black Papers, Manuscript Division, Library of Congress, Washington, D.C.

305. Letter from Hugo L. Black to William G. Symmers, December 10, 1968, Box 490, Hugo Lafayette Black Papers, Manuscript Division, Library of Congress, Washington, D.C.; and "CBS News Special: Justice Black and the Bill of Rights."

306. "CBS News Special: Justice Black and the Bill of Rights."

307. "CBS News Special: Justice Black and the Bill of Rights."

308. Box 1441, Folder 2, Harry A. Blackmun Papers, Manuscript Division, Library of Congress, Washington, D.C.

309. Box 1441, Folder 6, Harry A. Blackmun Papers, Manuscript Division, Library of Congress, Washington, D.C.

310. Box 1441, Folder 3, Harry A. Blackmun Papers, Manuscript Division, Library of Congress, Washington, D.C.

311. Box 1441, Folder 3, Harry A. Blackmun Papers, Manuscript Division, Library of Congress, Washington, D.C.

312. Box 1441, Folder 3, Harry A. Blackmun Papers, Manuscript Division, Library of Congress, Washington, D.C.

313. "Marshall Says He Never Heard of Bush's Nominee," *New York Times*, July 27, 1990, at http://www.nytimes.com/1990/07/27/us/marshall-says-he-never-heard-of-bush-s-nominee.html?pagewanted=1.

314. Mason, *Brandeis: A Free Man's Life*, pp. 620–621.

315. Margolick, "Phantom News Conference Where Burger Sets the Tone," p. A23.

316. Tony Mauro, "No Retirement Press Conference for Justice Souter," May 5, 2009, at http://www.law.com/jsp/scm/PubArticleSCM.jsp?id=1202430428707; "The Law: Chief Justice in Mufti," *Time*, April 19, 1976, at http://www.time .com/time/magazine/article/0,9171,914092,00.html; and Linda Greenhouse, "Rehnquist, in Rare Plea, Urges Raises for Judges," *New York Times*, March 16, 1989, at http://www.nytimes.com/1989/03/16/us/rehnquist-in-rare-plea-urges-raise-for-judges.html?pagewanted=1.

317. Murphy, *Wild Bill: The Life and Legend of William O. Douglas*, p. 485.

6. BECOMING NEWSWORTHY

1. Edward Smith, "Disappearing Act," *State Legislatures* 35 (May 2009): 26–31.
2. Richard Davis, *Electing Justice: Fixing the Supreme Court Nomination Process,* New York: Oxford University Press, 2005, p. 68.
3. Denis Steven Rutkus, "Supreme Court Appointment Process: Roles of the President, Judiciary Committee, and Senate," CRS Report for Congress, Congressional Research Service, Library of Congress, February 19, 2010, at http://www.fas.org/sgp/crs/misc/RL31989.pdf.
4. David Folkenflik, "Critics Question Reporter's Airing of Personal Views," National Public Radio, September 26, 2006, at http://www.npr.org/templates/story/story.php?storyId=6146693.

7. THE TWENTY-FIRST CENTURY AND THE FUTURE

1. Andrew Peyton Thomas, *Clarence Thomas: A Biography,* San Francisco: Encounter Books, 2001, p. 586.
2. Lee Epstein and Jack Knight, *The Choices Justices Make,* Washington: CQ Press, 1998, p. 37.
3. "O'Connor Doesn't Want Job," *New York Times,* May 27, 1988, at http://www.nytimes.com/1988/05/27/us/o-connor-doesn-t-want-job.html?pagewanted=1.
4. "Supreme Court Justice Stephen Breyer Interview," *CNN Larry King Live,* November 23, 2005, at http://transcripts.cnn.com/TRANSCRIPTS/0511/23/lkl.01.html; and "Justice Kennedy Remarks on the Supreme Court," Speech at the Forum Club of the Palm Beaches, May 14, 2010, at http://www.c-spanvideo.org/program/id/224222.
5. See Joan Biskupic, *American Original: The Life and Constitution of Supreme Court Justice Antonin Scalia,* New York: Farrar, Straus and Giroux, 2009, pp. 271–274.
6. Biskupic, *American Original,* p. 146.
7. Biskupic, *American Original,* p. 281; and "Justice Antonin Scalia," C-SPAN, May 4, 2008, at http://www.q-and-a.org/Transcript/?ProgramID=1178.
8. "Justice Kennedy Remarks on the Supreme Court."
9. "Most Americans Can't Name Any Supreme Court Justices, Says FindLaw.com Survey," January 10, 2006, at http://www.ipsos-na.com/news-polls/pressrelease.aspx?id=2933; and "C-SPAN Supreme Court Survey," C-SPAN, July 9, 2009, at http://www.c-span.org/pdf/C-SPAN%20Supreme%20Court%20Online%20Survey_070909_6pm.pdf.
10. Anita Hill, *Speaking Truth to Power,* New York: Doubleday, 1997; Jane Meyer and Jill Abramson, *Strange Justice: The Selling of Clarence Thomas.* New York: Plume, 1995; David Brock, *The Real Anita Hill: The Untold Story,* New York: Touchstone, 1994; Timothy M. Phelps and Helen Winternitz, *Capitol Games: Clarence Thomas, Anita Hill, and the Story of a Supreme Court Nomination,* New York: Hyperion, 1992; Andrew Peyton Thomas, *Clarence Thomas: A Biography,* San Francisco: Encounter Books, 2001; and Kevin Merida and Michael A. Fletcher, *Supreme Discomfort: The Divided Soul of Clarence Thomas,* New York: Doubleday, 2007, p. 212.

11. Virginia Lamp Thomas, "Breaking Silence," *People,* November 11, 1991, at http://www.people.com/people/archive/article/020111251,00.html.

12. Thomas, *Clarence Thomas: A Biography,* pp. 457–458.

13. Thomas, *Clarence Thomas: A Biography,* p. 481.

14. Merida and Fletcher, *Supreme Discomfort: The Divided Soul of Clarence Thomas,* pp. 5–6.

15. Thomas, *Clarence Thomas: A Biography,* p. 492.

16. Quoted in Thomas, *Clarence Thomas: A Biography,* p. 504.

17. Thomas, *Clarence Thomas: A Biography,* p. 591.

18. "Justice Kennedy Remarks on the Supreme Court."

19. Robert Barnes, "High Court: Justices Increasingly Speaking Outside the Classroom," *Washington Post,* April 5, 2010, at http://www.washingtonpost.com/wp-dyn/content/article/2010/04/04/AR2010040402464.html?nav=rss_politics.

20. Laura Krugman Ray, "Lives of the Justices: Supreme Court Autobiographies," *Connecticut Law Review* 37 (2004): 233–320.

21. William O. Douglas, *Of Men and Mountains,* New York: Harpers, 1950; *Go East, Young Man,* New York: Random House, 1974; *The Court Years: 1939–1975,* New York: Random House, 1980; and Bruce Allen Murphy, *Wild Bill: The Life and Legend of William O. Douglas,* New York: Random House, 2003, pp. 513–515.

22. Ray, "Lives of the Justices: Supreme Court Autobiographies," 308.

23. Sandra Day O'Connor and H. Alan Day, *Lazy B: Growing Up on a Cattle Ranch in the American Southwest,* New York: Random House, 2002.

24. Joan Biskupic, *Sandra Day O'Connor: How the First Woman on the Supreme Court Became its Most Influential Justice,* New York: HarperPerennial, 2005, pp. 323–324.

25. Biskupic, *Sandra Day O'Connor,* pp. 329–330; Sandra Day O'Connor, *The Majesty of the Law: Reflections of a Supreme Court Justice,* New York: Random House, 2004; and Sandra Day O'Connor, *Chico,* New York: Dutton Juvenile, 2005.

26. William Grimes, "The Justice Looks Back and Settles Old Scores," *New York Times,* October 10, 2007, at http://www.nytimes.com/2007/10/10/books/10grim.html?ex=1349668800&en=e743440de824b868&ei=5124&partner=delicious&exprod=delicious.

27. Robert Barnes, Michael A. Fletcher, and Kevin Merida, "Justice Thomas Lashes Out in Memoir," *Washington Post,* September 29, 2007, at http://www.washingtonpost.com/wp-dyn/content/article/2007/09/28/AR2007092801634.html; "Cable Exclusive: Justice Clarence Thomas Sits Down with Sean Hannity," Fox News, October 3, 2007, at http://www.foxnews.com/story/0,2933,298923,00.html; and "Book Parties and Festivals: Clarence Thomas, 'My Grandfather's Son'" C-SPAN, October 3, 2007, at http://www.booktv.org/Program/8744/Clarence+Thomas+My+Grandfathers+Son.aspx.

28. Bill Barnhart and Gene Schlickman, *John Paul Stevens: An Independent Life,* Dekalb: Northern Illinois University Press, 2010.

29. Herman Obermayer, *Rehnquist: A Personal Portrait of the Distinguished Chief Justice of the United States,* New York: Threshold Editions, 2009; and Chris Mondics, "A Friend Writes of His Years with Rehnquist," *Philadelphia Inquirer,*

September 8, 2008, at http://www.philly.com/philly/news/homepage/57680447
.html.

30. Antonia Felix, *Sonia Sotomayor: The True American Dream*. New York: Berkley
Hardcover, 2010.

31. Biskupic, *Sandra Day O'Connor*, op cit; and Biskupic, *American Original*, op cit.

32. Meyer and Abramson, *Strange Justice: The Selling of Clarence Thomas*; and
Phelps and Winternitz, *Capitol Games: Clarence Thomas, Anita Hill, and the
Story of a Supreme Court Nomination*.

33. Thomas, *Clarence Thomas: A Biography*, op cit; Ken Foskett, *Judging Clarence
Thomas*, New York: Harper Paperbacks, 2005; and Merida and Fletcher, *Supreme
Discomfort: The Divided Soul of Clarence Thomas*, op cit.

34. Merida and Fletcher, *Supreme Discomfort: The Divided Soul of Clarence Thomas*,
pp. 222–223, 287, and 343; and Biskupic, *Sandra Day O'Connor*, p. 249.

35. Biskupic, *American Original*, pp. 338–339.

36. Dennis Hutchinson, *The Man Who Once was Whizzer White: A Portrait of
Justice Byron R. White*, New York: Free Press, 1998; and John Jeffries, *Justice Lewis F. Powell: A Biography*, New York: Fordham University Press,
2001.

37. Jeffrey Toobin, *The Nine: Inside the Secret World of the Supreme Court*, New
York: Doubleday, 2007.

38. Jan Crawford Greenberg, *Supreme Conflict: The Inside Story of the Struggle
for Control of the United States Supreme Court*, New York: Penguin Press,
2007.

39. Jeffrey Rosen, *The Supreme Court: The Personalities and Rivalries That Defined
America*, New York: Times Books, 2006.

40. Rosen, *The Supreme Court*, p. 6.

41. Biskupic, *Sandra Day O'Connor*, pp. 333–334; and "Justice Kennedy Remarks on
the Supreme Court."

42. William H. Rehnquist, *The Supreme Court*, New York: Knopf, 2004; William H.
Rehnquist, *Centennial Crisis: The Disputed Election of 1876*, New York: Knopf,
2004; and William H. Rehnquist, *Grand Inquests: The Historic Impeachments of
Justice Samuel Chase and President Andrew Johnson*. New York: Harper Perennial, 1999.

43. "O'Connor Saddened by Attacks on Judiciary," *USA Today*, July 21, 2005, at http://
www.usatoday.com/news/washington/2005-07-21-oconnor_x.htm; Jack Shafer,
"O'Connor Forecasts Dictatorship: Why Didn't the Press Chase the Story?"
Slate, March 13, 2006, at http://www.slate.com/id/2137961; and Nina Totenberg, "O'Connor Decries Republican Attacks on Courts," National Public
Radio, March 10, 2006, at http://www.npr.org/templates/story/story.php?storyId=
5255712.

44. Hope Yen, "O'Connor: Court Should Follow Precedent," *USA Today*, May 20,
2007, at http://www.usatoday.com/news/washington/2007-05-20-1373990718_x.
htm; and Robert Barnes, "O'Connor: Corporate Campaign Funds Could Affect
Judiciary," *Washington Post*, January 26, 2010, at http://www.washingtonpost.
com/wp-dyn/content/article/2010/01/26/AR2010012603322.html.

45. "Supreme Court Justices Reflect on Judicial Independence," *PBS News-
Hour*, September 26, 2006; at http://www.pbs.org/newshour/bb/law/july-dec06/

independence_09–26.html; and Bill Mears, "Justice Ginsburg Details Death Threat," CNN, March 15, 2006, at http://www.cnn.com/2006/LAW/03/15/scotus .threat/.

46. "Justice Breyer: Burning a Quran May be Wrong, but It's a Right," CNN, September 15, 2010, at http://www.cnn.com/2010/US/09/15/US-Breyer-LKL/index.html? hpt=C1.

47. Antonin Scalia and Amy Gutmann, *A Matter of Interpretation: Federal Courts and the Law*, Princeton: Princeton University Press, 1997; Stephen Breyer, *Making Our Democracy Work: A Judge's View*, New York: Knopf, 2010; Stephen Breyer, *Active Liberty: Interpreting Our Democratic Constitution*, New York: Knopf, 2005; and Biskupic, *Sandra Day O'Connor*, pp. 332–333.

48. Joan Biskupic, "Ginsburg: Court Needs Another Woman," *USA Today*, May 5, 2009, at http://www.usatoday.com/news/washington/judicial/2009–05–05-ruth-ginsburg_N.htm.

49. Matt Sedensky, "Justice Questions Way Court Nominees are Grilled," Associated Press, May 14, 2010, at http://news.yahoo.com/s/ap/20100514/ap_on_re_us/us_supreme_court_kennedy.

50. Jeffrey Toobin, "After Stevens: What Will the Supreme Court be Like Without Its Liberal Leader?" *New Yorker*, March 22, 2010, at http://www.newyorker.com/reporting/2010/03/22/100322fa_fact_toobin.

51. Joan Biskupic, "Scalia's Comments on Torture Latest Taste of Bluntness," *USA Today*, February 13, 2008, at http://www.usatoday.com/news/washington/2008–02–13-scalia_N.htm; William H. Rehnquist, *All Laws But One: Civil Liberties in Wartime*, New York: Knopf, 1998; and "Supreme Court Justice Slams Death Penalty," Fox News, August 7, 2005, at http://www.foxnews.com/story/0,2933,164970,00.html.

52. Biskupic, *American Original*, pp. 145–146.

53. See Biskupic, *American Original*, p. 266.

54. Merida and Fletcher, *Supreme Discomfort: The Divided Soul of Clarence Thomas*, p. 228.

55. Thomas, *Clarence Thomas: A Biography*, p. 473; and Merida and Fletcher, *Supreme Discomfort: The Divided Soul of Clarence Thomas*, p. 227.

56. Toobin, "After Stevens: What Will the Supreme Court be Like Without Its Liberal Leader?"; and Adam Liptak, "At 89, Stevens Contemplates Law and How to Leave It," *New York Times*, April 3, 2010, at *http://www.nytimes .com/2010/04/04/us/04stevens.html?scp=1&sq=stevens&st=cse*.

57. "Chief Justice Says Goal is More Consensus on Court," *New York Times*, May 22, 2006, p. A16; and Toobin, "After Stevens."

58. Biskupic, *Sandra Day O'Connor*, op cit.

59. Biskupic, *Sandra Day O'Connor*, p. 289.

60. For a discussion of White's life, see Hutchinson, *The Man Who Once Was Whizzer White*, op cit.

61. Hutchinson, *The Man Who Once Was Whizzer White*, p. 5.

62. Hutchinson, *The Man Who Once Was Whizzer White*, p. 413.

63. Linda Greenhouse, "Telling the Court's Story: Justice and Journalism at the Supreme Court," *Yale Law Journal* 105 (April 1996): 1537–1562.

64. Letter from Irving Dilliard to Hugh L. Black, n.d., and Letter from Hugo L. Black to Irving Dilliard, October 24, 1957, Box 25, Hugo LaFayette Black Papers, Manuscript Division, Library of Congress, Washington, D.C.

65. Carl T. Rowan, *Dream Makers, Dream Breakers: The World of Justice Thurgood Marshall*, Boston: Little Brown, 1993, pp. 408–409.

66. Box 23, Hugo LaFayette Black Papers, Manuscript Division, Library of Congress, Washington, D.C.

67. Paul Y. Anderson, "Marquis Childs and Justice Black," *The Nation*, May 21, 1938, p. 579; and Frank R. Kent, "Douglas Boom Called Upsetting to Dignity of Supreme Court," unknown newspaper and date, Box 217, Robert Houghwout Jackson Papers, Manuscript Division, Library of Congress, Washington, D.C.

68. "Equality and Governmental Action," Speech delivered at the James Madison Lecture at New York University, February 11, 1964, Box 163, Folder 4, Arthur J. Goldberg Papers, Library of Congress, Washington, D.C.; and "Goldberg Calls on U.S. to Repay Costs to Those Cleared in Crime," *New York Times*, February 12, 1964, p. 35.

69. Biskupic, *American Original*, pp. 110, 301.

70. Adam Liptak, "So, Guy Walks Up to the Bar, and Scalia Says." *New York Times*, December 31, 2005, p. A1.

71. Biskupic, *Sandra Day O'Connor*, pp. 278–279.

72. Rosen, *The Supreme Court*, p. 6.

73. For a sample of the discussion about whether political coverage of the Court reduces the Court's legitimacy, see John R. Hibbing and Elizabeth Theiss-Morse, *Stealth Democracy: Public Attitudes Towards American Political Institutions*, New York: Cambridge University Press, 2002; and Vanessa A. Baird and Amy Gangl, "Shattering the Myth of Legality: The Impact of the Media's Framing of Supreme Court Procedures on Perceptions of Fairness," *Political Psychology* 27 (2006): 597–614.

74. Biskupic, *American Original*, pp. 320–326.

75. Hibbing and Theiss-Morse, *Stealth Democracy*, p. 201.

76. Barbara A. Perry and Henry J. Abraham, "Franklin Roosevelt and the Supreme Court: A New Deal and a New Image," in Stephen K. Shaw et al., eds., *Franklin D. Roosevelt and the Transformation of the Supreme Court*, vol. 3, Armonk, N.Y.: M.E. Sharpe, 2004, pp. 20–21.

Index

ABC News, 26, 134, 136, 151, 152, 178, 180
Abington School District v. Schempp, 148
abortion, 1, 3, 6, 7, 11, 19, 22, 24, 25, 32, 113, 119,
    120, 139, 143, 157, 166
Acheson, Dean, 88, 92
Adams, John, 37, 47, 186
Adams, John Quincy, 37
affirmative action, 11, 24, 32, 113
Alito, Samuel, 3, 12, 15, 20, 27, 158, 162, 163,
    167, 173
    commenting during presidential address, 8
Armey, Dick, 175
Armstrong, Scott, 25, 137

Baltimore Sun, 78, 136
Barbour, Philip, 57
Beckwith, David, 138
Bernstein, Carl, 25, 137
Biskupic, Joan, 179, 193, 208
    interviews with justices, 184–186
Black, Hugo, 3, 12, 87, 105, 116, 118, 121, 140,
    146, 164, 171, 191
    controlling interactions with the press,
        130–135
    feud with Robert Jackson, 106–108
    granting interviews, 149–150
    interaction with the press, 125–129, 187–191
    paying attention to press coverage, 120
Blackmun, Harry, 11, 12, 19, 26, 92, 109, 127,
    129, 133, 134, 136, 141, 144, 149, 151, 158,
    168, 179
    "the Blackmun effect", 161–168
    as a source for *The Brethren*, 137–139
    interest in press coverage, 116–118, 119–120
    interviews with, 149–151
    shaping press coverage, 186–192

Blaine, James G., 56
Blair, James, 35
blogosphere, 27
Bork, Robert, 21, 29, 101, 155, 157
    nomination of, 101
Bosch, Juan, 93
Bradley, Joseph, 72
Brandeis, Louis, 4, 11, 28, 88, 95, 98, 104, 109,
    116, 120, 129, 130, 146, 148, 152
    as presidential advisor, 89–90, 92
    interaction with the press, 133–135, 187–189
Brennan, William, 90, 121, 124, 129, 152, 164,
    179, 183, 188
    exerting influence over other justices,
        140–141
    interaction with the press, 132–133
Breyer, Stephen, 15, 16, 20, 21, 31, 164, 174, 191
    defending the court, 182–184
    interaction with the press, 172–173
Brown v. Board of Education, 3, 6, 13, 14, 24,
    119, 148
Bryant, William G., 62
Buchanan, James, 78
Burger, Warren, 26, 92, 96, 117, 120, 124, 129,
    130, 143
    criticism of, 137–139
    holding press conferences, 152–153
    press coverage of, 161–166
Burr, Aaron, 34
    treason trial of, 51–52
Burton, Harold H., 83, 90, 116, 119, 125, 140,
    189
Bush v. Gore, 7, 158
Bush, George H. W., 152
Bush, George W., 6, 8
Byrnes, James, 88, 92

237